BC   12

WITHDRAWN

Figural Choice
in Poetry and Art

FRONTISPIECE: *Simultaneous Windows (2nd Motif, 1st Part)*,
Robert Delaunay (1912).
Oil on canvas, 21⅝ × 18¼″.
Solomon R. Guggenheim Museum, New York.

Figural Choice in Poetry and Art

Albert Cook

Published for Brown University by
University Press of New England
Hanover and London, 1985

University Press of New England

Brandeis University   University of Connecticut   University of Rhode Island
Brown University   Dartmouth College   Tufts University
Clark University   University of New Hampshire   University of Vermont

Cover illustration: The Departure of the Poet, Giorgio de Chirico (1914). Private Collection, USA.

Illustrations: Frontispiece, *Simultaneous Windows (2nd Motif, 1st Part),* 1912, by Robert Delaunay, from the Solomon R. Guggenheim Museum Collection, New York, Carmelo Guadagno and David Heald, photographers. Figure 1, *Torso of a Young Man,* from Miletus, fifth century B.C., from The Louvre, Paris. Figure 2, *Birds Erect,* 1914, by Henri Gaudier-Brzeska, from the Museum of Modern Art Collection, New York, gift of Mrs. W. Murray Crane. Figure 3, *Torso Fruit,* 1960, by Jean Arp, from the Hirshhorn Museum and Sculpture Garden, Smithsonian Institution, Washington, D.C. Figure 4, *Between Leaf and Bird,* 1959, by Jean Arp, copyright 1984 by Founders Society, Detroit Institute of Arts (Founders Society Purchase, General Membership Fund). Figure 5, *The Departure of the Poet,* 1914, by Giorgio de Chirico, from a private collection. Figure 6, *I Saw the Figure 5 in Gold,* 1928, by Charles Demuth, from The Alfred Stieglitz Collection, 1949, all rights reserved, The Metropolitan Museum of Art, New York. Figure 7, *Gloucester Harbor,* 1852, by Fitz Hugh Lane, from the Cape Ann Historical Association, deposited by the City of Gloucester. Figure 8, Mycenean Seal, *Boar Hunt,* and Figure 9, Mycenean Seal, *Lion with Calf,* from the National Archeological Museum, Athens, reprinted by permission from *Corpus der Minoischen und Mykenischen Siegel.*

Printed in the United States of America

LIBRARY OF CONGRESS CATALOGING IN PUBLICATION DATA

Cook, Albert Spaulding.
Figural choice in poetry and art.

1. Poetics.   2. Art and literature.   I. Title.
PN1042.C584   1985   809.1   84–40582
ISBN 0–87451–333–2

For Mac and Katka Hammond

Contents

Illustrations   viii

Acknowledgments   ix

   I. Thought, Image, and Story:
     The Slippery Procedures of Literature   *1*

   II. The Range of Image   7

   III. Aspects of the Plastic Image: Rilke, Pound, and Arp   *38*

   IV. The Windows of Apollinaire   *64*

   V. Surrealism and Surrealisms   *86*

   VI. William Carlos Williams: Ideas and Things   *124*

   VII. Maximizing Minimalism:
     The Construct of Image in Olson and Creeley   *149*

   VIII. Expressionism Not Wholly Abstract: Ashbery and O'Hara   *167*

AFTERWORD:
Visual Aspects of the Homeric Simile in Indo-European Context   *203*

Notes   225

Index   251

Illustrations

Simultaneous Windows (*2nd Motif, 1st Part*)
Robert Delaunay   *frontispiece*

Torso of a Young Man   44

Birds Erect
Henri Gaudier-Brzeska   49

Torso Fruit
Jean Arp   60

Between Leaf and Bird
Jean Arp   61

The Departure of the Poet
Giorgio de Chirico   122

I Saw the Figure 5 in Gold
Charles Demuth   125

Gloucester Harbor
Fitz Hugh Lane   152

Mycenean Seal, *Boar Hunt*   222

Mycenean Seal, *Lion with Calf*   222

Acknowledgments

I should like to thank the following journals for publishing earlier versions of parts of this book: *Comparative Literature Studies* ("Thought, Image and Story"), *Journal of Aesthetics and Art Criticism* (a section of "The Range of Image"), *Quaderni Urbinati di Cultura Classica* ("Visual Aspects of the Homeric Simile"), *Dada and Surrealism* ("Pound and Arp"), *American Poetry Review* ("Surrealism and Surrealisms"), *Boundary 2* and *Sagetrieb* (parts of "Creeley and Olson"), *American Poetry* ("John Ashbery"), *Audit* (part of "O'Hara").

This book has been considerably helped by the acute editorial advice of Aaron Rosen, and of others who have read all or part of it, including Irving Massey, Peter Baker, Ernest B. Gilman, and Claus Clüver. I am grateful for bibliographical assistance—especially in gathering materials for the chapter on Homer—to my wife Carol. The book was evolved under favorable conditions, and with help from their libraries, at Brown University and Cambridge University, where I shaped an advanced draft into final form as a Fellow at Clare Hall. Two research assistants eased and improved the work, first Angelika Webb, and then Blossom S. Kirschenbaum, who also gave useful editorial advice. She also made the index.

It should be noted that all translations here are my own, except where otherwise indicated.

*Figural Choice
in Poetry and Art*

Thought, Image, and Story
The Slippery Procedures of Literature

The goal of accounting for literature, or for the literary element in discourse, is an elusive one. Taken generally, a definition gravitates towards the falsely exclusive pole of the purely aesthetic, and literature's fundamental spheres of reference to reality become attenuated. Or else, conversely, literature's qualities as plain discourse are enunciated, and the literary element effectually vanishes. When the question is taken more specifically, the critic easily falls into the trap of enumerating the obvious, in "levels" and the like.[1]

Questions raised by the whole hermeneutic debate, similarly, constitute a set of questions that are essentially preliminary. These questions may be bracketed, though, after awareness has been informed of the dialectical constraints they provide: of offering an epistemology that validates the possibility of interpreting on the one hand, and of pressing skeptical considerations that relativize it on the other.

It is possible, and indeed helpful, to ask the large question first: What is literature? Now lengthy answers to this question are endless. Prior justifications for the special nature, or mode of existence, of the literary work, and for its procedures and statements, could also be endless—which is a good strategic reason for bracketing such questions and asking directly what level of generality will work as a starting point.

I should like to start with a fairly general set of terms, and to define literature as an artful resort through words to, and usually a combination of, three fundamental approaches to the understanding of anything—conceptual thought, image, and story.

Thought is an activity that embraces an explicit range of procedures from the momentary inference and its arguable substructure to vast constructive systems, while it also includes implicit assumptions and world views consciously or unconsciously held. In so far as words are conceptual counters, thought in this coded sense for literature may be taken to be a *first* (to adapt Peirce's terminology), or the only recoverable record, partial or otherwise, of a first. Under the dominance of all this, and through a sort of implied analogy to the very sort of discourse I am conducting at this moment, we tend to treat thought also as an ultimate. Whether deconstructing the literary work through the interestingly revelatory process of displacing some of its constituents, or reconstituting it on the basis of its structured communication as a speech act,[2] there are those who will rest satisfied if we have given an account of the thought, realized or otherwise, that may be derived from the work. For the word itself, and also for the symbol, there are three conceptual components whose relations with each other offer a whole world of speculation to philosophy, as they have done for over two millennia.[3] These, to use current terms, are the signifier, the signified, and the object of reference. However we multiply the relations between the signifier and the signified, while banishing the object as irrecoverable; or however we simplify these relations by, in effect, refusing to talk about anything but the object in an insistence that after all qualifications, literature is firmly about life; in any case we are remaining on the terrain of thought. To do so is reassuring, inescapable, and fortified by a large measure of truth. It leads to the further invention of supposed atomic constituents of, say, narrative—the *isotopies* and *actants* of Greimas,[4] the *unités* of Barthes,[5] and so on. Such writers rest, after devising these tools for picking up the semantic constituents of a literary statement, without really addressing the question of where the statement is heading. Self-consistent description is taken for explanation. Or a whole mode of literature may be defined by describing a whole area of its concerns. Poetry has often been defined in this way, recently by Evan Watkins,[6] who sees poetry as composed of *being*—identified by him with *feeling*—, of *non-being* or structure, and of *becoming,* or the poet's dialogue with himself. Adapting a Hegelian dialectic of *Sein, Nicht-sein,* and *Werden,* this challenging set leads to a combination of thought elements: abstract itself, it reduces to abstraction, and it may be said to continue a line of assertion well phrased by Matthew Arnold: "Poetry attaches its emotion to the idea; the idea *is* the fact."[7]

Baudelaire, however, insisted on a different line, on correspondences, the "forest of symbols." From the Romantics through the Surrealists, Wallace Stevens, the proponents of deep image, and beyond, poets and others have insisted on the irreducibility of the image. Almost all recent theory of metaphor proceeds by translating metaphors into thoughts by teasing out the interrelations of the tenor and the vehicle. But most metaphors include images. If we take the very separation of tenor from vehicle as a special self-advertising way of presenting an image, then we have moved aside at one step from the knotty dialectic of accounting for image by working out the relation of tenor to vehicle. The image, indeed, will just not go away; it refuses to be replaced by thought—or for that matter to be comprehensively defined.[8] Even if image may be argued to be present at every stage of the perceptual process, this origination would not dictate, or even further, an interpretation of aesthetic images. This self-subsistence of the image encourages the poet, floats across at least the surface of philosophical discourse, and furnishes an analytic terrain for Bachelard.[9] We perceive through images, we construct a sense of our perceptions at least partially through images, and we guide the emotional currents of our lives through something like images. All theatrical events excerpt bodies from the flow of life and invent for them a sequence that frames them for being seen, as images. Poems use images, and when they do not, it may be said that they are avoiding them. Fiction strangely enlists images as a sort of ballast, and earlier narratives do something comparable. What else is the Holy Grail for the medieval romance? This image is stubbornly irreducible, as much so as the carriage of Vautrin or the house of Gatsby or the money pouch of Dmitri Karamazov.

> Wie sucht ihr mich heim, ihr Bilder
> Die lang ich vergessen geglaubt![10]
>
> Images, why do you haunt me,
> Whom I thought I had long forgot!

So even Chamisso. The modern poet's turn to theory only redevelops the mystery, as René Char, "L'intensité est silencieuse. Son image ne l'est pas. (J'aime qui m'éblouit puis accentue l'obscur à l'intérieur de moi)." (Intensity is silent. Its image is not. [I love that which dazzles me, then accentuates what is obscure inside me.])"[11]

Just how does an image, something connected to the visible world, bring the invisible into play? How can it be used to establish connections? To change them? How does an image especially gear with a person's repertory of presuppositions about images and about matters not reducible to image, if such there be?

Then there is story, the narrative, whether in poem, novel, or play—or for that matter in the skillful account of the historian. Hexter has shown the irreducibility of that procedure, too, in human communication.[12] Narrative will not resolve to analysis, and for fiction not to depth analysis either.[13] Starting the reader from his expectations at the beginning of a book instead of having him recollect it schematically at the end will highlight certain features, with Iser—but it will not account for the story. The conviction that a story has some overall sense and some final reference leads us either to weigh its details for some higher coherence, or else to give up the possibility of coherence by referring them to *vividness, color,* and the like, if not simply to *randomness.* But the essential character of the story form, of a radical narrativity that does not simply interweave sign systems, resists re-coding either as a thought coherence or as a random thoughtlessness.

Thought, image, and story cut across the literary genres, even when they are distinct themselves. But they are often not distinct. They also, and characteristically, combine in the literary work. The image, when it enters into combination with story, easily accedes to an atmosphere of terror and menace, as Irving Massey has shown in his study of metamorphoses—a fusion of image and story.[14] For Massey even the presentation of an image in a single line of verse is rooted in sequence, and so implicitly in story-as-sequence. A *figura* in Auerbach's reading is an image at two different points of real time, the modification of image through story. So, at the beginning of Wordsworth's *Michael* we are shown "the straggling heap of un-hewn stones," leading not only through coherence of images but also through story to the famous last line, "and never lifted up a single stone." Story tends to displace itself into the image, to trans-late itself into image; Apollo in myth is an image composed of a number of stories. And as Lévi-Strauss has shown, to use examples from a kindred art, the masks of the Pacific Northwest have behind them stories of origin, and they also replay elements of those stories in terms of image. Beyond this transposition of story into image, the different kinds of masks and coppers set up sequences of interrefer-ence—and also of evasion, "comme un mythe, un masque nie autant qu'il affirme" (like a myth, a mask denies as much as it asserts).[15] Allegory seems a spatialization, even a displacement into space; but Benjamin correlates it to time, to history.[16]

Image and thought combine, even if their combination cannot wholly be resolved into the single activity of thought. Modern "constructivism," in poetry or the visual arts, makes capital of in-sisting on the connection. As Charles Olson says:

> Of rhythm is image
> Of image is knowing
> Of knowing there is
> A construct[17]

When image and thought and story converge, in whatever real-ized proportion, we are reassured by a sense of plenitude above and beyond any messages, or even any sense of ineffable mystery, they may convey—as well as beyond the gaps and "absences" of the work, however elaborately constructed and deconstructed. Some such plenitude has usually been intended and it is achieved firmly enough to override various shifts, darknesses, and lacunae in the work—without replacing those lacunae by thought-constructs of easy coherence. The sense of plenitude persists in literary work even when—as with Céline or Beckett—it is based on notions and strategies of yawning vacancy. Accounting for that sense of plenitude in a literary work offers us our true goal, one we may approach in optimism, even if it keeps receding from us.

While we should find no reason to cease the currently fashionable practice of raising considerations that distance us from the work or impoverish its communicative effect, at the same time we should not abandon the complementary goal of accounting for the depth of understanding that is an inescapable part of what we assume, our *Vorverständnis*. Image and story, however resistant they may be to conceptual thought in our accounts of them, continue to combine with thought in the literary experience. They further, as well as evidence, our implied involvement in the plenitude achieved by the works we experience through their elusive means.

II

The Range of Image

A host of philosophical questions comes flocking in upon us the minute we raise the possibility that a common fundament exists on which the use of image draws in both the visual arts and verbal usage, or at least literary usage. And another host of such questions disappears, or at least recedes to a manageable distance, if we assume this possibility of a common fundament. For one thing, we realease ourselves from the trap of dealing solely with the logic of metaphor and shift to the question of the communicative force residing in images—a question that itself is not an easy one. So difficult is it, indeed, that some writers have taken to avoiding the very term *image.*

For another thing, we enable ourselves to deal more fully with the range of communicative properties, and not just with the iconographic references or contexts, in specific poems, as in specific paintings and sculptures.

These are heady possibilities, and they become headier when literature itself is seen not as the main route of intuitive communication but just an alternate route. We are of course on the ground that has been called aesthetics since the mid-eighteenth century, but an attention to communicative strategies and resources, as these center on image, may have the advantage of keeping the general questions of aesthetics also at some distance. Questions of aesthetics could be resumed in what ought to be a more powerful manner after some deductions have been made about aspects of what word and image may have in common.[1]

Contexts are often sensitized to images, and in many societies is found image worship or idolatry. In many others are found versions of iconoclasm—refusing images to the point where one breaks them— a term that may be extended to cover any contextual situation where the image breeds discomfort or invokes uncanniness. We could dwell on that profound question, and on several others that point to a ground beyond mere influence or analogic comparison.[2]

Lessing's distinction that the visual arts are spatial and the literary ones temporal has only limited application, since our mysterious ground of significance underlies that distinction. It does so iconographically, to begin with: the Laocoön, whether in words or in stone or in graphic presentation of paper, refers to the same point in the Trojan story—whether as a statue in Rome, an ornamented description in the *Aeneid,* or the graphic representation by Blake, with its heavy overlay of sloganlike commentary all around the central figure. It gathers up the same images. And it draws on the same deep sources of association—with snakes, and priesthood, and the sea, and fathers, and sons.

All of this is in what we may call black and white, though hues do fall over the stones. And if we add color, we have further significations, ones that enlist a surface of communication only to touch deeper chords. Red is not just a signal, blue is not just an associative cue for the sky or the Virgin. Colors may also be named, as is often done in modern poetry. Color is also a presence—Proust's yellow patch of wall in the Vermeer, the black of Kline. This for single colors, the diction of colors. When we get to the syntax, the harmony or combination of colors, we have entered a communicative universe whose muteness is only a surface manifestation. The blue square links to the yellow in Mondrian. Accounting, with Gombrich or Arnheim, for the constructive side of our perceptions will not get us to what it is we have then constructed.[3] Adrian Stokes distinguishes between the deep emphasis on separate colors on one hand and the interplay between colors on the other, finding in each emphasis different approaches to color which he associates with "carving" and "modelling" respectively.[4] Wölfflin divides painting, and architecture, and sculpture as well, into the plastic and the painterly—a distinction not so different from Stokes'.[5] These are valiant attempts to provide a large-scale simple vocabulary from the most fundamental presentational strategies, to carry us beyond the intricate philosophical questions raised by Husserl and Wittgenstein, among others, about how and what we perceive in a single color.[6]

It would be easy to find literary analogies to visual practices. A propos of *plastic* and *painterly,* we may note that Spenser is interested in the distinct moment and Milton in an interfusion, an opposition we could parallel in setting Browning, with his slippage of distinct moments, against Tennyson, that later master of interfusion. Or again, perhaps, Pound against Eliot—the "art in profile" of *Mauberley* as against the rich fusions of *Ash Wednesday.* Or the distinct and discrete Williams against the Stevens who wished his sea surface full of clouds to be a sort of endless merging.

Once we had attended to such effects, we would have the terms where we could begin to discuss not just aesthetics, or the principles on which such operations function, but also the theory of signification, the large and whole communications and expressions that take place therein. We would have a ground on which we would not just be thrown back on psychology to deal either with the paintings of Pollock, which are certainly more than just the record of an internal action, or the poems of O'Hara, which are certainly more than a marvelous rhetoric embroidering trivia.

Our goal, then, is some further understanding of what it is we understand when we apprehend the achieved work, verbal or visual. This book aims to approach that goal by drawing inferences from the visual features, the images, as we may continue to call them, of some poems, especially with reference to analogous works of visual art. Poems that enlist visual effects or refer to paintings, pictures that incorporate words or play with their titles, are not really hard cases, though films of the "feature film" variety, combining the verbal structure of a story and its dialogue with the montage of moving pictorial sequences, do offer an intricate challenge. But any image does, the more so if it has been raised and intensified to the point of artistic expression.

2

If we turn to the image as it is transmitted just by words, certain problems arise that cannot be solved by information theory, linguistics, or semiotics. The most complex verbal uses transcend such codes—especially when such uses reside wholly or partially in the presentation of images, even just a couple of images.

We have significant images as early as the wall paintings of Paleolithic man,[7] but the inclusion of images into poems in a structured way, in Greece at least, is a surprisingly late development. The expanded similes of Homer, for example, serve incidentally to the poem so far as the internal structure of the image is concerned, though their explanatory function in a given passage does contain complexities of the sort discussed in my concluding chapter.

The recent study of metaphor, in its attention to "pragmatics," tends to see the context in which an image is produced as somewhat inert.[8] Such separate explanations, we learn from Freud's analysis of dreams, would not do even for the flow of images in dreams, where a change of image may be used to indicate a change in logical relations.[9] Four normalizing cases for the verbal use of image from early Greece to the nineteenth century will show some inadequacies of such accounts. In the light of inadequacies, we may measure our distance from a full account of the linguistic process for which metaphor is only a special case of image.

High uses pose problems, as for example in Pindar:

> Golden lyre
>
> . . . . .
>
> You quench the speared thunderbolt
> of ever-flowing fire. Zeus's eagle sleeps on his
> staff, slackening quick wings both ways.
>
> Lord of birds; you shed a black-faced mist on his hooked head,

sweet lock of eyes; dreaming he ripples
his liquid back, held
by your buffets. And so powerful Ares
leaving far off the harsh edge
of spears charms his heart
with sleep, and your shafts enchant the minds
of gods, in the skill of Leto's
son and the deep-girdled Muses.

Such as Zeus has not loved are terrified hearing
the cry of the Pierides on earth and
on the unyielding sea,
and he who in dread Tartarus lies, the god's enemy
Typhon the hundred-headed
. . . . .
Sicily presses his
shaggy breast and heaven's pillar contains it,
whitening Aetna, year-long nurse of keen snow

from whose chasms belch up purest springs
of unquenchable fire and rivers pour forth
into day a glittering stream
of smoke, but in darkness from the rock
a red rolling flame carries to the deep
expanse of the sea in a crash.

(Pythian Odes 1.1–24)

The excited dwelling on detail in the descriptions of the eagle on
the sceptre and of the erupting Aetna arrests perception point for
point. At the same time it sweeps all the perceptions up into the
tensions of the assertions, along with the many incidental metaphors they include. These assertions in turn are, as it were, straining
at and into the elaborate and given framework of the poem, con-
stituting a priamel in Bundy's sense.[10] In the description of the
eagle itself there is no metaphor, only image. Though the quick
movement through images and the tone seem Aeschylean, at this
point we are given nothing like Aeschylus' condensed metaphors,
nothing like—to take one example—the *surizon phobon* (fear-

whistling) of the *Prometheus* (355), a comparison that combines synesthesia and metonymy as a way of indicating the psychological extremity of what is evoked.

Pindar is high-flown but not extreme. He is normative, and the images in their succession here function gradually to produce a "charm" of contentment that the progressive excitement of the pell-mell statements and the high elaboration of the meter would seem to belie. He will soon pass on to images of sailing that are directly and simply metaphoric—poetry is like sailing or running a life is like sailing. And then he will bring in exempla, condensed and riddling for what they signify, but simple in the structure of their relationship to the auditor. The listener is to be like Philoctetes in some ways, to avoid being like Phalaris in others. The orientation of such actions into a dim, generalized future refers to exempla out of a quasi-legendary past. This implies the tension the poem offers for these images—a vast but invented norm—a tension between the momentary point and the key constituent of a structured statement-in-the-making that dissolves into simple proverb at the end and crops up into gnomic statements throughout.

At this opening moment of *Pythian I* an image structure involving the cosmos is hyperbolically delineated, in such a way as to emphasize the presence in the cosmos of both chthonic and Olympian gods. All this, though, is extravagantly stated to be a response to a power that the poet himself exemplifies, though he does so through the agency of another god, the Apollo "Leto's son," whose festival defines the context in which the ode is uttered. Even at this point the sign system has been pushed, through the crowding images, to a self-transcendence where the secular and the religious are no longer discrete, nor are they fused. Nor can it be said that they have entered into a dialectical relationship, and it will not help to label the images seriatim as *signals* for the auditor or within the poem of music to Zeus, as *symptoms* in volcanic nature of the presence of music, as an *icon* of the relationship between ruling and dominated powers (Zeus and Typhon) as they are mapped from underground to sky, as a conventional *symbol* (the eagle), or as an act of *naming*.[11] The sign system lends itself only provisionally, as well, to such dual categories as Olympian and chthonic, poetry and worship, men and gods, and the like. On the one hand the whole pantheon is figured as yielding to the force of something similar to what the poet is producing, and Pindar elsewhere emphasizes his own flight, using the eagle as a metaphor for it (*Olympian* 2.88). On the other hand, the distance between men and gods remains firm, though at other points man is enjoined not to aspire to the other realm.

The poet here advertises, celebrates, and communicates a freedom to dwell over such images as eagle and volcano, to sketch in a large scene involving both of them, to switch the image-frame, to change the significative structure of the image into metaphor, to characterize the progression as emotional series (*thaumasion* 26–27), or as something like a logical formula,[12] a *logos,* to conclude by leaving image entirely behind him as only an overtone of his multiple-incremental gains. The fact of this freedom defines the bond of the auditor to the poet as something new, and it probably also serves to evoke a state in the auditor that draws on celebration, religious awe, and something like rhetorical-literary admiration all at once. If we were to trace this out step by step, phrase by phrase, in a response sequence, it would all seem quite varied and staccato; but our fundamental impression is one of overriding unity.

For Plato, of course, the word *logos* is important in the philosophical senses it quickly accrued after the powerful use of Heraclitus. But we should not make the oversimplifying mistake of looking back at Plato from the vantage only of modern philosophy, wholly occupied with continuing the activity of *logos.* The term *eidos,* too, bulks large in his system, a term we may render as "image." And images in our slightly different sense enter Plato's demonstration at crucial points of the discourse in a way quite different from the incidentally illustrative images of Locke or Kant.[13]

At a summary point in the middle of the *Republic,* offering a full and explicit analysis of the idea of the good that will guide his philosopher kings, Plato suddenly offers the image of the line. The line supposedly presents the capping proof, and more precise demonstration, of the homology he has just elaborately mapped (504A–509C) between the sun and the idea of the good, in accordance with which light corresponds to truth, objects seen to ideas, seeing to knowing, the eye to the mind, sight to reason, and seeing to think-ing.[14] The line is cut into proportional segments; it is divided be-tween the process of appearance (*doxa*) and that of thought (*noesis*), these being subdivided into imaging (*eikasia*), and trust (*pistis*), then into ratiocination (*dianoia*) and a higher thought (*noesis*) whose objects are the higher patterns or, as we may again render it, images (*eide*) (509D–513E). This mathematical presen-tation of the "four faculties" (*pathemata*) of the soul is not pre-sented as an aid to visualization only; it constitutes a sort of proof, in the hands of a philosopher whose mathematics always has a geometric and physical basis, and whose whole doctrine, according to a strong tradition in antiquity, finally took mathematical form.[15]

The myth of the cave, which immediately follows in the text (514–17), is an illustration "applied and fitting (*prosapteon*) to everything said before" (517B). As he introduces it, Socrates tells Glaucon to make an image of it, *apeikason* (514A).

The cave is, we may say, illustrative, and as such it has within the *Republic* a different referential structure from the line. Persons walking along a ramp in the cave hold up objects, and a fire behind them throws shadows of the objects on the wall for those whose legs and necks are chained away from seeing either the fire or the objects directly. Still less may they see the sun up outside the cave where those analogous to philosophers may mount and go through a process analogous to becoming educated (*paideia* is in question) to higher thought. At the same time the cave powerfully revises into a sort of eternal primitive time the stages of evolving political states presented earlier in the *Republic*. And while the cave illus-trates the line, it does not correspond to it. The line demonstrates the philosopher's idea of the good; the cave portrays through a complex image the difficult physical and social conditions under which a philosopher may try to attain it.

The *Republic* closes with another myth that has still another referential structure, the myth of Er. Plato had early adduced the principle in accordance with which no single thing is comparable to the way the just man is to be presented, and therefore, many things are needed to express it (488). The myth of Er, as a myth of the afterlife incorporating Greek traditions and not merely invented like the other two complex images, looks to a future in which we may no longer separate the real from the imagined.[16] We do not live in a cave, but in some sense, Plato asserts, we are to see the Sirens atop their spindles in the astronomically bounded afterlife. In the myth of Er Plato concludes by creating a convergence between his three areas of authority, abstract statements, and myths with mathematical correlatives. All these come together in music, in the harmony of the spheres—the term *harmony* being both geometric and musical—a music the very Fates also are singing.

Dante, too, is a thinker, a philosophical poet who presents his ideas through a progressive network of images. The fourfold system of signification, in which the literal sense is distinguished from the allegorical, the moral, and the anagogical, is made to provide in his hands a convergence for all four senses. The randomness of ordinary medieval allegory has been left behind. His "fiction" is "composed" to use his own words.[17] So for any given image, even if we are unable to provide one or more of the four senses, that particular sense is still present in the conception as a formal blank or zero degree of signification. The bearing of such coherent complexity refers to the entire work for its solution, and then to the conception of the entire work. The passage Dante himself used in the letter to Can Grande constitutes the clear image, enlisting sight and sound but not synesthetically, of souls singing a psalm in a boat while an angel-pilot automatically moves it:

> Da poppa stava il celestial nocchiero
> Tal che parea beato per iscripto
> E più di cento spirti entro sediero.
> *In exitu Israel de Aegypto*
> Cantavan tutti insieme ad una voce
> (*Purgatorio* 3.43–47)

As he says, "if we look to the letter only, there is signified for us the exodus of the sons of Israel in the time of Moses; if to the allegory there is signified for us our redemption performed by Christ; if to the moral sense there is signified for us the conversion of the soul from the lament and misery of sin to a state of grace; if to the anagogic, there is signified for us the exodus of the holy soul from the servitude of this corruption to the freedom of eternal liberty" (*Epistulae* 10.145–54). All of this, of course, is standard. What I wish to throw into relief is the implication of this mighty, comprehensive procedure as a test for a theory of the significance that may reside in images. As though aware of such questions, Dante repeats the expression *significatur* or *significatur nobis* four times. If the senses may be separated out for the psalm sung by the passengers, their very singing presents too full a convergence for a more than formal separation of the senses. And when dealing with angels—creatures who are not only images but real, eternal beings for Dante—we can no longer distinguish between the fact of beatitude and the light and beauty that amount to it in the angel's presence, any more than we can distinguish between appearing *beato* (blest), and having the word itself written all over the creature, *beato per iscripto* (blest in writing).

It does not matter how arbitrarily we reconstruct, or deconstruct, Dante's images. In his intentional universe of discourse their complexities and contractions—he characterizes them both of these ways (*Ep.* 10.185, 235)—serve a coherence which in turn serves a dimension of speculation that does not merely refer its signifiers back to their starting point. If they are not taken as dealing with explaining the world, they are not being dealt with at the base of their assumption.

Dante is at pains to make sure we are aware of the constant presence of a rational substructure. In later poetry that he might have characterized as an attempt to reproduce angelic speech, to be *beato per iscripto,* the rational substructure is bypassed and we are given a direct "logic of images." Rimbaud enters such a realm even in his haunting poems of childhood, and more thoroughly than in the colors he assigns to vowels.[18] The quasi-allegorical *Le Bateau Ivre* launches a line of sheer disconnected images where a million birds in the superlative condition of being gold evoke an invocation that links them somehow to an energy of the future: "Million d'oiseaux d'or, ô future Vigueur." A separation between tenor and vehicle cannot be made here, nor an allegorical tenor be assigned to the capitalized *Vigueur*. Nor can a classification scheme be introduced where the possibility of a scheme has been obscured, and there are also no categories offered whereby we may deduce that this metaphor is a category mistake. The absence of a verb between them prohibits our resting firmly upon a predication connecting the gold birds with the vigor—or excluding that connection. And both can be read, either of them metaphorically, with the two verbs in the preceding line: "Est-ce en ces nuits sans fond que tu dors et t'exiles. / Million d'oiseaux d'or, ô future Vigueur?"

Series of connections, at the same time, are mounted by the logic of images, as for example in the sequence of poems that announces its own special and archaizing magical properties, "L'alchimie du verbe."

In this group, characterized as "Délires," and further as a section of "Une Saison en enfer," the poems are framed by what amounts to a third characterization, a prose account of their modality: "J'écrivais des silences, des nuits, je notais l'inexprimable. Je fixais des vertiges." All this framing qualifies the immediately ensuing poem away from the pastoral reminiscence that firmly sets the tone; "Loin des oiseaux, des troupeaux, des villageoises, / Que buvais-je, à genoux dans cette bruyère," "Far from birds, flocks, villagers, / What did I drink on my knees in this heather." What he drank was a gold liquor that made him sweat, and the last lines make it, too, fade in reminiscence: "Pleurant, je voyais de l'or—et ne pus boire—." The armorers in the next poem work in the sun of the Hesperides, and prepare *lambris précieux*. The next, "Le Chanson de la plus haute tour" is called an *espèce de romance;* it names the thirst of the first poem and touches on something of the exaltation of the second. The fourth poem, "Faim," turns from liquid to rocks for the diet but still mentions Solomon as an echo of the Babylon of the second poem, and it ends with a nourishing liquid, "Le bouillon court sur la rouille, / Et se mêle au Cédron." "The broth runs on the rust / and mixes with the Kedron." The next poem, more delighted in tone, declares that eternity has been found as sea mixed with sun—a version of the Hesperides, and the phrase "braises de satin" continues the note of luxury. The sixth and last poem, "ô saisons, ô châteaux! Quelle âme est sans défauts?" touches on images and ideas. that appear in all five prior poems.

Much has been written about these mysterious poems, of course, and it is not my intention to extend any specific interpretations, but rather, by way of indicating the faint correspondence of images and nascent coherences from poem to poem, to raise the question of what sort of significative function they declare they are performing.

For Rimbaud, as for the three other writers I have drawn on, the image, whether in the form of metaphor or no, is not just used to signify. It is also used to focus and to center; it has a normative function. Yet as these examples spendidly demonstrate, there is no one normative function under which we can subsume their practice, no algorithm that can describe any one. In order to make sense of an image in any one of these writers, we must make sense of his entire work, and beyond that of the conception of signification it implies. One could not proceed to these complexities by analyzing them back into simple communicative forms because the symbols themselves in each instance depend on the entire conception of the complex individual communicative act.[19]

3

Symbol is the honorific word, stressing as it does either the strong communicative function in the image or its expressive connection to some complex or powerful area of reference. The term is used by anthropologists for some image or image-laden act that draws together a wide range of phenomena.[20] And of course the poets of the Romantic experience and later invested the symbol with considerable hypostatic power The images in the visual arts may be called symbols, though their relative lack of involvement in unambiguous lexical references and syntactic combinations makes them at once more direct and more mysterious than verbal presentations.

Using *image* as a central term will narrow our focus away from the large communicative and expressive questions raised by *symbol.* More crucially, it will serve to hold our attention on what it is that stands at the heart of these communicative and expressive questions. *Image,* too, for all its complexity, is less slippery than a term like *metonymy,* that current jack-of-all-work which is also a jack-in-the-box of tautology, since references named in a sequent language must perforce be contiguous to each other, and almost any kind of contiguity can be called metonymy.

Valéry, very much in line with his contemporary Husserl's distinction between empirical and abstract ideas,[21] deduces an unwavering and subtle principle of recursive form behind the arts of poetry and architecture, enabling it to frame and even to exalt its images through an instinctive proportionateness. Gombrich emphasizes the manipulation of constructive cues in the activity of the viewer, who is energically asked, as though all art were Op Art, to put together the harmonies of recursive form.[22] Principles of organization, however, illuminating as they may be, leave in obscurity the force and direction of the image as it transcends the lexical summary of its significations. Semioticians like Mukarovsky, Eco, and Lotman, by different means, though they isolate the transcendence of prior codes in the achieved art work, all direct their attention to the interaction of codes. A great deal can be said about the handling of codes, and the discursive nature of language itself leads the questioner to ask how the images are manipulated by the codes. Indeed, what follows here is largely a discussion of what may be deduced from such manipulations about the significative properties of the image. Moreover, the manifest self-presentation of the image, as theorists of both "Symbolist" poetry and "Expressionist" art had been insisting all along, accords the image, even the color, a finality that resists discussion. If we are to talk about images without undue schematism or immediate hypostatizing, the means must be found to keep that finality steadily in view.

And while the finality is kept steadily in view, an apprehended sense that resists finality resides between the image and the meanings it encodes, or the chords that it strikes. Between *discourse* and *figure*—to adopt the terms of J. F. Lyotard[23]—there may be seen to operate, as Lyotard's intricate discussions manipulate them, the large oppositions of modern epistemology: absence and presence, sense and reference, self and other, desire and object. All of these terms, however, could be made to circle the image.

Such a process involves not only Romantic and post-Romantic

poets.[24] The very presence of intellection, in Donne or Cavalcanti, serves to draw tight a systemic net around a presentation of images whose finality comes into only ornamental qualification and intensification through "rhetorical," and even through musical, manipulation. When we have got past rhetoric and music, we are left with image.

Patently musical and rhetorical are, for example, the concluding lines of a poem by a notable thinker-in-images, Andrew Marvell's "Upon Appleton House." Yet the music and the rhetoric are transcended in and by its final image, which is not of Appleton House or its grounds but of some seemingly incidental salmon fishers, who come to occupy the whole last stanza. Moreover, the image has a religious force as well, but not a direct one. Indeed, as in other matters connected with religiosity, the religious force of an image cannot be decided as a case of simple presence or simple absence. Such a notion would be too simple even for early cultural uses. Homer, firmly grounded in an Olympian religion, aims his images differently from those in the Rig Veda. Still different is the interaction between a scriptural command against graven images in the Old Testament and the enlistment of deep images in Hebrew prophecy and Wisdom literature. Nor does the Confucian Anthology, though its particular connection to an early religious impulse is obscure, correspond in any imaginable way to these religious investments of image from other cultures.

Similarly, the formulae applied to Romantic and modern poetry— "the gradual disappearance of God," "the transfer of function from religion to art"—are too crude to do justice to the religious implications of their manipulations of image. The religious presence is considerably and variously modified in Pindar, Plato, Dante, and Rimbaud—to list the figures whose use of image I have discussed above. The religious dimension has not disappeared or been transferred in modern poetry either, for all the indirectness of its "numinous" presence. The considerable dialectic surrounding Rilke's angels, the submerged religiosity in Trakl, and the condensed religiosity in the images of Celan, involve extremely indirect, but also extremely numinous, force in the images.

Between the direct uses of Dante and the oblique modern ones, we may take Marvell as instanced in this particular passage, the Milton of *Paradise Regained,* and Emily Dickinson, as cases where a distinct, original, and considerably manipulated theological application of images appears.

In an epoch much given to elaborate allegorization and emblemizing, in literature and in art,[25] the traditions of the "Renaissance imagination" still do not offer very helpful cues for explaining the effect of such a strange image as that of the salmon fishers. These salmon fishers are less than allegory or an emblem, or a rich metaphor, in structure, while more in the comprehensiveness, and in the very elusiveness, of their effect:

> But now the *Salmon-Fisher's* moist
> Their *Leathern Boats* begin to hoist;
> And like *Antipodes* in Shoes,
> Have shod their *Heads* in their *Canoos.*
> How *Tortoise* like, but not so slow
> These rational *Amphibii* go?
> Let's in: for the dark *Hemisphere*
> Does now like one of them appear.

The twilight invocation to retreat is Vergilian, a pastoral note permuted with the "witty hyperbole" of Cleveland, whose tone Leishman traces in Marvell generally.[26] Specifically Marvell borrowed the shod head and the antipodes from Cleveland, as Leishman informs us, but Cleveland simply uses it for a witty description of a lawyer's hat:

> The Calot Leather-cap strongly pleads,
> And fain would derive the pedigree of fashion.
> The antipodes wear their shoes on their heads,
> And why may not we in their imitation?
> ("Square-Caps" 17–20)

For Marvell's powerful image we can find, really, only a partial iconographic predecessor in Cleveland. Indeed, part of the force of the image resides in its novelty, in its implied arbitrariness, its total freedom from iconographic context. And even from iconographic usage. The freedom, in fact, reinforces the hyperbole: Marvell is high-flown enough to be arbitrary. Yet in the tone the pastoral "checks" the hyperbole; we are offered a decrescendo in the form of something intensely visible, human beings so strange in their appearance that we must turn normal categories topsy-turvy somewhat along the lines of medieval *adunata:* the "Heads" are "shod" as feet normally are, and in that which is normally a conveyance rather than a bit of gear, a conveyance several times larger than a shoe (as the "Calot Leather-cap" is not), and so itself anomalous. These boats are not only upside down: they are walking; they move spasmodically in air above their passengers instead of evenly below them in water. These are logical contradictions. Another such contradiction enters the language explicitly: the fishers are not only antipodal. The antipodes contain people who act not contradictorily at all, but merely in an opposite but homologous manner on the other side of the world. They are also amphibious. That final description comprises a double contradiction or "paradox" (the term used in LX, line 473): they are *"rational* amphibii," whereas in nature itself amphibii are only nonrational. And they are amphibii, whereas men are solidly terrestrial. The visual image of a sight to be seen in nature verges on the counternatural, perhaps with intimations of the supernatural, wholly muffled here.[27] And there is a latent contradiction between antipodes on the other side of the globe and the hemisphere we are told we can see, which the fishers resemble.

The amphibious image is prepared for in stanzas LIX-LX, where the flooding of the fields and its attendant paradox earlier in the poem are described, a description culminating in a simpler form of the salmon association. Here, though, it is not complexly darkening salmon fishermen in their natural activity that are brought into view, but salmon in an unnatural position:

> How Boats can over Bridges sail;
> And Fishes do the Stables scale.
> How *Salmons* trespassing are found;
> And Pikes are taken in the Pound.

This image relates to the tradition of *adunata* or topsy-turvy images. It may also be felt to anticipate a procedure in Surrealism, or even that of Proust's fictional Elstir, who in his paintings causes land and water to interfuse.

In the image of the salmon fishermen Marvell moves us out to the edge of Appleton House's extensive domains. We are made to envision to the verge where land gives way to water. Thus, by implication, we have begun an encyclopedia, or at least a terrestrial sphere. Two stanzas earlier a wide conspectus of space and time is touched on: "Thessalian Tempe's seat," "Aranjuez," "Bel Retiro," "Idalian grove," "Elysian Fields." These are by way of comparison. The final comparison is not of Appleton House to any other fine country location, actual or mythological, but rather of one of the salmon fishers as night falls to the "dark hemisphere." The topsy-turvy man comes to look like the whole visible darkened sky. But the resemblance obtains only because he is wearing on his head, as of all men only these professionals would do, an object having a large curvature that extends beyond him symmetrically. The sky, of course, is immeasurably larger than the fisherman's overturned coracle. The vision expands; or rather, in the evoked darkness, the scale is erased by which one could distinguish between expansion and contraction in space. A similar operation has been performed in time, because "Upon Appleton House" begins with a century and more of the history of the mansion, which was converted from sacred to secular uses after a nun had been induced to leave a convent. But the end of the poem treats only the end of the day. There is even, in these salmon fishers, an apocalyptic note, a suggestion of some final universe, and perhaps of the Flood. They are moist, whereas men are normally dry. And they move at a speed like amphibious sea creatures, "tortoise-like but not so slow." The poem itself, too, Marvell's longest poem, is at once faster than the progress of the day that it invokes and yet rather deliberate in the buildup of its couplets.

The salmon fishers are distinct but plural in their first odd visual presentation. They are blurred but singular in the second and last one that merges them into a geometric figure representing the arched vault of the visible, darkening cosmos. At the edge of the world, they are perceived at the center of it. They carry with them all the mythology that clings to the exotic other who is a semblable:

the antipodes. And, in that connection, they evoke many "symbolic" functions: the social classes (salmon fishers are far more humble than Marvell or Lord Fairfax, owner of Appleton House); the related distribution of labor into "natural" and "cultural," food gathering against composing verses and ruling men; the role of the fisher in folklore, as that role includes the most famous fishers of all, the Disciples who were the Fishers of Men (there are religious data at the beginning of the poem, a religious use for Appleton House in its first phase).

Salmon fishers here are associated with three hemispherical figures, only one of which is metonymically related to them: the overturned "canoe," the tortoise, and the hemisphere of the night sky. This series brings to expression a macrocosm-microcosm relationship for the fishers, while their "moistness," their immersion in the element where they gain their living, carries with it some subliminal suggestion of the primal Ocean that Marvell elsewhere refers to, where world and amniotic fluid and ground of conception are one ("The Mind, that Ocean where each Kind / Does streight its own resemblance find"). Yet at the same time it is the odd, arch point of the poem that these fishers are disjunct. They stand at the edge of the poem, as of our perceptions. They have nothing to do with the large, fixed house, the vast but delimited grounds, that are the poet's nominal subject. They are an off-focus refocusing of the mysteries he wishes to figure forth by trailing richly off with this intense image he slips upon us as he thrusts it upon us.

Unlike "The Garden," this poem offers few metaphysical speculations. Yet I would submit that this strange final image of the salmon fishers is a condensed piece of metaphysical thought not just decipherable into its component resumptions of antithesis. The very insistence on its oddity, and above all on the firmly visual inferences of its presentation, subverts any role it might have of encoding nodal complications of signification. These, we may say, are part of its rhetoric. Beyond all this rhetoric the image itself persists, in its fusion of exaggeration and understatement, so fully that it at once caps and undermines the mere praise of a noble house. It is as symbolic as anything in Rimbaud or Mallarmé. And it has its religiosity, as does the work of the other two also. Mallarmé, particularly in the

Tombeaux, expresses pieties summed up through images, by means of a style that constantly displays strong marks of a meditation bearing elements of the devotional.[28] Rimbaud's image-encoded thought carries a religious orientation and frame.[29] The salmon fishers are *there,* at once outside and within the coherent rhetorical circle of the poem.

4

Milton, too, like his contemporary Marvell, powerfully transmuted his images in an attention to religious implications. How much he did so will be apparent if we apply some conventional senses of the term *image* to his latest work, *Paradise Regained.* First, the image can be taken to mean an item of imagery in the sense of Caroline Spurgeon, an image joining a number of similar ones in the course of a work to produce a pattern of embedded visual congruences. Barbara Lewalski finds several of these in *Paradise Regained*—rocks versus air, light versus dark, hunger versus food, and a martial imagery that might be opposed to peace.[30] One could augment this list: vegetation versus desert waste, for one. These images tend to enter into patterns of opposition, patterns that certainly exist on a larger and more explicit scale in *Paradise Lost,* where, to begin with, the anguished dark and turmoil of Hell stands in large contrast to the light and jubilation of Heaven. The situation is more complicated as well as more ample in *Paradise Lost,* because in Paradise itself the two contrasts interpenetrate—the contrast of present to future in the garden, and the contrast of past to present in our vision of the garden. In the main action of *Paradise Lost,* the ensuing structure of paradox tends to twist out of shape, and a protracted analysis of image congruences would certainly show this. So would the sort of analysis of image effect by sequential presentation, about which Stanley Fish sensitively teaches while trying to lead us down the garden path of the reader's infinite regress.[31]

In a second sense of image, an image taken singly and by itself will have its own internal rhetorical and propositional structure. This is, of course, a vast and intricate topic; but without getting deeply into the logic of the questions it generally raises, one may notice a difference in the number of single images between the two poems. *Paradise Lost* is obviously the more lush, and it also happens to enlist more frequently that protraction of image known as the epic simile.

The most pronounced and climactic of the similes in *Paradise Regained* is the comparison of the confounded Satan to Antaeus and then to the Sphinx (*PR* 4.562–76). These similes compare one defeat to another; "But Satan smitten with amazement fell," and Milton's somewhat amplified account of the other two defeats follows. The account is also somewhat abstract. It contains elements that could be called visual, but it does not dwell on, and itself amplify, visual detail and visual correspondences, as do the similes in *Paradise Lost.* The same may be said of another comparison of one abstraction to another, earlier in Book Four. This is a comparison of one kind of persistent trouble to another. These similes are consciously Homeric, but they consistently avoid the pronounced visualization and vehicle spillover of the Homeric similes:

> But as a man who had been matchless held
> In cunning, over-reach't where least he thought,
> To salve his credit, and for very spight
> Still will be tempting him who foyls him still,
> And never cease, though to his shame the more;
> Or as a swarm of flies in vintage time
> About the wine-press where sweet moust is powr'd,
> Beat off, returns as oft with humming sound;
> Or surging waves against a solid rock,
> Though all to shivers dash't, the assault renew,
> Vain battry, and in froth or bubbles end:
> So Satan . . .
>
> (*PR* 4.10–21)

The visual gets no deep hold here. We have "froth or bubbles," alternate items. In *Paradise Lost,* on the other hand, a shift from one visual, or sensible, state to another is often a spiritual shift as well as a physical, accompanied by many plasticities of poetic attribution.[32] In this passage, too, many senses are present, but their effect is not of profusion. Rather, a sort of coordination holds them in check—as the Savior has been held in check from indulging in food or yielding to images of power. *Sweet* relates to taste, *swarm* to sight, *humming* to hearing, and it may even be said that *wine-press* implies touch. Smell alone is left, and smell would be strong for one standing near a full winepress, though smell is unmentioned here. *Dash't* could imply either sight or sound, and the alternatives tend, again, to mute each other rather than to allow an amplification of image.[33]

Moving away from figurative language, there is a third sense of image as a sort of overall focus at a point in the poem. Christ stands in an actual landscape of which an image is constructed, as do Adam and Eve. He is in a wilderness, they are in a garden. At points in both poems an overall focus is offered to the protagonist. Satan shows Christ a view of Rome (4.25–42). Michael shows Adam a view of the whole earth (*PL* 11.375–422) from a hill, and this situation is explicitly compared to the situation of *Paradise Regained:*

> It was a Hill . . .
> Not higher that Hill nor wider looking round,
> Whereon for different cause the Tempter set
> Our second *Adam* in the Wilderness
> To show him all Earths Kingdoms and their Glory.
> (*PL* 11.377–84)

The use of overall focus in general, and its enlistment within a dramatic context, are specially characteristic of Milton's poetry, though also a feature of epic style generally. More common to all poetry is local focus—the naming, without recourse to figurative language, of something in the course of the poem that has visual properties. This fourth kind of image is a sensitive area for Milton from the beginning. I have elsewhere noted the originality of the visual imagery even in his youthful translations from the Psalms which amplify their Hebrew original in a visual direction.[34] The poet who says his Swain "twitch'd his Mantle blew" in the final rhyme of *Lycidas* is placing a strange and powerful emphasis on the color blue which cannot be wholly accounted for by studying the rich iconography of that color in Renaissance usage.

The term *iconography,* of course, may refer not only to such

particular significations but to the staple subject chosen by the poet,
a fifth sense of the term *image*. This is what Roland Frye, who docu-
ments it elaborately for Milton, calls "the vocabulary of visual
images."[35] Milton, like a painter, presents us with an image of
Adam and Eve being tempted and expelled from the Garden. These
are conventional subjects, shown on the sculptured portals and
pillars of scores of medieval churches, as well as notably in the
works of painters from Masaccio to Rubens. The Temptation of
Christ is much less common: it seems to resist visual representation,
just as Milton keeps in check for *Paradise Regained* the visual elements that are noteworthy elsewhere in his poetry. To be sure, the
Temptations might be included in a very large repertory of images
for the Life of Christ. They appear twice at Chartres, for example:
once in a group of thirty-eight scenes on the West portal and once
in a window on the South aisle of the ambulatory that represents
separately each of the three Temptations. Or Milton could have seen
his third Temptation on a panel of the North gate of Ghiberti's
Bronze Doors.[36] Still, Chartres is a sort of iconographic encyclopedia, as are the Bronze Doors. The Temptations are singled out
as little there as they are in Crashaw's Latin epigram on them:

> Ergo ille, Angelicis, o sarcina dignior alis,
> Praepete sic Stygio sic volet ille vehi?
> Pessime! nec laetare tamen. tu scilicet inde
> Non minus es Daemon, non minus ille Deus.

> So he, O burden more worthy than angels' wings,
> Thus by Stygian bird thus he will wish to be borne?
> Wretch, still do not rejoice. Clearly for that
> You are no less Demon, he no less is God.

In one sense this single quatrain of Crashaw's resumes *Paradise
Regained*. Yet it is not only short; it is one among many statements,
like the panels at Chartres. Milton has chosen to make a single
statement about the whole redemption, and he has chosen to center
it on a moderately infrequent iconographic subject. He has taken
his license from the typological identification between an Old Testament figure and Christ (which might be called, incidentally, a sixth

sense of *image,* Auerbach's *figura*).[37] Still, Job does not enter into typological comparison as often as David, say. The long tradition of classifying Job as a brief epic would still not dictate that for his brief epic Milton choose that point of Christ's life most analogous to Job. Nor is Milton's style much like that of the Book of Job, as this deep student of the Bible would have known well.

There are many differences between *Paradise Regained* and Job— so many that Milton's "humanist" adduction of the Biblical "brief epic" is more honorific than it is illuminating about his own poem. With regard to imagery, Job offers a poetry much stranger and more condensed than anything in *Paradise Regained.* It is a high example from a tradition distinct from either of the two Indo-European traditions, themselves arguably quite divergent, that I shall discuss in the afterword to this volume.

> Hast thou given the horse strength?
> Hast thou clothed his neck with thunder?
> Canst thou make him afraid as a grasshopper?
> The glory of his snorting *is* terrible.
>   [Lit. "terror," *"e'mah"*]
>   (Job 39.19–20, King James version)

The second of these lines synesthetically merges a tossing mane with an audible portent over the whole sky. The third line is almost Picasso-like in its disengagement of rapid visual effects from two animals whose similarity is, strikingly, the more purely visual for having only this point of contact: the legs of a leaping horse, taken globally, look like the legs of a leaping grasshopper. The fourth line links two Hebrew abstractions, *glory* and *terror,* through a single sensual attribute, *snorting.* None of these effects can be paralleled in *Paradise Regained,* or in Milton generally.

In what must correctly be felt to be the figural as well as the tonal consistency of *Paradise Regained,* the distinction between allegory and mimesis is too crude. The poem's visual images of Rome and Jerusalem, for example, have both allegorical and mimetic properties. Rome and Jerusalem stand for something, they are allegorical; they are at the same time real places, their depiction is variously mimetic. And the actual presentation has many subtleties throughout, for which we have really so far just tried to lay out the

defining conditions. The effects remain to be accounted for. Take
the description of Rome, or part of it:

> He brought our Saviour to the western side
> Of that high mountain, whence he might behold
> Another plain, long but in bredth not wide;
> Wash'd by the Southern Sea, and on the North
> To equal length back'd with a ridge of hills,
> That screen'd the fruits of the earth and seats of men
> From cold *Septentrion* blasts, thence in the midst
> Divided by a river, of whose banks
> On each side an Imperial City stood,
> With Towers and Temples proudly elevate
> On seven small Hills, with Palaces adorn'd,
> Porches and Theatres, Baths, Aqueducts,
> Statues and Trophees and Triumphal Arcs,
> Gardens and Groves presented to his eyes,
> Above the highth of Mountains interpos'd.
> By what strange Parallax or Optic skill
> Of vision multiplyed through air, or glass
> Of Telescope, wee curious to enquire:
>
> (4.225–42)

Satan's further description adds hyperbole to this one, as well
as qualification. He speaks of a microscope, the narrating poet of a
telescope. The laws of "Parallax" employed, and named but not
explicitly identified, introduce perspectival techniques of the science
of the day. These laws resemble those of a common aid to perception that Renaissance painters used in constructing proportionate
imagery, the *camera obscura*. Some painters active in England during Milton's time used it, as did Vermeer, who was also Milton's
contemporary.

The bare naming of "Porches and Theatres" and so forth in this
account accords with the figurative curtness of *Paradise Regained*,
and it is not entirely foreign to the proportionate literalness in Vermeer's nearly contemporaneous *View of Delft*. The names offer
minimal images, the type images of the architectural staples that
they designate, strung together in only a metrical order to label the

shapes of the buildings of Rome as they might be seen. The scale is reminiscent of such paintings as the topographic view in the Sala del Mappemundo of the Palazzo Pubblico in Siena, which Milton might have seen, or the similar panoramas of Italy in a corridor of the Vatican. In this passage the image has been reduced to topographical inventory. Correspondingly, little use is made of the hyperbaton found elsewhere in the poem, a hyperbaton whose capacities for distorting images Fish has so actively described.

The images, or the lexically implied proto-images, of this passage are quite far over on the general side of the general-to-specific scale that Wayne Shumaker has devised for Milton's imagery.[38] Yet they do not just happen to be general, any more than the brief description of Jerusalem happens to be figural. Milton's theology, taken all around, is fairly conventional: his originality appears in the poem through the instinct that deploys images for local effect and for overall focus.

The antistyle of *Paradise Regained*, in fact, by varying and at the same time restricting its deployment of images, undercuts the traditional distinction of styles. In *Paradise Regained* Milton is grand, medium, and low all at once. On his theological ground, as in his handling of images, he manages to get past the Renaissance criteria of stylistic decorum for these three styles as expounded by Bembo, Tasso, and others.[39] These criteria justify the use of *durezza* in Tasso, and they sanction, as Prince has shown us, the abruptness of Milton's sonnets—and indeed their virtual absence of imagery. So their models, the sonnets of della Casa, have little recourse to imagery. But in *Paradise Regained*, again, Milton has managed to modify this abruptness while retaining it, and he has done so by virtue of modulating his presentation of images.

In this particular negative sense, of removal from the three classical styles, Milton in *Paradise Regained* may be said to capture something of the style of Isaiah and Job. Or, in visual analogy, he may be said to offer at once the space-filling solidity of Poussin (d. 1665), and the effects of mysterious light and dark of Rembrandt (d. 1669). Wylie Sypher's suggestive alignment of Milton with Baroque and late-Baroque procedures in architecture and painting, even if we accept it, can be said to succeed in naming only organizational constituents of the poem. In the case of Milton the particular mix offered by the poem, its particular structure of vision, is distinct not only for the given poet but, as Sypher does assert of Milton, from poem to poem within the work itself.[40] Spenser's presentation is steady, where Milton's is variable, even within the limits he sets himself. Spenser is uniformly figurative, Milton only incidentally so in presenting his images, general or specific. The images in Milton tend to separate, and yet the underlying vision coordinates them to what he would have us register. Milton cannot, in *Paradise Regained,* be assimilated to the method of "mosaic," the laying of separate image next to image, the *intarsie* that Galileo finds in Tasso. In Milton's final "brief epic," we are left with the effect of the poem, to which the images of the poem, rudimentary as they are, remain mysteriously intrinsic while at the same time residually intractable to the critical approaches we may bring to bear upon them.[41]

5

In the many developments of premodern usage, Emily Dickinson offers an especially powerful example of a poet who thinks in images. So, for that matter, does her contemporary Whitman, who has a deep visual streak, cast the very first form of the project that grew into *Leaves of Grass* as an expansive, potentially encyclopedic descriptive list of paintings in a gallery, the long unfinished poem "Pictures." And in his mature work he approaches at times the Luminism of the artists who were his contemporaries. As for Dickinson herself, like Milton, she uses poetic imaging for theological clarification, but she does so much more explicitly, and, perhaps correspondingly, with much less recourse to baroque modifications of the image. There is, then, a systematic as well as a historical reason for her relative simplicity. Where poets like Novalis and others invested their religious thought in a hypostatization of the symbol, she manipulates her images so as to produce a theological dialectic. As Geoffrey Hartman has pointed out, a form may occasionally be traced in her work of the three-step process that Wordsworth foregrounds more explicitly, whereby the image first is perceived, and then blanks out, and then is retrieved in some altered, more revelatory form.[42] Dickinson thereby engages in a sort of imaginal syllogism, put at the service of the apperception of last things. In this practice, I have tried to show elsewhere, "The relation in these poems between the metaphoric and the literal is potentially to be superseded by a heavenly perspective and its concomitants of different rules for signification."[43]

There is considerable slippage in Dickinson's work from one image to another, but this slippage itself both exemplifies and examines the central slippage in human life, the slippage towards some other state. In this way, as for Wordsworth too, the process of thought is subjected to a total imaginal reorientation.

This may happen in very short compass indeed, as in poem 633:

> When Bells stop ringing—Church—begins—
> The Positive—of Bells—
> When Cogs—stop—that's Circumference—
> The Ultimate—of Wheels.

The sound of bells and the spatial measure, the circumference of wheels, are here at once paralleled and differentiated, while being firmly rooted in the perception of their characteristic activity, a ringing in one case and a spinning in the other. Bells are deduced to be the opposite, or preliminary, of a "Positive." *Church* is the "Positive" of bells, and so their ringing would be something like a negative. As sound to sight, so bells to cogs. As church to mechanisms, so a "Positive" to an "Ultimate." The dizzying series here, based on an imaginal process, has the air of providing entries for some theological lexicon of the true spiritual function of the things of this world. The things imaged are attached to four abstractions, themselves set up in a double opposition, a "Positive" and whatever its opposite would be, as against an "Ultimate" and whatever its opposite would be.

This powerful attempt at definition-through-images, as by a more strenuous Wallace Stevens, may be observed operating at greater length and with more explicit deductive rhetoric in poem 575:

> "Heaven" has different Signs—to me—
> Sometimes, I think that Noon

Is but a symbol of the Place—
And when again, at Dawn,

A mighty look runs round the World
And settles in the Hills,—
An Awe if it should be like that
Upon the Ignorance steals—

The Orchard, when the Sun is on—
The Triumph of the Birds
When they together Victory make—
Some Carnivals of Clouds—

The Rapture of the finished Day—
Returning to the West—
All these—remind us of the place
That Men call "Paradise"—

Itself be fairer—we suppose—
But how Ourself, shall be
Adorned, for a Superior Grace—
Not yet, our eyes can see—

Here the progress of the day is not even; noon comes before dawn. And the traditional devout ascription of divine significance to the visible world is here at once affirmed and amplified by considerable qualification in the very first line, with its puzzling quotation marks, " 'Heaven' has different Signs—to me—." The *sign* is a conventional enough theological term, with a history going back through St. Paul to the Old Testament, not to mention its Greek derivation from Homer on.[44] Here the first statement is of a differentiation. A special temper, and even a special kind of signification, haunts each of the moments singled out. "Noon / Is but a symbol of the Place," while at dawn we have "a mighty look" that "runs round the World." Very soon, by virtue of the light's being perceived, we move into one of Dickinson's preternatural psychological observations, "An Awe if it should be like that / Upon the Ignorance steals—." Just as it might be if we had no clocks, or no other barriers of measurement between ourselves and the raw experience, we cannot tell, at this point or in stanza three, whether we have moved to a further stage, as noon is further than dawn. It is possible that we are being treated only to further aspects of the same perception. It is all the same, for in any case names like *Noon* and *Dawn* have now dropped away in favor of celebratory participations, *Triumph, Victory,* and *Carnivals.* The first two words have a Biblical usage, and the last is easily assimilable to the religious celebration.

The famous "Because I could not stop for Death" derives the sense of the afterlife—and the fact that it is the afterlife—from a series of progressively more revelatory imaginal perceptions, finishing with one that still links eternity to what lies beyond the horses' heads, "Since then 'tis Centuries, but each / Feels shorter than the Day / I first surmised the Horses Heads / Were toward Eternity—" (712). There is a final dash, as though to mark the onward pointing of the horses' heads. Each century *feels* shorter not than the day of death, but the day on which death registered; a capital change of the same nature, we may say, as the humble yet awesome observations that Dickinson aligns in the poem we have just looked at.

Poem 601 is based on a cliché of the nineteenth-century popular imagination, Naples and the nearby Vesuvius, seen not through Leopardi, certainly, but probably through popular prints:

> A still—Volcano—Life—
> That flickered in the night—
> When it was dark enough to do
> Without erasing sight—
>
> A quiet—Earthquake Style—
> Too subtle to suspect
> By natures this side Naples—
> The North cannot detect
>
> The Solemn—Torrid—Symbol—
> The lips that never lie—
> Whose hissing Corals part—and shut—
> And Cities—ooze away—

The identifications of the other poems are subsumed in this one (or conversely they in it). The saying, See Naples and then die, may also underlie the poem, which makes the existence of the volcano near a city something like evidence that can be adopted in a repository of ultimate resemblances, so as to validate the metaphor that life is like a sleeping volcano. The mouth of the volcano becomes "lips that never lie." For it to speak is for it to utter doom, "Whose hissing Corals part—and shut— / And Cities—ooze away—." These hissing Corals remain, as well, imaginal. Their message is our visual and audible perception of them, and not any words, the strange portent of "hissing Corals." And even the death is not a flashing moment, but the aftermath of an eruption, a slowing lava flow, "Cities—ooze away." But the word *ooze* is not fixed in place. As often with Dickinson, the word yields and totters before alternative possibilities. Here *slip, slide,* and *melt* are her variant readings. The word itself suffers something akin to the approximations of her imaginal thinking.

6

This book attempts to come at the choice of such figures by keeping in view the fundament of image making at least partially shared by the verbal and the nonverbal arts. There is, to begin with, inside the *langue* at a given stage, an implied power and range of visual possibility. Taking early examples, I have examined the similes of Homer as realizations of a context present in some ways in early Greek visual artifacts. I have contrasted them with the similes of the Rig Veda, generally but loosely thought of as comparable because they derive from the same large linguistic tradition. This long look at work that is still at some distance from imaginable origins I mean to serve as a comprehensive background to the modern confrontations of what are still arguably similar problems. Since many readers will wish to consider at this point the imaging in modern poetry, I have placed the chapter "Visual Aspects of the Homeric Simile in Indo-European Context," which is initial in both a historical and a systematic sense, as an afterword.

Prevailingly, indeed, I do discuss several modern poets in whom the theory about metaphor, intricate imaginal procedures, and (persistently but less obviously) a special access to the visual arts move to the center of large-scale cognitive and musical strategies. Rilke,

Pound, Arp, Apollinaire, Breton, Char, Éluard, Celan, Williams, Merwin, Ashbery, O'Hara, Olson, and Creeley are among those whose activities as poets make balanced sense only if a proper latitude, without prior postulates, be accorded the figural choices they have splendidly bound in words.

This book broaches three areas: the theory of image, the analogues for enlisting the significances of images between poetry and the visual arts, and the structural preconceptions of some poetry, mostly modern. While these three areas mutually illuminate each other, I am convinced that they best do so in a loose presentation. I do not, then, offer a lock-step sequence of logical demonstration, nor do I produce the single key of doctrine that such a demonstration would imply. I am not sure there is such a key available. At the same time I would not wish to imply a decentering impulse, or a simple lack of center, to the signifying power of images. On the contrary, it is the strength of such radiant centers to resist partial extrapolations. Images, rendered significant, provide not provisional accommodations but convincing access.

III

Aspects of the Plastic Image
Rilke, Pound, and Arp

> That is, I knew sculpture was buried, was become the art underneath us all, had gone down to be our sign—by a sort of inverted archeology—that each of us had now to come up live, like those stone images scholars are digging up in so many places; that only by ourselves can we find out—by no outside medium or means whatsoever—the round all men have been rifled of.
>
> —Charles Olson

The image at once hides and offers its act of communication. In the special case of metaphor, the image makes this feature, its simultaneous concealment and display, the axis of what it has to say. We may try to come at the special powers of the image by asking what the common ground may be in the work of three modern poets for whom the nonverbal, tangible images of sculpture have played a crucial role.

The common ground, that is, between poetry and sculpture, would be our question, and not the common ground, vestigial at best, among Rilke, Pound, and Arp. In asking these questions we would have to avoid, in so far as possible, the play of assessing likenesses and differences between poetry and sculpture, of turning them into a metaphor for each other, whereby middle Pound would become the poet as sculptor or late Arp a poet in stone.

Rilke married a sculptor, lived with her in a bare landscape about which he wrote art-critical essays, and at her behest approached the sculptor who was her mentor.[1] He moved first into the orbit of Rodin and then lingered in his city preponderantly for the time of all his main creative development, age twenty-six through thirty-nine, from before the *Buch der Bilder* till the first drafts of the *Duineser Elegien.* The big shift in his style he attributes to Rodin,[2] and terms like *image* (*Bild*) and *thing* (*Ding*), after association with the sculptor, become subtler and more central as he toughens into the *Neue Gedichte,* the second part of which is dedicated to Rodin.

There is the oft-told story of Rodin's injunction to study an object closely, an injunction that resulted in hours spent before the panther in a cage at the *Jardin des Plantes,* and then in *Der Panther.* Beyond such acts of concentration, the whole statement that constitutes a poem is framed, set off for salience in the first place, as a sculpture is. Sculptures with holes that let the environment through, sculptures that advertise their being slapped into place, sculptures that eschew what had come to seem the natural curvature of stone and bronze for harsh angularity, or that try to flatten out into nearly two dimensions—all these emphasize their framing. The distance between object and what surrounds it is characterized by Rilke as a sort of mutual estrangement, implying a sense of the strain in framing that all these modernist gestures are trying to incorporate into the work itself:

> Es giebt Bildwerke, welche die Umgebung, in der sie gedacht sind, oder aus welcher sie gehoben werden, *in* sich tragen, aufgesogen haben und ausstrahlen. Der Raum in dem eine Statue steht, ist ihre Fremde,—ihre Umgebung hat sie *in* sich.[3]

> There are sculptures that carry *in* themselves the environment in which they are thought or out of which they are lifted; they have sucked it up and radiate it. The space in which a statue stands is its foreign country. Its environment it holds *in* itself.

Now in Rodin's work there is a smoothing of contour and sometimes a roughening of interior that goes as far as it can towards seeming to melt the frame. A sculpture like *The Kiss,* without rising to abstraction, blends the sculptor's tactile mastery of the body into an englobing whiteness that seems to permit a diffusion, to try to dissipate the very strangeness it evokes. Something of this effect must have been Rilke's intention for "Requiem," since he dedicated it to Clara Westhoff:

> Seit einer Stunde ist um ein Ding mehr
> auf Erden. Mehr um einen Kranz.
> Vor einer Weile war das leichtes Laub . . . Ich wands:
> Und jetzt ist dieser Efeu seltsam schwer
> und so von Dunkel voll, als tränke er
> aus meinen Dingen zukünftige Nächte.
>
> (1:469)

> For an hour now there is one thing more
> upon the earth. More by a wreath.
> A while ago was light foliage . . . I wound it:
> And now this ivy is strangely heavy
> and as full of darkness as if it drank
> out of my things the future nights.

The funeral wreath is seen as sort of improvised sculpture that turns from light to heavy once it becomes a "Ding." The heaviness is "strange," and its darkness draws from other things the dimension of time—a reference, it would seem, to its funeral character, but it is the poet's things from which it drinks the future nights.[4] All this description of the subliminal feelings attendant upon seeing such a made object rises into a long, circling meditation that hovers between definition and visualization.

In this confrontation of a purposeful object with its surrounding circumstances, Rilke asserts at one and the same time a flow between life and death and a flow between the visible and the invisible. These qualities are brought together, too, much later, in his long letter about the *Duino Elegies* in which he speaks of the bees of the invisible,[5] without exploring further the relation between the visible (*Sichtwerk*) and the spiritual (*Herzwerk*).[6] In the

Elegies and in the *Sonnets to Orpheus,* he returns, via this sort of distinction, to the *Zwischenraum* between life and death, an intermediate space partaking of both, and graced with angels. What has been digested in these later poems is the increment of a longstanding sculptor's insistence on the object, while he takes for granted a melting of the object into the frame of the surroundings. Contrasting *Sonnets to Orpheus* with the earlier *Orpheus. Eurydike. Hermes* will bring out how thoroughly this view has become internalized. Long subjection to Rodin, supplemented by the deliberate study of Cézanne, has enabled the poet to evoke a surrounding space that is vibrant and at the same time total—the goal of the sculptor attained without either lodging flintlike words into place word by word or directing the attention fixedly to hard objects. In this light the water of Roman days gets antique sarcophagi that are oddly flowing like a song through them, a process linked with the persistence of these objects in the speaker's feelings:

> Euch, die ihr nie mein Gefühl verliesst
> grüss ich, antikische Sarkophage,
> die das fröhliche Wasser römischer Tage
> als ein wandelndes Lied durchfliesst.

> You who never leave my feeling
> Do I greet, ancient sarcophagi,
> who through the joyous water of Roman days
> flow like a wandering song.
> (*Sonnets to Orpheus* 1.10.737)

The spirit that dissolves the most perdurable objects into a sort of perceived transience, and exalts transience into a trembling permanence, dominates the *Sonnets.* Breath is defined as a kind of solid (2.1; 1. 751), and the vague addressee is enjoined to "dance the orange" (1.11; 1. 748). The glorious overflows of our destiny are compared to stone men arched like tree trunks under balconies by the close of high portals, sculpture merging into architecture as both merge into time ("die herrlichen Überflüsse unseres Daseins . . . als steinerne Männer neben die Schlüsse / hoher Portale, unter Balkone gebäumt!" 2; 22; 1. 765). In the last lines of the sequence one is asked to treat water as permanent and stone as transient.

Rilke worked up to poems about a delimited object, the panther, the swan, the ball. Before that, and throughout his career, he also reverted to traditional iconographic objects, incidents in the life of the Virgin, Adam and Eve, the sculptured angels of Chartres. The *Buch der Bilder* (Book of Pictures) announces its iconographic intention in its title, and the resolute attention to a deductive process, making the image yield senses, can be equated with an attempt to keep it from the rigidities of metaphor, to let it flow free, like the goal of sculpture rather than like sculpting. He says of sculpture that its speech was the body ("Ihre Sprache war der Körper" 5: 146). And other objects, the *Dinge* of his continuous meditation, are conceived in a continuity between natural objects and human artifacts that carry the trace of a threatened, open life ("trug an sich die Spuren eines bedrohten offenen Lebens" 5:210). He sees it as a crucial task to come to an understanding with things ("eine Verständigung zu finden mit allen Dingen" 5:365). The sculpture is conceived of as a transformation of movement, and duration as a transformation of time's transience, through the mediation of the forced and peaceful *Ding:*

> Die Stille, die um die Dinge ist. Alle Bewegung legt sich, wird Kontur, und aus vergangener und künftiger Zeit schliesst sich ein Dauerndes: der Raum, die grosse Beruhigung der zu nichts gedrängten Dinge.[7]

> The stillness about things. All movement subsides, becomes contour, and from past and future time something abiding comes to conclusion: space, the great repose of things forced to nothing.

Even a blind man is perhaps a thing, as all things move around him in "Pont du Carrousel" (1:393). Things are compared to the bodies of violins, full of murmuring darkness ("Die Dinge sind Geigenleiber / von murrendem Dunkel voll," "Am Rande der Nacht" 1:400). The angel of the Ninth Elegy is to be told of things, how happy and innocent they are in belonging to us (1:719). In *Der Panther,* a poem whose careful notations Rilke attributed to what he had learned from watching Rodin at work, at the conclusion it is an image that passes through the eyes of the caged beast:

Dann geht ein Bild hinein,
geht durch der Glieder angespannte Stille—
und hört im Herzen auf zu sein.

(1:505)

Then an image goes on in,
goes through the tensile stillness of the limbs—
and ceases in the heart to be.

This plays back within the animal what the viewer himself has
projected upon it, but almost entirely without the metalinguistic
circularity such reflexivity usually evokes. The animal is a favored
object for the sculptor at all times, and certainly for the nineteenth-
century predecessors of Rodin, though not for Rodin himself. Here
the panther is conceived of as digesting the image through his
entire body: it dissolves in his heart, but then he himself (as the
poem does not say) in effect becomes the essence of the image,
since what has happened to the image finally defines him. He is
an unmetaphoric carrier of image rather than an image himself:
the movement of attributions to him makes him something akin to
the inner meaning and force of an animal sculpture.

The second part of the *Neue Gedichte* is dedicated to Rodin. It
opens, as the first part had, with a sonnet to a particular torso of
Apollo (figure 1). The force of the first poem is associated with
poems in a way that makes the head of this early Apollo an equivalent for poems through failing to be an antidote for them:

so ist in seinem Haupte
nichts was verhindern konnte, dass der Glanz
aller Gedichte uns fast tödlich träfe;

(1:481)

So there is in his head
nothing that might hinder that the glare
of all poems hit us almost mortally.

In the second poem, *Archäischer Torso Apollos,* an extension of
the panther strategy, in which the perceptions of the very object
perceived are accounted for, moves the sculpture up to its crucial

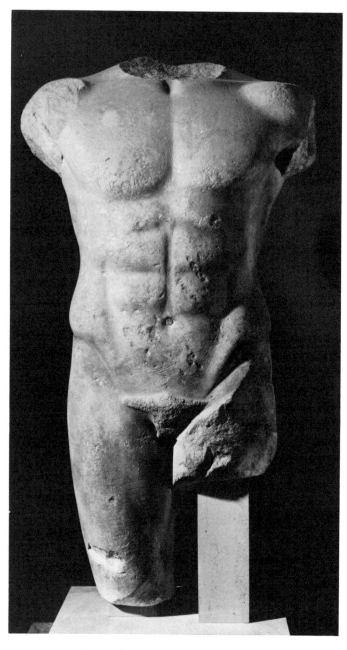

FIGURE 1. *Torso of a Young Man,* from Miletus, fifth century
B.C. Louvre, Paris.

impression on the silent observer, "Du musst dein Leben ändern" (1:557), a statement that is more than the tag conventional for an *ekphrasis*:

Archäischer Torso Apollos

Wir kannten nicht mehr sein unerhörtes Haupt,
darin die Augenäpfel reiften. Aber
sein Torso glüht noch wie ein Kandelaber,
in dem sein Schauen, nur zurückgeschraubt,

sich hält und glänzt. Sonst könnte nicht der Bug
der Brust dich blenden, und im leisen Drehen
der Lenden könnte nicht ein Lächeln gehen
zu jener Mitte, die die Zeugung trug.

Sonst stünde dieser Stein entstellt und kurz
unter der Schultern durchsichtigem Sturz
und flimmerte nicht so wie Raubtierfelle;

und bräche nicht aus allen seinen Rändern
aus wie ein Stern: denn da ist keine Stelle,
die dich nicht sieht. Du musst Dein Leben ändern.

Archaic Torso of Apollo

We didn't know his unheard-of head
wherein the apples of his eyes ripened. But
his torso glows still like a candelabra,
in which his looking, scarcely turned down,

is held and gleams. Otherwise could the bend
of the breast not blind you, and in the soft turn
of the loins a smile could not go
to that middle, which bore the genitals.

Otherwise this stone would stand distorted and short
under the transparent plunge of the shoulders
and would not glimmer like the fell of a beast of prey

and would not break out of all its boundaries,
out like a star: for there is no place
that doesn't see you. You must change your life.

The elaborate contrary-to-fact condition, dominating the central nine lines of the sonnet, prepares the way for the turn of the last half-line. The many negatives strip language away like the unmentioned space around the fragmentary sculpture.[8] Every single attribution is not allowed to stand but serves to lead the mind through a logical series of an apprehension whose sudden emergence is already implied in the assertive visual presence of the sculpture. The "durchsichtiger Sturz" of the shoulders has to be opaque in literal fact: it is only "transparent" if the two directions are permitted between the sculpture and the beholder. *That* transaction is the only true, comprehensive metaphor in the poem; and it is not exactly a metaphor, but rather a foreshortened account of an obscure apperception. The other near metaphors are resolutely subsidiary and ancillary: the dead metaphor of "the apples of his eyes," the extension of it in the nonce metaphor "ripened," and the similes of the candelabra and the fell, one each for torso and for loins. It is the eyes, ours as well as his, that ripen as they play over the sculptured torso. This is, in fact, more unlike a candelabra than it is like one. The dissimilarity displaces onto the perceptual movement from *glüht* to *glänzt,* the first suggesting a soft deep light, the second an intense surface light. This movement describes the way the sculpted *Apollo* sees in terms of our seeing it. Between *glüht* and *glänzt* his gaze is registered as *zurückgeschraubt,* an attribution that is caught up and progressively released by *glänzt.*

When men are silent, things say amen ("Und wenn die Menschen schweigen, werden die Dinge 'Amen' sagen"; 5:446). There is a central piety launched by Rilke, in which both poems and sculptures participate. He attends in this sonnet and effectually elsewhere to the hieratic quality in the deferral of perception, the fruitful displacement between the perceiver and his object. The fixedness of the work of art magnifies and freezes this deferral, through displacement.

Rilke tends to define time and space in terms of each other, allowing poem and sculpture to be reversals of each other rather than simple echoes or analogues. Space, time, motion, and rest are set into an order that subverts the simple opposition of Lessing between the temporal verbal arts and the spatial visual ones:[9]

Alle Bewegung der Welt verwandelt sich in Kontur, und die Zeit, auf-
genommen von der grossen Gleichzeitigkeit des Raumes, zeigt ihren gan-
zen Kreis und kehrt in sich selbst zurück.

(5:258)

All the movement of the world transforms itself into contour, and time,
taken up by the great synchronicity of space, shows its whole circle and
returns back into itself.

And as Rilke says of painting, at a time when Cézanne was about
to displace Rodin in his absorbed attention, "In den Gedichten sind
instinktive Ansätze zu ähnlicher Sachlichkeit" (in poems are instinctive dispositions to a similar objecthood).[10]

2

Pound went through much trial-and-error before he enabled himself to approach a long poem that was to become *The Cantos*.[11] He
did so through his associations with a theorizing sculptor, Henri
Gaudier-Brzeska, and with a painter-writer whose paintings had a
Cubist air, Wyndham Lewis.

Imagism tends to slip away from definition, and to vanish as a
movement, Hugh Kenner has shown. But we may isolate in it a
special emphasis on what Pound was to call *phanopoiea*, the component of image in poetry.[12] The revisions of other poems, and of
his own "In a Station of the Metro," strip the presentation down to
nearly uneditorialized visual designations, poetry aspiring to water-
color, the impression of an isolated quick take.

Still, in Gaudier's phrase "sculptural energy is the mountain."[13]
Where Gaudier stressed combinations of planes and masses, Pound
defined poetry, while writing about Gaudier, as a final sort of
algebraic combination, much the way van Gogh had described
painting:[14]

Fourthly, we come to Descartian or "analytical geometry." Space is
conceived as separated by two or by three axes. . . . One refers points to
these axes by a series of coordinates. . . . Great works of art contain this
fourth sort of equation. They cause form to come into being. By the "image" I mean such an equation; not an equation of mathematics, not something about a, b, and c, having something to do with form, but about *sea,
cliffs, night,* having something to do with mood.

The image is not an idea. It is a radiant node or cluster; it is what I can, and must perforce, call a VORTEX, from which, and through which, and into which, ideas are constantly rushing.[15]

Space and its axes are here equated to the rushing of ideas through a set of visual images more painterly than sculpturelike— *sea, cliff, night.* And Pound here will shortly talk about a painting, Wyndham Lewis's *Timon,* saying at the end—it is a sort of backhand announcement—"I see nothing against a long vorticist poem."[16] Earlier he had defined desiderata in terms of making distinctions among groups of painters, separating the Futurists as speeded-up post-Impressionists from the Cubists and Expressionists, singling out Kandinsky's *Über das Geistige in der Kunst* for particular recommendation.[17]

"These new men have made me see form," he said. He aspired to "a sort of poetry where painting or sculpture seems as it were just coming over into speech."[18] The *Cantos* are organized on a "complex" pattern rather than the "simple" one which Pound declared sculpture to have by contrast with "say, one of the more complex designs of Lewis' 'Timon.' "[19] Pound has bits of perception or memory or opinion or visualization flow into the arbitrary organization of a single Canto. He makes his achievement hinge on a sort of evasion of the emblematic structure of, say, Dante's *Paradiso,* though he invokes that poem repeatedly in his own, and by implication labels it an image of quasi-vorticist bearing.[20] It is as though he were carrying out in a more volatile medium Gaudier's program for sculpture:

I SHALL DERIVE MY EMOTIONS SOLELY FROM THE ARRANGEMENT OF SURFACES, I shall present my emotions by the ARRANGEMENT OF MY SURFACES, THE PLANES AND LINES BY WHICH THEY ARE DEFINED.[21]

And just as Pound revised the linking coherence of sequent argument out of his first versions of *The Cantos,* so Gaudier also, in another impulse, revised the line out of his formulation, "Line is nothing but a decoy." And, more compactly, "Sculpture consists in placing planes according to a rhythm."[22] (See figure 2.) According to another of his distinctions, "Sculptural feeling is the appreciation of masses in relation. Sculptural ability is the defining of these masses by planes."[23]

FIGURE 2. *Birds Erect,* Henri Gaudier-Brzeska (1914).
Limestone, 26⅝ × 10¼ × 12⅜".
The Museum of Modern Art, New York.

Masses in relation will provide a fair definition of *The Cantos,* in which the fixity of the Chinese ideogram, a sort of punctuating compacted mass, offers a tonic measure for multiple relations, since it contains two or three images within itself, but leveled to a single locution like *dawn.* As the sun over a horizon line, its elements are drawn to a coherent simplicity within itself, like Pound's definition of sculpture. We must come at the texture of *The Cantos* as to a surface, not allowing the complexities of relation to imply a corresponding complexity of metaphoric structures. We may look closely at this process by inspecting the different "planes" of image presentation in a stretch from the middle of one of *The Pisan Cantos* group—a group with its own particular structure to be set globally against the longer Jefferson units or the shorter planes of *Rock-Drill* (named for a sculpture of Epstein's).

> As Mabel's red head was a fine sight
> worthy his minstrelsy
> a tongue to the sea-cliffs or "Sligo in Heaven"
> or his, William's, old "da" at Coney Island
>   perched on an elephant
> beaming like the prophet Isaiah
>   and J. Q. as it were aged 8 (Mr. John Quinn)
> at the target.
>
>   "Liquids and fluids . . . !"
>   said the palmist. "A painter?
>   well ain't that liquids and fluids?"
>   [To the venerable J.B. bearded Yeats]
>
> "a friend," sd / mr cummings, "I knew it 'cause he
> never tried to sell me any insurance"
>
> (with memorial to Warren Dahler the Chris Columbus of
> Patchin)
>
> Hier wohnt the tradition, as per Whitman in Camden
> and an engraving 596 Lexington Ave.,
>   24 E. 47th,
> with Jim at the checquer board by the banana cage

"Funny looking wood, James," said Aunt F.
"it looks as if it had already been burnt"
      [Windsor fire]

   "Part o deh roof ma'am."
   does any museum
contain one of the folding beds of that era?
And now, why? Regents Park
   where was the maison Alma-Tadema
   (with a fountain) or Leighton House
      for that matter?
and the mass of preraphaelite reliques
   in a trunk in a walled-up cellar in Selsey
"Tyke 'im up ter the bawth" (meaning Swinburne)
"Even Tennyson tried to go out
     through the fire-place."

which is what I suppose he, Fordie,
      wanted me to be able to picture
when he took me to Miss Braddon's
   (I mean the setting) at Richmond
But that New York I have found at Périgueux
   si com' ad Arli
in wake of the sarascen
     As the "Surrender of Breda" (Velasquez)
was preceded in fresco at Avignon
   y cavals armatz with the perpendicular lances
and the red-bearded fellow was mending his
   young daughter's shoe.
              (LXXX:507–9)

"Toute description est une vue," Barthes well says,[24] but in the serial presentation here we are offered almost nothing that would pass as a description, only suggestive surfaces, like the girl with the red hair who happens to be Aubrey Beardsley's sister and so part of a milieu; or we have emblematic characterizations, the elder Yeats as Isaiah atop an elephant. So we are referred for a *vue* to the connections of the units. *Mabel's red head* connects on one plane with personal reminiscence, on another with the Persephone and Beatrice figures through the poem, since she is "worthy his minstrelsy." On another plane she connects with any instance of beauty, *was a fine sight,* and in a more subdued mode with the many references to painting in this Canto. *Williams's old 'da* connects with art too, since the father of the poet Yeats was a painter. The Coney Island makes it connect to all the swiftly sketched characterizations of decadent city life, which still permit the sort of celebration that the personal reminiscence here touches on, a reminiscence sharpened by the presence of the narrator in a prison camp. We almost have narrative here, in the form of something approaching a snapshot: the picture includes John Quinn, the patron of the arts; a redheaded girl; and a creator of the arts, J. B. Yeats; and the poet, first watching one atop an elephant, then in a shooting gallery.

The jump to connecting the Bible with art in the next "liquids and fluids" section could not be a snapshot; it offers a plane at a different, more abstract angle. The next plane, a testimonial comment from another poet about a modern activity relating to the pervasive topic of usury, is still more succinct, though the parenthesis of identification sharpens the reminiscence while connecting to New York City via an elided reference to Patchin Place, where Cummings lived.

All the references tend to be elided. Near narrative is broken off, while image is only one possible plane, reaching its flattest in swift visual notation, as a passage earlier in this Canto "with a sky wet as ocean / flowing with liquid slate . . . the red and white stripes / cut clear against the slate . . . the blue field melts with the cloud flow." Narrative and image, taken together, offer—exhaustively, we may say, if abstraction be added—the possibilities for any verbal presentation whatever. Here the angles of each are blunted; narrative is not allowed to be complete, while image is faced off at a different angle all the time. *Jim at the checquer board by the banana cage* is a snapshotlike image smoothed so as to offer none of the delectation in the sky description above. It is also an anecdotal item. And it is a vortical presentation of discordancies, checkers not going with bananas; hence it is abstract, and the game being played also is. *Antiques,* again, connects with city, art, and reminiscence, as do the Swinburne and Tennyson of the end, reduced to comparable anecdote, feeding back again into art as it connects with history.

If we ask a main question, What relation obtains between the multiplicity of connections and the ruminative but at the same time blunted mode of presentation? we are thrown back not so much on the sculptural analogy, since this goes far beyond Gaudier, as on the abstract substratum of the sculptor's ideal project (see figure 2).

"The poet, whatever his 'figure of speech,' will not arrive by doubling or confusing an image."[25] It would have seemed that the whole strategy of *The Cantos* was to double and confuse images. Taking our cue from this declaration, we may see that, on the contrary, to connect is not ever to double: each plane is kept distinct, by being unmetaphorical. That procedure permits the anecdotal its just pause. Nor is it confused, though curtailed. Each figure remains virtual: the steel dust patterns into a rose but never activates those floral attributes. The virtuality can allow for the inclusion not only of ideograms, translated passages, bits of quotation, digested history, but also of musical notation and even the playing cards of Canto LXXXVIII. The figural strategy never becomes so complicated that another one cannot take over and change the angle. The planes remain in relation, because they have been made to be what they are, carefully limited to their differently angled surfaces.

3

Arp was both a poet and a sculptor who expressed himself not so much indifferently or alternately or supplementally as indeterminately in either medium. In the same way he hung back a little from the Dada café celebrations, while dwelling on the Movement through his life and expanding something in it more steadily than any of the other participants. Not only the near nonsense of Dada can claim him but the depth-associativeness of the Surrealists among whom he spent many hours in the twenties and among whom he has often been counted. Even the abstractness of Mondrian's De Stijl both provides a living association for him and stands as an analogy to the self-purification of his mature sculpture.

Arp's duality of medium allowed the method of the poems to furnish titles for the sculptures, while the method of the sculptures, or rather that impulse which lay at the inception of both poetry and sculpture, held the poems to images that were at once Dadaist, Surreal, and abstract. In the face of the nonsense poems of Hugo Ball, the babble of Raoul Haussmann's *Lautgedichte,* and the verbal shock tactics of Tzara, Arp's justifying definition of Dada points up his own work more centrally than that of the others:

Der dadaistische Glaube Ohnesinn ist kein Unsinn, kein Ulk. Der dadaistische Glaube Ohnesinn ist ebensowenig Unsinn wie die Pflanze, die Kinderzeichnung, die Musik, die Schönheit, die Liebe, die Hoffnung, der Kreis, das Quadrat, die Farbe.[26]

The Dadaistic belief *no sense* is no nonsense, no lark. That *no sense* is as little nonsense as a plant, a child's drawing, music, beauty, love, hope, the circle, the square, color.

The list he offers here will characterize his own poems or his sculptures, but not those of any of his Dadaist associates. The poems manage an access to abstractions like hope and music, to figures like square and circle, and to particular colors, while drawing as minimally as possible on the rhythmic resources germane to poetry. In them the line seems to serve mainly as a field of demarcation for the named objects. So the sculptures, in their nearly wordlike conjunctions of *egg-plank* and *navel-bottle,* or even *infinite amphora,* eschew the more violent disjunctions of, say Picabia—who was also a poet—and Schwitters' *Merzbilder.*

Arp speaks of Rodin as being "far from the mechanical erotomachia of our century"[27]—and his own forms, when they round into slightly more abstract equivalents for the sculptures of Rodin that have love as a subject, take on an earnestness that betrays no kinship with the Dada-like work of Duchamp and Man Ray. Their light humor does not go as far as Duchamp's *Fresh Widow,* which plays on near homonymy with *window,* being a window of many panes, painted black; or with his *La Belle Haleine, beautiful breath* instead of *beautiful Helen,* playing again on near homonymy. (The work shows Duchamp himself in drag on a bottle of perfume.)

Fresh Widow and *La Belle Haleine* are a lark, playing the possibility of poetry off against the actuality of sculpture. Arp manages to balance both possibility and actuality by keeping the impulse to poetry and the impulse to sculpture in the same resolute frame. "Dada advises you to lay eggs in the mirrors of others," he says ("Dada ratet Dir in den Spiegel der Anderen Eier zu legen," 2: 183).[28] An artistic process is likened to a natural process that belongs to another creature than humans, to the birds of romantic inspiration that also served Arp's friend Klee as a near allegory.

Eggs enter into many combinations for Arp.[29] They point to the possibility of psychoanalytic decipherment; but they also advertise that possibility. By doing so they remind us, as it were, to hold back: to remember that the psychoanalytic interpretation is not the message of either art or poetry, but rather a part of the code. "Our deeds are those of dreamers, of enigmatic swimmers," he says ("Unsere Taten sind die von Träumenden, von rätselhaften Schwimmenden," 2:132). The parity of the riddle with our acts is maintained by the impermeability of the image, named or sculpted.

And Arp's main device is to blend the image by juxtaposition in poetry or title; in sculpture, finally, by blending together limb and fruit or jar and sky, preserving an essential form through concretion, as he calls it, trying to produce by art the economical symmetries that D'Arcy Thompson deduces in nature.

The term *Surrealism*, like that of *Dadaism*, provides a rubric but does not explain or offer a sure derivative for the presentation of image. Arp, at his simplest, offers Surrealist contradiction (Breton), image confusion (Éluard), and wisdom-aphorism (Char), all at once: *Flower Hammer, Plant Hammer, Navel Bottle,* and *Egg Plank* are near paradoxes, titles given to sculptures that knot the visual world into a riddle to which at the same time they offer a near solution. In poems, by a frequent procedure, nouns are set against one another for puzzle but not for nonsense. The cloud pump sees nature, in effect, as a sort of producing machine. *Schwarze Eier,* black eggs, do exist in nature: most notably in the caviar always placed atop chickens' eggs in the common German restaurant dish *Russische Eier.* And if black eggs are paradoxical, it is simply so—eggs are usually white. It is the painter who may change their color, or the sculptor with access to either paint or some material like basalt.

In the one line from the poem of that title that names them, "schwarze eier und narrenschellen stürzen von den bäumen" (black eggs and fools' bells plunge from the trees, 1:41), an effect of visual blurring is suggested, a fantasy of seeing what leaf shapes, eggs, and bells have in common—a sort of near concretion. And if we are here led to visual solutions, at the same time in logic we are on the terrain of Breton, since eggs do not fall from trees and bells are not left in trees. So with "die edelfrau pumpt feierlich wolken in säcke aus leder und stein" (the gentlewoman festively pumps clouds in sacks of leather and stone; 1:33; 2:101)—a line that Arp used twice in his poetic career. Each of the items named by the nouns possesses a rotundity and physical presence that could lend itself to sculpture. Clouds are not kept in sacks except by mythical beings. Women do pump, but on farms; gentlewomen are those who do not pump—except perhaps in the topsy-turvy feast of fools, on some festive occasion, *feierlich*. Sacks are often made of leather; they may never be made of stone: the material doesn't lend itself at all to the requisite flexibility. Only the worlds do, and whatever visual possibility underlies the material impossibility. They force on our attention their comic nature; they are a serious joke, like the sculpture of an egg board. They pump clouds. Only incidentally do they jumble material and object, does the stone sack anticipate Claes Oldenburg.

Visual logic undermines conceptual illogic, and vice versa—through a less solemn mediation of the visible and invisible than Rilke's, as in the title, "Weisst du, schwarzt du," the title poem of a collection (1:126–31). White and black are opposite colors, but *weiss* is only a noun meaning white. *You white, you black* is no more a verb sequence in German than it is in English. *Du weisst* is a simple expression, often colloquial and parenthetical, as in "you know." "You know, you black."

These are the barely named colors, but colors always have, for the sculptor, the possibility of depth, and even of change as the light plays over them. As Arp says in a later poem:

Das Schwarze vergisst, dass es fliegen kann
und sieht den davonschwebenden Flammen
immer schwärzer werdend nach

(2:84)

Black forgets that it can fly
and looks at the disappearing floating flames
becoming ever blacker

These lines can be taken for a sportive but literal description of an eye playing over a three-dimensional black surface. The strange conjunctions he sets forth for "Puppen" (dolls), still may be taken to describe dolls, and to avoid at the same time Rilke's mystique about them, while drawing on something like the aura of those folk sculptures: "Mein Kopf ist ein Schneeball / Meine Arme und Beine sind schwarze nasse Zweige" (My head is a snowball / My arms and legs are black wet twigs, 2:211). Or take the combinations with which begins the poem "Konfiguration" (1:196):

das weisse haar der steine. das schwarze haar der wasser.
das grüne haar der kinder. das blaue haar der augen.

the white hair of stones. the black hair of water.
the green hair of children. the blue hair of eyes.

In this list of items only children really have hair, and it is not green. But the other items all have the color named: stones are white, water is black, eyes are blue. Yet in no case do they have hair. Arp stays with the color-hair-of-x formula to make it graze logic, not moving on as Breton does with his "white-haired revolver." And the white hair of stones is a possible visual illusion in a certain kind of fairly common light, since white serves as the fundamental color of stone. The poem ends, more succinctly but comparably, by mixing three of these four colors with two abstract moral adjectives, "blau grün schwarz feig und treu" (blue green black cowardly and loyal), following on a straight designation, the same one of the poem's opening but with the surrealist genitive dropped, "die weissen haare" (white hair).

The effect in a whole poem is one of focusing, of what he later called concretion in characterizing his sculptures. The hair-formula phrase above is repeated over and over in the poem, and gradually varied till it leaches out in its conclusion. So he dwells on the clouds in the poem of that title:

Wolken

In wogenden Räumen spuken Wolken.
Mit weichen Händen weichen Armen und übertrieben
                weichen Gebärden
führen sie süss duftende Monde an ihren Mund.
Schmachtend verzehren sie die Monde.
Ein Mensch zeichnet Wolken auf ein Blatt Papier,
und füllt die Wolken mit kleinen Kreuzen aus.
Ein Vogel lässt sich stumm vor ihm nieder
und schaut ihn aus bodenlosen Augen an.
Stumme Vogel sind Boten von Verstorbenen.
Sie lassen sich furchtlos vor den Menschen nieder
und überbringen ihnen in ihren bodenlosen Augen
hell leuchtende Funken Grüsse aus dem Totenreich.
Eine Wolke liegt nackt im Dunkel.
Sie schläft und träumt.
Eine Wolke liegt nackt im Dunkel.
Sie ist schön wie meine Geliebte.

                                                    (2:39)

Clouds

In surging spaces haunt clouds.
With soft hands soft arms and exaggerated soft gestures
they bring sweet-smelling moons to their mouth.
Pining they consume the moons.
A person draws clouds on a sheet of paper
and fills the clouds in with little crosses.
A bird lets itself down before him dumb
and looks at him from bottomless eyes.
Dumb birds are messengers from the dead.
They let themselves down before men without
fear and bring them in their bottomless eyes

brightly shining sparks of greeting
from the kingdom of the dead.
A cloud lies naked in the darkness.
It sleeps and dreams.
A cloud lies naked in the darkness.
It is beautiful like my beloved.

The last line makes this poem, very likely, still another of the many elegies Arp wrote for Sophie Tauber, to preserve and center and keep alive all his profound feeling by subjecting it to a mockery that never becomes too severe. And the means of mockery is the visual attribution: the sight of clouds, the act of painting them, expresses what it avoids. The threshold of the visual is kept in view but not crossed. Birds do fly out of the clouds at times, but they do not alight dutifully before men. These birds are those of Klee in a more somber key, but without losing the visual hinge on something in perception that founds integrity on a refusal to do much more than name and combine visual entities.

The principle of simple juxtaposition is the principle of the collages that Arp was one of the first to make, as he was also one of the first to compose "found poems" (*Weltwunder,* 1917, 1:46–49). These, together with the first noun pairings of *black eggs* and *cloud pump,* and *Navels Tables Legs* (1:181), emphasize the separateness of elements in the visible world so forcibly as to seem to lament the impossibility of joining or fusing them. As if they were disjunct, three-dimensional sculptures. The corresponding, and opposite, principle of seeking the underlying visual structure, the concretion that will fuse objects without losing their identifying contours, was the increasingly dominant principle of Arp's mature sculpture.

As the poems have found a way to jell Surrealistic predications, so the late sculptures—with titles like *Idol of the Hares, One-Eyed Doll, Bird Masquerade, Leaf or Bird, Star Amphora, Torso-Amphora, Torso Fruit* (figure 3), *Between Leaf and Bird* (figure 4), and *Flower Resting*—manage to jell their contours between the objects they suggest, without either blurring or overlapping, and also without abstraction. So their procedure is the inverse of Brancusi's, though the actual sculptures seem to be shaped on the

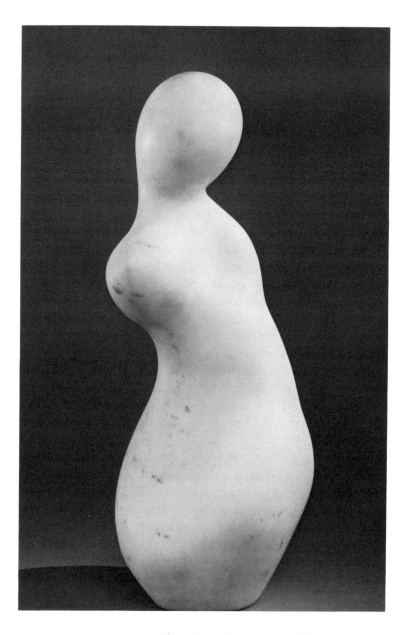

FIGURE 3. *Torso Fruit,* Jean Arp (1960).
Marble, 29½ × 12 × 11½ ″.
Hirshhorn Museum and Sculpture Garden,
Smithsonian Institution, Washington, D.C.

FIGURE 4. *Between Leaf and Bird,* Jean Arp (1959).
Black granite, 34 × 15 × 10″.
Founders Society, Detroit Institute of Arts.

same principle, till we notice their protuberances and multiplicities of plane. As William S. Rubin puts it, "Brancusi's sculptural process is centripetal, paring away to the simplest, most economical forms; Arp's is centrifugal, the work appearing to grow organically from a nucleus."[30] It also appears to refer while eliding references, in that way going beyond the term *biomorphism* and such Romantic formulations of organ utility as Goethe's. As Arp put something like the biomorphic fusion in a poetic statement:

> Lichterloh lösten sich Farbenbeete aus Farbenbeeten
> Sophie liebte die Harmonie, das göttliche kugelförmige Wesen,
> von welchem Empedokles sagt,
> dass es an der ringsum herrschenden Einsamkeit
>   seine Freude habe.
> ("die Engelschrift" 2:59)
>
> Blazing color beds loosed themselves from color beds.
> Sophie loved harmony, the godly spherical being,
> of which Empedocles said
> that it has its joy in the solitude that
>   reigns round.

Again, a sculpturelike inference, and an elegiac reference to his dead wife, and the rhetorical register of nearly scholarly quotation, all neutralize each other, along with the quasi-mystical half-Greek doctrine of a harmony that locates everything, only momentarily and only for the word, in color. The Romantic loneliness and solitude stands on a par with the color, and the term retains its identity of naming, *Farbenbeete,* through its possible transformations.

The programmatic summary of his views begins with an image that keys to his sculptures. It ends in a list that sorts more with his poems, though painting and sculpture are the nominal subjects:

Art is a fruit that grows in man, like a fruit on a plant, or a child in its mother's womb. But whereas the fruit of the plant, the fruit of the animal, the fruit in the mother's womb, assume autonomous and natural forms, art, the spiritual fruit of man, usually shows an absurd resemblance to the aspect of something else. Only in our own epoch have painting and sculpture been liberated from the aspect of a mandolin, a president in a Prince Albert, a battle, a landscape. . . .

I remember a discussion with Mondrian in which he distinguished between art and nature, saying that art is artificial and nature natural. I do not share his opinion. I believe that nature is not in opposition to art. Art is of natural origin and is sublimated and spiritualized through the sublimation of man.[31]

Once again the lexicon is psychoanalytic, but the syntax takes us, as in an Arp sculpture, towards a sort of unity, this time the unity between nature and art that it is the natural work of the "absurd resemblance" in an image to substantiate. In that work, poetry and sculpture are means towards an end for which the terms *art* as it suggests ornament and *Kunst* as it suggests artifice are somehow felt to fall short, and may be embraced just because they do so. Falling short that way becomes the special kind of human perception that embraces the human limitation and turns it back on itself. So the poet-sculptor is empowered to do what he attributes to the Kandinsky who was on the verge of leaving Expressionism for a symbolic abstraction, to create "autonomous compositions directly out of their most intimate joy, their most personal suffering, out of lines, planes, forms, colors."[32]

Or out of words. Rilke, Pound, and Arp all show, in different ways, the force that may be harnessed by opening the mind to sculpture and its approximations.

The Windows of Apollinaire

It was through association with painters, through thinking about painters, and through applying a verbal equivalent for the theories of painters, that Apollinaire was able to give an extra dimension to his fluid, personal, pre-Surrealistic style. The "calligrammes" that followed on this realization—an extension of the concrete poem or painting poem exemplified by Mallarmé's *Un Coup de dés*—were only a special development of the possibilities inherent in the "simultaneism" that he had suddenly realized in December 1912 with *Les Fenêtres.*

Just a month before, in applying what he had worked out for the rhythms of *Vendémiaire,* he had suppressed all punctuation in the proofs of *Alcools.* The poem whose importance for that book he had signaled by placing it first, *Zone,* was actually written last, in October 1912. He brings to a high pitch in *Zone* the fluidity of mood and multiplicity of personae that a singleness of purpose overrides by embodying it in the implication that a recollective associativeness can be given free rein.[1] Simultaneism is still only implied in the disjunction from one association of personal recollection to another, right through to the new note of the last line's mysterious invocation-attribution:

J'humilie maintenant à une pauvre fille au rire horrible ma
    bouche

Tu es seul le matin va venir
Les laitiers font tinter leurs bidons dans les rues

La nuit s'éloigne ainsi qu'une belle Métive
C'est Ferdine la fausse ou Léa l'attentive

Et tu bois cet alcool brûlant comme ta vie
Ta vie que tu bois comme une eau-de-vie

Tu marches vers Auteuil tu veux aller chez toi à pied
Dormir parmi tes fétiches d'Océanie et de Guinée
Ils sont des Christ d'une autre forme et d'une autre croyance
Ce sont les Christ inférieurs des obscures espérances

Adieu adieu

Soleil cou coupé

I now humiliate before a poor girl with a horrible laugh my
    mouth

You are alone morning is coming
The milkmen clink their cans in the streets

Night goes away like a beautiful Métive
It is Ferdine the false or Léa the attentive

And you drink this alcohol burning like your life
Your life that you drink like an *eau-de-vie*

You walk toward Auteuil you want to go home on foot
To sleep among your fetishes from Oceania and Guinea
They are Christs in another form and of another belief
They are the lower Christs of obscure hopes

Goodbye goodbye

Sun neck cut

    The rumination here is constant, sustained by the tenderness of
the poet to himself, the loves that mingle with the sounds of a

morning in which he finds himself alone walking home to his actual apartment in a near suburb. The primitive objects he has collected in accord with a vogue shared by his painter friends are simple appurtenances of the apartment where he will sleep late. They have a theological existence, too, that can be willfully assimilated to the religion the poet has taken the posture of at once manipulating and celebrating. The *adieu* works for the poem, and also for the time of early morning when he is going to bed. The abruptly named and treated *Soleil cou coupé* retains its connection to the narrative line: the sun indeed metaphorically has its neck cut when the speaker who has been up all night goes to bed instead of staying awake in the daylight. The sun further connects to Christ; the speaker's religion is somewhat truncated, or the religion of the fetishes would be a truncated Christianity next to the glories of a Christ celebrated earlier in the poem, in congruence with the topos of Christ as the sun—"la flamboyante gloire de Christ" ("le Christ qui monte au ciel mieux que les aviateurs . . . Pupille Christ de l'oeil"). Logical undercurrents, a deeply articulated coherence, govern the progressions here, even though *Soleil cou coupé* may also be taken to stand richly apart from the poem, to qualify and summarize it by an image wholly different from those it has evoked. The image is wholly traditional in the tenor and wholly innovative in the shocking vehicle, since the sight of a blood-red sun may be taken to resemble the look head-on of a freshly beheaded torso.[2]

Except for such possibilities in this stunning final grace note, the movement in *Zone* retains the logical connections of sequence, just as much as does one of his earlier poems in this effusive free-verse style, this Whitmanism in which brio has been substituted for solemnity: the *Poème Lu au mariage d'André Salmon* (July 13, 1909) keeps the links firm in a final associative crescendo:

> Réjouissons-nous non parce que notre amitié a été le fleuve
>   qui nous a fertilisés,
> Terrains riverains dont l'abondance est la nourriture que
>   tous espèrent
> Ni parce que nos verres nous jettent encore une fois le
>   regard d'Orphée mourant

Ni parce que nous avons tant grandi que beaucoup
      pourraient confondre nos yeux et les étoiles
Ni parce que les drapeaux claquent aux fenêtres des
      citoyens qui sont contents depuis cent ans d'avoir
      la vie et de menus choses à défendre
Ni parce que fondés en poésie nous avons des droits
      sur les paroles qui forment et défont l'Univers
Ni parce que nous pouvons pleurer sans ridicule et que
      nous savons rire
Ni parce que nous fumons et buvons comme autrefois
Réjouissons-nous parce que directeur du feu et des poètes
L'amour qui emplit ainsi que la lumière
Tout le solide espace entre les étoiles et les planètes
L'amour veut qu'aujourd'hui mon ami André Salmon se
      marie.

Let us rejoice not because our friendship
      has been the river which has fertilized us
Riverbanks whose abundance is the nurture all hope for
Not because our glasses throw us one more time the look
      of a dying Orpheus
Nor because we have grown so much that many could
      confound our eyes with the stars
Not because the flags flap at the windows of citizens
      who have been content a hundred years to have life
      and trivial things to defend
Nor because founded in poetry we have rights on the
      words that make and unmake the Universe
Nor because we can weep without being ridiculed and
      know how to laugh
Nor because we are smoking and drinking as before
Let us rejoice because the director of fire and poets
Love that just like the light
Fills all the solid space between the stars and planets
Love wishes my friend André Salmon to marry today.

The very extravagance of the anaphora here, as reinforced by
the excessive rhythmic sweep of the long lines, is made to seem to

be straining to crest itself for perpetually increased climaxes. The metaphors, too, are extravagant—friendship as a river,[3] glasses that throw the look of a dying Orpheus, words that make and unmake the universe, love as a director of fire and of poets. Yet the connections are firmly classical, a catalogue that is a logical series in the subsidiary, classical rhetorical figure of *climax*. This is mixed with anticlimax, because the occasion for celebration is at once humbly particularized beside the grand theological ultimates, rising to echoes of the end of the *Paradiso* in the penultimate lines. And it is also truly climactic if marriage be taken to subsume all these activities and the poetry of late-adolescent poets be seen, in one light, as a kind of bachelor rite superseded by the deep maturity of sexual fulfillment and commitment. The elation that Apollinaire evokes here will not rest to assert the priority of either of these notions; marriage and the high function of poetry are equally if successively exalted. Still, neither at this splendid beginning nor in the culminating achievement of *Zone* do the individual images break through the classical framework; in both poems, though more obviously here, they are rhetorical, if personal. They are public and private at once in a refurbished version of a traditional mode, one whose logic remains in *Zone* after its rhetoric has been obscured.

Les Fenêtres, however, suddenly presents a sequence in which the rhetorical pitch is retained while the rhetorical connections have been wholly loosened. The personal inner voice of *Zone* has transposed its fluency into a kind of objectivity without losing any of the force found in the ranging long-line poems of *Alcools*. In the two months since writing *Zone* Apollinaire has turned around the style of *Cortège, Le Voyageur, L'Émigrant de Landor Road* and *Vendémiaire*. The newer mode is hinted at only in the one-line poem he inserted in the proofs of his book, *Chantre* (Cantor):

> Et l'unique cordeau des trompettes marines
> And the unique string of the marine trumpets

This re-renders the voice of a religious or poetic singer as that in trumpets which can be strung on a single line, and in an orderly fashion (implied by one sense of *cordeau*). To this self-referentiality of the one-line poem is superadded a term of strong poetic association, the sea. These superimpositions of sense, along with this objectivity, may be associated with the "simultaneism" of the painters Robert and Sonia Delaunay—or the Orphism, to use the term Apollinaire himself applied to their painting. He was living in their apartment during those two months,[4] and the major turn in his style is most emphatically represented in the poem dedicated to Robert Delaunay, given the title of several of Delaunay's paintings, and first printed as the introduction to the catalogue of his show in Berlin:

Les Fenêtres

Du rouge au vert tout le jaune se meurt
Quand chantent les aras dans les forêts natales
Abatis de pihis
Il y a un poème à faire sur l'oiseau qui n'a qu'une aile
Nous l'enverrons en message téléphonique
Traumatisme géant
Il fait couler les yeux
Voilà une jolie jeune fille parmi les jeunes Turinaises
Le pauvre jeune homme se mouchait dans sa cravate blanche
Tu soulèveras le rideau
Et maintenant voilà que s'ouvre la fenêtre
Araignées quand les mains tissaient la lumière
Beauté pâleur insondables violets
Nous tenterons en vain de prendre du repos
On commencera à minuit
Quand on a le temps on a la liberté
Bigorneaux Lotte multiples Soleils et l'Oursin du couchant
Une vieille paire de chaussures jaunes devant la fenêtre
Tours
Les Tours ce sont les rues
Puits
Puits ce sont les places
Puits
Arbres creux qui abritent les Câpresses vagabondes
Les Chabins chantent des airs à mourir
Aux Chabines marronnes

Et l'oie oua-oua trompette au nord
Où les chasseurs de ratons
Raclent les pelleteries
Étincelant diamant
Vancouver
Où le train blanc de neige et de feux nocturnes fuit l'hiver

O Paris
Du rouge au vert tout le jaune se meurt
Paris Vancouver Hyères Maintenon New-York et les Antilles
La fenêtre s'ouvre comme une orange
Le beau fruit de la lumière

The Windows

From red to green all the yellow dies
When the aras sing in their native forests
Pihis giblets
There is a poem to be done
     on the bird with only one wing
We will send it by telephone
Giant traumatism
It makes one's eyes run
There is one pretty one among all the
     young girls from Turin
The unfortunate young man blew
     his nose in his white necktie
You will lift the curtain
And now look at the window opening
Spiders when hands wove the light
Beauty paleness unfathomable violets
We shall try in vain to take our ease
One will start at midnight
When one has time one has liberty
Periwinkle Monkfish multiple Suns
     and the Sea-urchin of the setting sun
An old pair of yellow shoes in front of the window
Towers
Towers are streets

Wells
Wells are market places
Wells
Hollow trees which shelter vagabond goat-maids
The Octoroons sing songs of dying
To their chestnut-colored wives
And the goose honk honk trumpets in the north
When raccoon hunters
Scrape the pelts
Gleaming diamond
Vancouver
Where the train white with snow and fires of the night flees
      the winter
O Paris
From red to green all the yellow dies
Paris Vancouver Hyères Maintenon New York and the
      Antilles
The window opens like an orange
The beautiful fruit of light

                   (Trans. Roger Shattuck; revised by author)

As Apollinaire said of this poem, "I have done as much as possible to simplify poetic syntax, and I have succeeded in certain cases, notably in one poem, *Les Fenêtres*."[5] The simplification of syntax works to place each of the statements in parallel position to the others, much like the wedges of color in the "windows" painted by Delaunay (frontispiece). Apollinaire evens out syntax as Delaunay abolishes perspective.

"Du rouge au vert tout le jaune se meurt." This opening line by itself states a principle about the interaction of color, an entry in a long discourse sustained by Goethe and Runge and maintained to this day.[6] And at the same time this kind of abstraction aims its statement not only at a general maxim, but also at a specific possibility of description. It indicates the actual colors in the "windows" of Delaunay, who was fond of reds, greens, and yellows. And it may also indicate the actual light coming in the window of the studio where Delaunay said Apollinaire composed the poem.[7] These possibilities of shuttling between generality and notation of visual facts

are resumed suddenly in the run beginning *Et maintenant voilà.*
Beauté pâleur insondables violets may be taken as the effects on the
speaker-beholder when the light, or else the painter himself, has
"lifted the curtain" and "woven the light." Of his painting *Fenêtre
Simultanée* Delaunay himself later emphasizes this very color, "le
violet . . . contrastes simultanées."[8]

In the same place Delaunay associates joy with a mobility of perspective, "une sensation de mobilité, de joie." The attempt begun
in Cubism, baptized in a joke five years earlier by Matisse (as
Apollinaire notes),[9] emerges in the Orphism of Delaunay, and in
the suspended logic of Apollinaire. The mythic birds of this poem
are freely invented while being divorced from any narration of
myth other than their existence. The young women are presences
on a par with the nose-blowing young man or the train presumably
headed south ("fuit l'hiver") while caught in the snows and fires of
a night whose Fauvist colors (the line suggests a painting by
Vlaminck),[10] are not completely divorced from the object always
held somewhat in view, a painting of windows by Delaunay.

The white of the snows has earlier been keyed in the white of the
young man's necktie. Yellow is picked up not only in the repeated
color-line but in the old pair of shoes—by the window. All the
colors here can be taken for reference to the paintings under nearly
surrealized discussion. The other colors come singly, the violet, the
maroon-chestnut of the Chabines, and finally that color which com-
pletes the complementarity of red, yellow, and green—orange.
Orange is a combination of red and yellow. It is a counterpart to
the mix of blue and yellow producing the named green. And
orange is also the strong afterimage of blue, a color combined for
green but not mentioned here.

The dense associations of the cities and places the nostalgic narrator evokes in *Zone* are here condensed to the connotations of their
bare names, given in a series whose amplification enters rapidly into
a simultaneity of effect that records and induces joy, as the special
length of that line emphasizes, "Paris Vancouver Hyères Maintenon
New-York et les Antilles." Not all of these places are in the un-
wintry clime where the train is heading, and so the connection can-

not be firmly made to a sequence. But some of them are, and so the connection cannot be severed either.

2

The collection in which *Les Fenêtres* was to have been given an important place, already set up in proof by August 1914 and long deferred by the war, was entitled *Et Moi aussi je suis peintre.* As I have indicated, there was ample justification for the assertion in this title, and we may find further analogues and congruences of purposes in what Delaunay himself was setting out to do, as he himself and as Apollinaire described it; "Le style est toujours synthètique," Delaunay says.[11] The adjective may be said to comprise a number of the features in his painting, and in Apollinaire's *Les Fenêtres.* Painting is synthetic because it puts together colors and organizes spaces on a canvas; this particular style of painting is especially so for confining itself to the purity of such procedures, forcing the purity beyond space and color-matching to a sort of exaltation or joy. The writing of this poem, too, is synthetic in its resolute disavowal of natural syntactic connections and sequences, in its insistence on the separability and richness of each integral line, and also in the play of mere association across the lines, from color to color, or bird to bird or place, or gesture to gesture as they are named. The self-transcendence of the means, Delaunay says, amounts to a sort of Expressionism,[12] thereby pointing to the work of German painters with whom he was in intimate contact. In being purely expressive, Apollinaire's poem may also be said to have pushed an Expressionism that makes *Alcools* resemble, say, Georg Heym, to a point where it retains the strong emotion of such poetry, while at the same time attaining an impersonality that would seem to rule out the possibility of strong emotion.

Of how this can happen in painting Delaunay provides a theoretical justification, "la lumière dans la nature crée le mouvement des couleurs. Le mouvement est donné par les rapports *des mesures impaires,* des contrastes des couleurs entre elles qui constitue "la réalité' " (light in nature creates the movement of colors, the movement is given by the relations *of unequal measures,* the contrasts of the colors among themselves which constitutes "reality").[13] The force of this statement for German painting, for Expressionism, is indicated by the fact that Klee translated this essay for *Der Sturm*. Its adaptability for Apollinaire is striking if one takes the colors in *Les Fenêtres* and the light that is repeated to be the last word of the poem as a verbal equivalent for this procedure. If *words* and *references* are substituted in this quotation for *lights* and *colors*, we have a fair description both of the movement of *Les Fenêtres* and its effect. The *rapports des mesures impaires* applies even more directly to the unequal line lengths of the verses, the measures, in the poem than to the uneven size of lozenges, say, in a painting of Delaunay, since in a sense a painting presented to the view is analogous not to many lines of verse but to one. It cannot be broken up; the yellow stands next to the green. Whereas in a poem, we move on to a line, and the minimal lines and names offered through the center here, the rich opposites of *tours* and *puits* with their arbitrary, dangling definitions, are separate and distinct, absolutized in their inequality. This phrasing impressed Apollinaire, since he twice borrows it to describe Delaunay's aims. He speaks, without explicitly naming Delaunay, of "sensations artistiques uniquement dues à l'harmonie des lumières impaires,"[14] where the uniqueness of effect to be derived from the procedure is emphasized. And he praises Delaunay as a source of an "harmonie des lumières impaires."[15]

Apollinaire speaks, further, of color as an ideal dimension that includes and creates the others ("la dimension idéale, c'est la couleur. Elle a par conséquent toutes les autres dimensions . . . la couleur ne dépend plus des trois dimensions connues, c'est elle qui les crée").[16] In speaking of this "fourth dimension" he is being so metaphorical that his inclusiveness can be, with the license he has taken, extended to the effect of the grouped locutions, the single lines, of *Les Fenêtres*.[17] We may take our cue from another of Apollinaire's statements about color in Delaunay and elsewhere. He declares that there is at once a development in color and a simultaneous presentation; and development would seem to suit the spatial art of painting (in spite of our perceptual reconstruction of the work) as little as simultaneous presence does the art of literature. ("La couleur est forme et sujet . . . elle est purement la thême qui se développe

. . . est fonction d'elle-même, toute son action est présente à chaque moment.")[18]

Now Apollinaire achieves something like this effect by so suspending the sequence from line to line in *Les Fenêtres* that, except for occasional runs of two or three lines, we are not even able to assert a clear or abrupt disjunction. (In this he is pre-Surrealistic, again, and also more inclusive than those Surrealists who foreground their abrupt disjunctions.) The train of snow and night fires may be fleeing the Paris of the following line, or it may not. It may be fleeing from or traveling towards the Vancouver of the preceding line. Paris and Vancouver are picked up, in inverse order, in the next line but one. But the anaphoric connection is interrupted by another repetition, that of the first line of the poem, "Du rouge au vert tout le jaune se meurt." The possibility of applying that line to the color of cities—Delaunay painted several lozengelike cityscapes at the same time that he was painting his series of *Fenêtres*—cannot be ruled out, since it runs a gamut from most general (an abstraction about the effect of color) to quite specific (a description of one or more paintings by Delaunay). Moreover, one cannot get to Paris from Vancouver by train, let alone New York or the Antilles. And since the function of simply naming them the first time was tied to no syntactic statement, but rather the bare locution (differentiated by *O* preceding Paris), the list of the antepenultimate line arranges them in a different order than the ones we may attribute to those first occurrences.

The poem at most points, then, resists an attribution of logical sequence. In *Zone,* however, randomized and associative as that poem is, a connection from section to section can always be picked up. There are thematic recurrences in *Les Fenêtres*—noises, fauna, places, even distances—but these, in their distinctness from each other, may be compared to a segment of yellow in the upper left-hand corner of a painting that picks up a segment in the lower right, and all the more powerfully if the color is attached to no representational object, not even a Cubistically rendered one.

We may then attribute to the new poetic effect Apollinaire had achieved the terms he applied to Delaunay's painting. *Les Fenêtres* verges on a simultaneism because in being suspended from either asserting or denying sequence to individual lines we are forced to concentrate on them. We thereby enter a mood of exaltation—all the significations are gathered up in a sort of rapturous affirmation—that may well be called Orphism—a term Apollinaire had given (*Le Cortège d'Orphée*) to his earlier bestiary illustrated by Raoul Dufy. The animals of *Les Fenêtres*—ara, pihi, one-winged bird, periwinkle, monkfish, sea urchin, raccoon—are divorced from even bemused allegorization but caught up in rich, momentary metaphors. Consequently we may also apply to his lines the even more specific term Orphic Cubism, something he declares to be an "entirely new, powerful reality."[19] Cubism, however, though it allows for a freedom of color, has a restrictive side.[20] To become purely Orphic, to free himself from those restrictions, Delaunay eschewed representation. There were poets who eschewed representation too—the Dadaists in one of their more extreme moments. But Apollinaire, for all his excitation about vogues, never imitated them, and he offers no single nonsense poem. Instead, he finds freedom, again, in the detachment of significations from even the random sequences of his earlier poems. "Quand on a le temps on a la liberté," and this casual statement, in one dimension a tautologous assertion about scheduling a day, may be taken in another dimension to be a declaration about the very poem before us, whose liberty is bound up with its mastery of the time in its own sequences.

"Du rouge au vert tout le jaune se meurt." There is no painting of Delaunay's composed of only three color bands, and so when applied to him this statement must be applied to the effect across just a segment of a painting. Turning this "constructive" effect of color interaction to one of Apollinaire's richer lines, we may find, within the isolation of the individual lines, an analogue to this effect. We may also find it moving over the whole poem; moving from Vancouver to Paris in the poem, no function is given to the snow-white night-fire train; it has "died," and indeed the line about colors is repeated right after the naming of Paris, which has also died by comparison with it (though one may aspectually apply mobile red, green, and yellow to the "feux nocturnes" of the trains). The old yellow shoes by the window may be taken anecdotally, "seen" visually, or loaded with significance. They are reminiscent of paintings by van Gogh that have turned out to have considerable theoretical suggestiveness.[21] These shoes are as suspended from, "die" towards, the towers, as they do towards the rich, much more complicated preceding line. The three lines offer a momentary decrescendo. And across the first of these lines there plays a blaze of metaphorical color: "Bigorneaux Lotte multiples Soleils et l'Oursin du couchant."

Monkfish, sea urchin, and *sun* are the only nouns except for *Tours* (suggesting the city), willfully capitalized in the poem, suggesting a mode of possible allegorization for them, as then also for the periwinkles (*bigorneaux*).

Most extravagantly metaphoric is the last of the series, "l'Oursin du couchant," a physical image that turns the setting sun into a spiny blaze of color—in itself an implicitly Cubistic image because the bare name leaves open the two possibilities that we are meant to visualize either the purplish, spiny exterior of the sea urchin or the richly red-orange interior. We then must juxtapose them much as Picasso juxtaposes front and side view of a face in the *Demoiselles d'Avignon* (1907). Reading backwards, the sea urchin is the last of the series begun with the periwinkle, it is a stationary mollusk; like the monkfish it comes from underwater and not from the rocks of the tidal zone. In this line it has not only become the vehicle end of a metaphor; it has also been powerfully displaced, from underwater into the heavens. It is a special and double metaphor, first through its capitalization, then through its figurative attachment to the sun. And at the same time the first of these, the allegorical capitalization, dies into the second, the figure, much as yellow (also a color of the sun) dies in the opening statement. For that matter— since the generalization holds—the yellow dies in the very next line, as all yellows, for their recessiveness, may be taken to do and as this yellow may be assumed specifically to do as it is eclipsed by the red of the sea urchin that precedes it or the greenish cast to the water of the wells mentioned three times in the lines that shortly follow.

Third in the series is not a sea creature but a group of suns, "Soleils," assimilated to the sea creatures by its inclusion in the series, by the common capitalization, and by the fact that the last sea creature, the "Oursin," is itself a metaphor for the sun. The

"Soleils" may be yellow; the "Oursin du couchant" is not, and the yellow may be said to die in it with the dying day.

The opening aphorism has been spelled out and also emblazoned. Added to all this play of "light" across the line is another grammatical alignment: The singulars and the plurals alternate—*Bigorneaux, Lotte, Soleils, Oursin;* and this alternation cuts across that between possibly literal (the first three) and certainly metaphorical (the last), as well as across that between sea creatures (the first, second, and fourth) and suns (the third and, in its figure, the fourth). The suspension of punctuation here works not just to emphasize rhythm, as Apollinaire claims. Taken with the bare nominalization here, it furthers the syntactic suspension.

From line to line, too, there is a sort of free play. Here an abstraction is followed by the rich list we have been reading out; and the rich list is followed by a plainly described object in a setting:

> Quand on a le temps on a la liberté
>
>> Bigorneaux Lotte multiples Soleils et l'Oursin
>>   du couchant
>> Une vielle paire de chaussures jaunes devant
>>   la fenêtre.

If the yellow of the shoes is not their natural color but one derived from the sun, then this line, too, picks up the "Soleils"; it is one of them; metaphorically a sun. And when the sun goes down, at the "Oursin du couchant" the color will die—which it will anyway, even if the shoes are a natural yellow, for the color will not show in the darkness of the midnight that has somewhat contradictorily preceded these lines ("On commencera à minuit"). *On commencera* is doubly future, in tense and in the verb of beginning. The possibility of reading the beginning on through the other lines allows that future to cast an air of prospective anticipation over all that is being said, a further play. So it must be secondary that the movement from the height of towers to the depth of wells inverts the movement from the depth of sea creatures to the height of suns. Or from one hollow (wells) to another (hollow trees). The runs are so playful anyway that a kind of parity subsists between defensible architectural observations ("Les Tours ce sont les rues") and nearly surrealistic propositions ("Puits ce sont les places"). Wells can be squares, or places, only if they are thought of as catch basins for the sunlight always in question when windows are the subject. Or if the well, as in certain German towns, prominently figures in the center of the public square. Or if, tautologously, a well must exist in a fixed place as a word must in a poem, to say nothing of a patch of color in a painting. All these possibilities play across the bare illogic of the proposition: it boldly challenges ordinary language to say that a well is a public square.

As we proceed the gaps get greater, the sequences faster:

> Et l'oie oua-oua trompette au nord
> Où les chasseurs de ratons
> Râclent les pelleteries
> Étincelant diamant
> Vancouver

The resolution, revelation, and possible summary, come in two lines that themselves are nascent equivalents for each other.

> La fenêtre s'ouvre comme une orange
> Le beau fruit de la lumière

Ten months before writing this poem, in February 1912, Apollinaire had praised the "mots en liberté" of the Futurists. Now, in the presence of painting, and through something akin to the principles of the art criticism he had been writing regularly for years, he has found a way to put individual words into further liberty.

3

Baudelaire and Mallarmé both wrote poems entitled "Les Fenêtres"[22] To these could be added Laforgue's two poems about stained-glass windows and Corbière's "Portes et Fenêtres." Mallarmé's windows encapsulate many psychological motions, including the exaltation through reflection of the beholder, "je me mire et me vois ange" (I look at me and see me an angel). Through the poem, however, for all the density of its attributions, there is a classical fixity of perspective, a steady look through the window or inferences about the look, first of the dying man "las du triste hôpital" of the opening, and then of the speaker who imitates him by looking. The first attitude does not differ in posture from the dying man of Tennyson's "Tears, Idle Tears," for whom "the casement slowly grows a glimmering square." Much fantasy accrues to both of Mallarmé's window-gazers, but the line between fantasy and reality is not erased, as it is in Apollinaire. And in Baudelaire's prose poem, written as it happens after Mallarmé's early one, the perspective is also fixed; these are windows to look through; first one looks out ("Celle qui regarde du dehors à travers une fenêtre ouverte"), then one looks at the closed window ("ne voit jamais autant de choses que celui qui regarde une fenêtre fermée"); and then at a window, whether from inside or out, that contains a lighted candle. Then the interest of what is seen through a window is valued above what has been seen through a window.

In *Les Fenêtres* of Apollinaire, window and sun are not differentiated. There is an iconography of windows in painting, beginning with the embrasures of Ghirlandaio, the elaborate near windows of early Netherlandish painting from Dirck Bouts to Jan van Eyck and Rogier van der Weyden; through the light-admitting windows of Vermeer and Rembrandt; to the broadly open windows of Apollinaire's contemporaries, Vuillard and Bonnard and Matisse. The elaborate nineteenth-century garden in the paintings of Vuillard is cleanly differentiated in space from the elaborate nineteenth-century living room whose French windows or large casements open upon it. Interpenetration of the spaces is subordinated to differentiation. In Matisse the space is less differentiated, and the window begins to become a "beau fruit de la lumière." Finally in Delaunay the windows are windows in name only; color and light confound each other, just as in the program Apollinaire extols. We cannot tell whether we are seeing through to a kaleidoscopic exterior or being dazzled by light breaking as it enters an interior: window and sun share each other's attributes. We know from the title only that we are dealing with a window.[23]

It is a window that resembles another, earlier iconographic tradition, that of the stained-glass window, a window meant not to permit a view but to structure the light as it enters into designs or into emblematic representation of religious symbols, Biblical history, and other referential figures.

Taken as a window, the painting of Delaunay looks like a stained-glass window rather than a window to see through; and yet inner and outer are fused: the painting is both and neither, and its Orphism presents a sort of model of intersubjectivity. So does *Les Fenêtres* of Apollinaire, where the elements of narrative, of image, and of logical proposition; of fantasy and reality; of rumination backwards and progression forwards, have lodged themselves into colorful bits of locution to become indistinguishable. Apollinaire has carried off, like Delaunay, what he asserts to be the task of both poet and painter, to change the appearance of nature in the eyes of men, "les grands poètes et les grands artistes ont pour fonction sociale de renouveler sans cesse l'apparence que revêt la nature aux yeux des hommes."[24]

4

There is a limit, and also a sort of virtuality, in identifying a common aim between poetry and painting. Apollinaire himself declared in a 1907 review of Matisse, before he had subjected himself deeply to the influence of the other art, that poetry and painting have nothing in common. One could, moreover, follow Lyotard and others in the highly intricate enterprise of distinguishing the implications of the sign systems in both verbal and visual structures.[25] Still, it is not just impersonality that Apollinaire has gained by writing about, and towards, Delaunay. He has also managed what he claims for Cubist painting, that it is not an art of imitation.[26] Yet it is not antimimetic either: the wells and towers and sea urchins and trains come somewhat into locutionary force from this angle; they are imitated without being delineated. Failing ot ask what is happening through the analogue of painting, staying a comfortable margin on the safe side of the limit between the two arts, would leave untested the very ground that is most important for this poem, the ground it shares with its artistic subject as it appears in the élan of introduction for the exhibition catalogue where the poem was first printed. Taking a cue from Apollinaire's description of Duchamp,[27] we can say that in what seems at once a directness and evasiveness in *Les Fenêtres,* "la littérature disparait de son art, mais non la poésie" (The literature disappears from his art, but not the poetry). Certainly a joke is not isolated and framed in this poem, as in the Dadaist or Surrealist *Fresh Widow* of Duchamp, a plain paneled window with panes covered in black as though for mourning.

The liberty Apollinaire achieved here of lines that are neither attached nor detached was shortly to afford him the balanced "concreteness" of painterlike poems, the *Calligrammes.* In the more involuted of these, like "Lettre-Océan" and "Coeur, Couronne, et Miroir," a richness of separable locutions is expanded round, teased into, and qualified by a variety of physical shapes. Nearly all these *calligrammes* surpass the programmatic post-Dada simplicity of most modern concrete poems, which sacrifice the profusion firmly gained in *Les Fenêtres* and retained throughout Apollinaire's career.

The emblematic arrangement of letters into shapes, from the egg of antiquity to the Easter Wings of Herbert, matches the statement of the poem by a single diagram and the artifice of the poem by still another display of virtuosity. The arrangement of words in *Un Coup de dés,* while not at all emblematic, is not yet "concrete." It simply uses up and renders significant the total white space of the page by utilizing the relative positions, intervening distances, and type sizes of its words—in addition to the usual sequence—for reverberant meaning. Most neo-Dadaist "concrete" poetry, via the irony of eschewing and advertising itself as object through the implicitly minimalizing display of its objecthood,[28] resolves to simple paradox. The word *love* is turned into a painting, colored and displaced in a broken circle; the word *rain* is printed to look like rain seen through a window or rain falling. Thus a simple juxtaposition of the momentary presentation with the lexical source comes to a dead heat of simple paradox or simple pseudomimesis. This point is nearly always reached in concrete poems—it is a sort of convention for them, and also a "Parnassian" limitation—however far apart the word constituents may be in their lexical moorings, however distorted their presentation. At the same time the terrain is vast that Mallarmé opened up between poetry and visual space by the simple process of bringing the white spaces of *Un Coup dés* into conjunction on the page with the size and positions of individual letters and words.

That intermediate terrain allows concrete poetry to converge and interact with conceptual art in a varied dialectic that Duchamp exploited and that many others have profoundly manipulated.[29]

Apollinaire's "Il pleut," however, powerfully works this terrain by stringing out utterances about other things than rain: each of the five strings of utterances touches distantly on the sort of Romantic associations to the mood of the rain that Verlaine evoked in his famous poem. "Il pleut des voix de femmes comme si elles étaient mortes même dans le souvenir" (It rains women's voices as though they were dead even in memory)—stringing this Nerval-like statement out into a single strand of "rain" enables Apollinaire to impersonalize it, to ironize it with a less heavy hand than Baudelaire had ironized Romantic attitudes. He can inspect it and share it at once.

Having less than the virtuosity and match of the Renaissance emblem, a freer space than that envisioned by Mallarmé, and little of the minimalist intent in concrete poetry, Apollinaire's *calligrammes* only play with the idea of being art objects, mixing that play into the modality of their statement. They are far from squarely encapsuling a self-recoding proposition into their visual features. "Coeur Couronne et Miroir" bends its words into three complementary pictures, similar in deriving from a royalist context; it then puts them together as three playfully exalted claims for the poet. "La Mandoline l'oeillet et le bambou," "The Mandolin the Violet and the Bamboo," arranges a less complementary triad, and the relative lack of complementarity becomes part of the poem's exuberance, spilling over into the statement, where the regular knots of the bamboo are called the links of a chain. "Lettre-Océan," in the public form of holding up a private letter to Apollinaire's actual brother Albert in Mexico, mixes varied type faces, phrases arranged in a sun wheel, postmarks, and schematic wave diagrams, while through these forms play aphorisms, observations about common scenes in Paris, and the standard phatic phrases of epistolary correspondence.

One could say of these transmimetic poems—these superrealistic achievements, to retranslate once again the word Apollinaire coined —that as he says in "Arbre," "La seule feuille que j'aie cueillie s'est changée en plusieurs mirages," (The only leaf I have gathered has changed into many mirages). Or, resuming the line of "La Chanson du mal aimé" in *Les Collines:*

> Et la lumière se déploie
> Et ces clartés la transfigurent
>
> Mais ce sont de petits secrets
> Il en est d'autres plus profonds
> Qui se dévoileront bientôt
> Et feront de vous cent morceaux
> À la pensée toujours unique
>
> And light deploys itself
> And these clarities transfigure it
>
> But there are little secrets
> There are others more profound
> That will soon be unveiled
> And will make of you a hundred pieces
> For the thought that is always one

The little secret is one that Delaunay, who often thereafter quotes Apollinaire, phrased for his own use of color, an effect that Apollinaire had invented for poetry, making words—as well as colors—a function of themselves, so that they are at once form and subject, their action present at every moment, "La couleur est forme et sujet . . . elle est purement la thème qui se développe . . . est fonction d'elle-même, toute son action est présente à chaque moment."[30]

One may find here and there in a somewhat more rhetorically sequenced poetry based on some disjunctions, what seem like, and may be, echoes of *Les Fenêtres,* as in Eliot's *The Waste Land:*

> Tours . . .
> Paris Vancouver Hyères Maintenon
>   New York et les Antilles
>
> Falling towers
> Jerusalem Athens Alexandria
> Vienna London

or

Tours
Les Tours ce sont les rues
Puits
Puits ce sont les places
Puits

And upside down in air were towers
Tolling reminiscent bells, that kept the hours
And voices singing out of empty cisterns and exhausted wells.

Less incidentally, and more certainly, much of the modern poetry in France and elsewhere has adapted a transmimetic mode of the seeming suspensions that cannot be found in the personal bravura of *Zone.* Such a transcendental use of sequence comes into triumphant statement first in *Les Fenêtres,* not just through the marvelous images of a new Rimbaud but through a new extension of the suspensions of Mallarmé. The new syntax, the new mode of signification, comes hand in hand with that of the paintings it celebrates, parallels, and describes.

V

Surrealism and Surrealisms

DALI SUFFOCATES
IN DIVING HELMET, UNSCREWED
BY BRITISH POET[1]

It is almost equally perplexing, or limiting, to define Surrealism broadly so that it covers a large variety of cases, and to define it so specifically that the theory and practice of one poet or painter—say André Breton or René Magritte—may be taken as a norm from which others diverge. Certainly if Surrealism be seen as a movement, the way Breton and others have insisted it be seen, then the practitioners immediately fall into precursors like Lautréamont and Apollinaire, main defenders of the movement like Breton and Éluard, recruits like Miró and Max Ernst, sometime associates like Arp and Max Jacob, and the defectors, themselves of various persuasions, like de Chirico and Char. Beyond these are the hosts of derivative poets and painters in Spain, South America, and Germany, or the third-generation figures derived in turn from them, like the American "deep image" poets. Even such a complex of historical affiliations would leave out analogous cases, like the Dadaists and post-Dadaists in poetry and painting, from Marcel Duchamp to those of the New York School of poets who specialize in absurd or explosive frames for their work. And what of filmmakers like Buñuel? What of Ionesco, whose *Cantatrice Chauve* contains standard juxtapositions of a Breton type under a title that could well have been invented by the author of *Le Revolver à cheveux blancs?*[2] In one sense, in fact, Ionesco inverts Breton's title and performs upon eroticism a transposition that harmonizes with the aims of Surrealism. Can one dissociate from the movement a Samuel Beckett whose intellectual development took place in Paris during the very years when Surrealism most dominated the artistic landscape?[3] The particular humor of Beckett's late plays, their very tempo, owes something not just to Pirandello but to such specific forms as those of Vitrac and Audiberti. The family situation in *Endgame* extends and solemnizes *Victor ou les enfants au pouvoir;* Hamm's parents have lost control, and correspondingly, as in Vitrac, the coordinates by which we recognize "comedy" and "tragedy" seem to have been replaced by a dream logic.

The label *Surrealism* shifts over time, in fact. In this connection it is instructive to look at the catalogue for the Surrealist show at the Museum of Modern Art in 1936. There Grosz is shown along with Dali, and figures too eclectic for the movement like Picasso, and others who since have drifted out of our association with Surrealism entirely, like Giacometti, Henry Moore, and Picabia stand alongside Magritte, Miró, Ernst, and Tanguy.[4]

Does not Delaunay's Orphic Cubism, as it explores the psychological range of color, repeat nonverbally the chromatic delirium of Surrealist poems, the irrational associations of other more typical paintings?

Gauguin had argued for the release of color from mimetic association, and the release was to be the sort of spiritual release Breton later promulgated in valorizing free association.[5] Kandinsky systematizes such effects of color, as the German Romantic Runge had done long before, in *Über das Geistige in der Kunst.* Kandinsky's own non-objective paintings contain figures in them not so different in their color and spatial relations from the slightly more figurative contemporary works of Miró. Even Mondrian, according to Robert Motherwell, thought of his squares of primary color on a white field as designating an ideal universe rather than as moving his forms in an ideal internalized space.[6] Mondrian saw his lines as thick two-dimensional areas like a road, not as abstract markers. Klee, too, has often been classified as a Surrealist, but his vast treatise on painting, *Das Bildnerische Denken,* speaks a great deal more about the psychological impression of various lines in combination and various colors in combination than it does about contradiction, the unconscious, or the spiritual in art. And when he does expound on them,[7] he sounds a great deal more like Kandinsky and even Gauguin than he does like Breton.

Matisse, around 1910, just as Surrealist practice was beginning to be formulated, liberated his own colors spectacularly from assignment to a given object and let them spread across the canvas like the atmosphere of a dream or the signature of the *bonheur* for which he aimed.[8] The colors are saturating and omnipresent beyond the limited visual cues of the waking world. Breton does not, as it happens, include Matisse in *Surrealism and Painting,*[9] but he does include marginal figures like Picasso and Duchamp, as well as precursors like Le Douanier Rousseau.

Breton would give equal powers to poetry and to painting in evoking a Surrealist universe.[10] Wallace Stevens would insist on the irrational as something not to be assigned so restrictedly to that label.[11] "We are at the moment so beset by the din made by the surrealists and surrationalists," he says, "and so preoccupied in reading about them that we may become confused by these romantic scholars and think of them as the sole exemplars of the irrational today."

This essay, written in 1937, at the heyday of the Surrealist movement's spread through the Western world, seems to have Breton in mind, or at least something like what Breton argues for. We may indeed take Stevens' term as a starting point, detach it from the movement, and restore the term *surrealism* in its common usage as the axiomatization of the irrational in art or poetry.

Even if we keep our view so general, following Stevens, that it will cover cases beyond those that have ever been considered Surrealistic, like Stevens' own work, still we will encounter difficulties peculiar to just this theoretical enterprise. The difficulties derive from the aspiration of such works in themselves, rather than from the usual difficulties of defining such terms as *allegory* and *symbol*. Such terms themselves undergo transformation when they enter a surrealistic, or even an irrational area of verbal usage. Steven says of the statue in his own "Owl's Clover" that it is a "variable symbol." Since Stevens aims this remark at the irrational, we cannot thread our way towards his sense by matching the predications of this poem's thousands of lines, all of which are aimed at the statue in its "rhapsodies of change"—to quote one of its myriad statements. Even the beginning section poses and evades the problem. In that double movement it shadows the irrational while offering rationality:

> Another evening in another park,
> A group of marble horses rose on wings
> In the midst of a circle of trees, from which the leaves
> Raced with the horses in bright hurricanes.

The poem opens by pointing its disquisitions about "The Old Woman and the Statue" away from its own occasion. An endless regress has been undertaken, and yet the next section posits an intent; "So much the sculptor had foreseen" are the very next words.

The practice in Stevens, or for that matter in Pasternak, of offering up definitions of the image, tends towards the opposite of enlightening definition. Nor can deconstruction cover the case, because the poet always has a special illumination in view. Rather, he bends the expression round on itself and opens up the possibility that a self-sufficiency in the image will evade the very comprehension it aids—a surrealistic result without what might have been called a Surrealistic procedure. It is not only, in Tynyanov's words— speaking of Pasternak's poetry specifically—that "The insurgent word tears itself loose from the thing. Thus Khlebnikov's 'self-valuable (*samovitoe*) word' converges with the 'hyperbolic word' of Mayakovsky."[12] Pasternak oscillates between the inexorably logical and the sound-speech (*zvukorech*), never resting at either of these poles that Tynyanov sets up for them:

The slantwise images, flying soaked in rain
From a highway that extinguished my candle
I cannot prevent from falling rhythmically
And tearing towards rhyme from hook and wall.

What if the universe has a mask on?
What if there are no expanses such
That someone wouldn't volunteer
To stuff their mouth with putty for the winter?

But things tear off their masks,
They lose control and shed their honor,
When they have a reason to sing,
Where's an occasion for a shower.

In this untitled poem the word translated *images* is *kartina,* the minimal word for a picture, or a canvas on which a picture would be painted—the canvases Pasternak would have seen daily in Leonid Pasternak's studio. Word interacts with picture, figuration with signification. Two different words are used for *mask—maska* and *lichina* (guise). The word translated *control* is *vlast* (power). To lose power is to gain it, when poetry relinquishes naming for evocation. This poem is a fantasia along the lines of Verlaine's poem about the rain. In it the language theorizing about images resembles Stevens while the effect resembles Breton—and still we do not quite have the surface excitation, the committed archness, or the floating signification of an emphatic Surrealism.

The modes of approach that would supplement each other in defining Surrealism and related artistic practices also contradict one another. And this is the quandary these radical procedures present to the formulating critical intelligence. If the line is erased between the dream life and the waking, if the irrational is enthroned—if a psychological approach dominates the definition, then logical contradictions become inconsequential. On the other hand, the careful logical approach, via the breaking of successive frames, as Hedges characterizes Surrealism, or the erasure of logical classes, is hard to retain inside the dream frame.[13] Either the psychological approach or the approach through logical connections among signifiers is hard to harmonize with a third approach that is nevertheless related to them, the approach through the theory of signification—from signifier and signified to referent.

Surrealism offers an "absolute" metapor. Generally there is not only a floating signifier, a variable symbol, but a floating signified, in such poems. This can be said of the poems of Merwin, or Char, or Neruda, as well as of Breton, and of the concretions of Arp as well as of the forms of André Masson. The signifiers do not float in the lines of Wallace Stevens above, however, nor do they do so in Pasternak's poem, for all the self-referentiality of both works. Signifier doubles back upon signifier in both poets, and yet Stevens points at a real statue and Pasternak at real rain. In Surrealism we pass from discourse like Mallarmé's "Le vierge, le vivace, et le bel aujourd'hui" (The virgin, lively, and beautiful today), where the abstractions converge on an actual sunlit time, to Éluard's "La terre est bleue comme un orange," where an initial relative concreteness is immediately subverted to sink, or leak, into a dreamlike associativeness.

This Surrealistic situation is further complicated when Char wishes to use such slippery images as Éluard's to produce aphorisms of wisdom or even when, in certain paintings of houses in early twilight, like *L'Empire de la lumière,* Magritte holds the nonrepresentational features of the painting to elusive effects of light and avoids entirely the juxtaposition of forms which is usually his signature.

An attempt to set definitions for Surrealism is also complicated by the presence of free-floating images in the works of poets who adhere to a rational frame for the poem but who permit it to be invaded by images whose signification cannot be referred easily to the argument of the poem. Such uses are in one way derivatives, in another way opposites, of the modernist practice where description is turned into a metaphor of human psychological activity—descriptions of a fish or a wounded bear, of ballet dancers or pelicans. Such quasi-Parnassian poems as these exercises in extended metaphor order perceptions in a single key of connection between signifier and signified: the metaphor, while submerged, remains rational. But consider this from Elizabeth Bishop after she had lived many years

in a South America where a surrealist aesthetic dominated the
world of poetry:

> The seven ages of man are talkative
> and soiled and thirsty. Oil has seeped into
> the margins of the ditch of standing water
>
> and flashes or looks upward brokenly,
> like bits of mirror—no, more blue than that:
> like tatters of the *Morpho* butterfly.
>
>   ("Under the Window: Ouro Preto")

Nothing in the persuasiveness of this calm voice can carry us
from the abstraction of that first sentence, with its strange triad of
adjectives, to the careful visual notation of the second. And the
very extravagance by which remote visual effects are imported to
focus just how the oil looks, culminates in opening a world where
relations other than visual cannot be established. The comparison
of oil to mirror, erased for the more accurate comparison to a torn
Morpho butterfly, does not relate oil to mirror to butterfly in any
way other than visual. There is no "absolute metaphor" here; rather,
the metaphor collapses back into pure tenor: used for purely visual
purposes, the mirror asserts a status of near equality with the oil,
and the butterfly fragments stand in a conclusion whose absolute-
ness refuses to be conclusive. The eye and the psyche move into per-
ilous conjunction, and we verge on the pure logical coordination
that the dream images analyzed by Freud possess. The age-old association of psyche and butterfly can neither be avoided nor applied.
Much of the poem up to this final point had sounded like random
notation. This conclusion aims its words towards the never-realized
possibility of a depth commentary on such randomness.

A similar effect is found in the final image of a poem dedicated
to Elizabeth Bishop, Robert Lowell's "The Skunk Hour," though
the analogue to Surrealism in his poem is less pronounced:

> I stand on top
> of our back steps and breathe the rich air—
> a mother skunk with her column of kittens
>   swills the garbage pail.

> She jabs her wedge-head in a cup
> of sour cream, drops her ostrich tail,
> and will not scare.

These are also the very last lines of *Life Studies,* a sequence in which the poet ponders at length his depth-psychological relations to his mother, borrowing his entitling metaphor from painting. In the context the mother skunk works as both analogy and contrast. And yet the blacks and whites of that final image—the black of the night and of the skunk's body, the white of the tail stripe and of the spoiled sour cream—do not assimilate easily to either analogy or contrast. They stand forth absolutely, turning the visual not into a metaphor but into a terrain for a life where to pause on the black stairs at night may lay one open to sights of the sort that normally one reserves for dreams.

William Stafford is a master of a corresponding oneiric vagueness:

Across Kansas

> My family slept those level miles
> but like a bell rung deep till dawn
> I drove down an aisle of sound,
> nothing real but in the bell
> past the town where I was born.
>
> Once you cross a land like that
> you own your face more: what the light
> struck told a self; every rock
> denied all the rest of the world.
> We stopped at Sharon Springs and ate—
>
> My state still dark, my dream too long to tell.

The recapitulative sentences seem rational, and the comparisons almost—not quite—do the work of locating their tenors. A mild but persistent near surrealism keeps the poem at once seamless and angled to other possibilities than the merely coherent.

Like the Lorca of a Spain where he has spent years in retreat, here suggested by his title, Philip Levine tends to conclude a poem with a series of images built on colors that assail our inability to tease their randomness into an order:

> He hates me. It's 20 years after;
> he's the brown son of a black bridge-builder
> who will die in Chicago,
>
> and I'm in a Volkswagen with three
> blue-eyed kids eating oranges. We
> keep our hands in our pockets.
>
> ("Yo Soy Americano")

Addicted like Levine to the anaphora of the Hispanic Surrealists, Robert Bly at top pitch manages a political logic and unconscious depth worthy of comparison to Blok's *The Twelve,* forcing image to suggest the drift of a state in ways that surpass much of Neruda's *Canto General:*

> There is a black silo inside our bodies, revolving fast.
> Bits of black paint are flaking off,
> where the motorcycles roar, around and around,
> rising higher on the silo walls,
> the bodies bent toward the horizon,
> driven by angry women dressed in black.
>
> ("The Teeth Mother Naked at Last")

These images operate somewhere between interior and exterior, and so between dream and waking, and in visual analogue between the still photograph and the surrealist film.

The images of this poem by James Wright are conventional, drawn seemingly from the iconography of lonely American experience. Yet these "deep images" slip over, one to another, into some dreamier world of signification than even the simply evocative. The horse and the meadow, to begin with, are uneasily linked to the derailed freight car:

Outside Fargo, North Dakota

Along the sprawled body of the derailed Great
   Northern freight car,

I strike a match slowly and lift it slowly.
No wind.

Beyond town, three heavy white horses
Wade all the way to their shoulders
In a silo shadow.

Suddenly the freight car lurches.
The door slams back, a man with a flashlight
Calls me good evening.
I nod as I write good evening, lonely
And sick for home.

The title locates the poem precisely in a place, but the last sentence of the poem renders the location of the speaker into a geographic Möbius strip. There is slippage betwen the present tenses of the nodding writer. It does not make sense either for him to write *good evening* in response to a spoken greeting or for him somnambulistically to write down words that he does not say he spoke. The act of writing, as he deepens into the nascent sleep of the poem ("nod"), can be extended back from the last sentence to the beginning of the poem, which subverts that present tense. This has the air of being written in another place than Fargo, North Dakota, and a third place is indicated when the writer speaks in the last line of being "sick for home." There is no reason to rule out the possibility that the third place and the first place are the same—that home is Fargo, North Dakota. Loneliness hovers, and logic quietly dissipates. These deep images are partly derived from the German pre-Surrealism of Trakl (who derived them in turn from the pre-Surrealist Rimbaud) and the common practice of Spanish Surrealism. They have returned their more flamboyant significations to the apparent tightness of an imperturbable narrative line. An account is given of one moment, or of a couple of moments, notable for being heavy with images and at the same time troubled in feeling. Yearning is a conventional response to trains, to open space, and to being in a strange place; these sentiments, through no mere designative strategy, are felt to invade the factual label Great Northern, but the name of the railroad remains at the same time firmly designative.

2

As for the contradiction inherent in the surrealist mounting of images, any image in a poem enlists contradiction. It does so explicitly in metaphors and in such metaphoric tropes as the simile, when some discrepancy between tenor and vehicle must obtain if the metaphor is to be felt as one at all. Even metonymy involves explicit contradiction in so far as the entities aligned, whatever their resemblance, must differ; in the world of the poem they must "resist" each other, if they are different at all.

At the same time the possibility of contradiction is implicit in the very naming of an image, one that is not metaphoric. Three horses in James Wright's poem, quoted above, fail to enter any order other than narrative. But the poem posits some order other than the narrative, for which the deep image of the horses, wading up to their shoulders in the barn's shadow, seems to stand. Between the explicitness of naming the white horses (their reference), and the implicitness of what they must mean (their sense), a contradiction would arise if the act of the poem were not calmly resolving that contradiction. This is a procedure like that in metaphor, where the discrepancy between two referents, the tenor and the vehicle, is at once evoked and resolved. But in the depth images of Wright the act of evocation-and-resolution—contradictory in itself as it enlists contradictions—pervades the poem "surrealistically."

In William Stafford's poem both procedures work together: there are metaphors, farfetched ones. And also there are bare images named in a sequence that reassures. The resolution of contradiction, operating in two registers at once, carries with it a tone of calm, and a sense that the plain depth of the world is there for all to receive and understand.

This mood is not far from the plenary presentation of the visual object, painting or sculpture, which isolates one or more images more or less selected from an iconographic tradition, presenting them for evocation and sensual delight. In this sense Surrealist and near-Surrealist poetry moves towards not just designative words but the poetic effects of words. In Victorian "literary" painting, of the sort where a betrayed girl watches her lover over a fence with another girl, the painting is not obviously poetic: the figures in the painting refer to an easily understood, typical story. This is a variant of genre painting, an appreciation of the twists of social custom. The mode of such painting is really the illustration of a nonexistent text. When Magritte, however, puts a carnival mask on an apple, or live toes on a shoe, or when he gives a bird the roots of plants, the contradiction of images enlists a structure like that in metaphor, except that in the wordlessness of painting the implicit persistently remains so. The act of resolution is itself enigmatic. It is . . . surrealist. So when Miró aligns star, bird, moon, and woman the same size on the same field. Or Arp compares forms and erases scale in *Still Life: Table, Mountain, Anchors, and Navel.*

"La terre est bleue comme une orange"—One color cancels another, and both stand in initial contradiction to *la terre.* Pindar, however, happened also to call the earth blue (*kuaneos,* fragment 33B4). Earth is, to be sure, *round* like an orange, and the possibility of so rational a statement shadows the actual line. But it is the color of the orange that is named, *blue,* and not the shape. The fruit orange has a color that is its same name, *orange.* In fact this first line of a poem by Éluard conforms to the Surrealist "color contradiction" sentence pattern, as "Je t'aime à la face des mers / Rouge comme un oeuf quand il est vert" (I love you in the face of seas / Red as an egg when it is green) (Breton, "Tiki"). The initial impression of contradiction in Éluard's line remains after we have noted that blue is the afterimage of orange; in the color experiment an orange disc stared at and pulled suddenly away will leave the illusion of a blue disc behind. Of the primary colors, yellow and red combine to make orange, leaving blue as the solitary third, an opposite as well as a sort of visual complement. Moreover the Fauvist palette, as in Matisse's *Reclining Nude,* uses rough blues and orange or reddish orange for earth colors. Such painterly use embodies still another contradiction, since blue is a sky color or cool, and orange is an earth color or warm. Éluard's line, then, could also be glossed, "The earth is celestial (blue) as it is terrestial (orange)"—an implication which in turn would well exemplify the

Surrealist erasure of the boundary between dream life and waking, the invisible life and the visible. Nor is Matisse far from such intentions, since at the time it was his aim, as stated, to get away from the visual registering favored by the Impressionists.[14] Breton himself sees contradiction, but not in the light of Duchamp, who uses it to point up the absurdity of the universe. Rather it serves to aid perception in a revolutionary new order:

Le surréalisme est le "rayon invisible" qui nous permettra un jour de l'emporter sur nos adversaires. "Tu ne trembles plus, carcasse!" Cet été les roses sont bleues; le bois c'est du verre. La terre drapée dans sa verdure me fait aussi peu d'effet qu'un revenant. C'est vivre et cesser de vivre qui sont des solutions imaginaires.[15]

Surrealism is the "invisible ray" which will one day allow us to carry it over our adversaries. "You have stopped trembling, carcasse!" This summer the roses are blue; the wood is of glass. Earth draped in its greenery has as little effect on me as a ghost. It is living and ceasing to live that are imaginary solutions.

In painting the distinction between analytic and synthetic, applied by Apollinaire to Cubism, could also be applied to Surrealism according to the kind of contradiction found in the work. De Chirico is synthetic, in a single mood. There is no real contradiction between a girl with a hoop and a simplified Renaissance building, between shadows and an even sky. The contradiction resides between the implicit meaning of such a scene and its apparent disconnection from what stands before our eyes. The same would also be true of Magritte, who is, however, analytic in the sense that contradictory elements appear on the surface of the painting. The label *La Lune* applied to a shoe, or *Ceci n'est pas une pipe* to a pipe, comprises at least two contradictions: that between a word and the wrong referent, and that between a word and a wordless object.

Where to classify Miró is a puzzle: the woman and the bird might occur in the same landscape as the star (synthetic), but on a different scale (analytic). The fact that they are abstracted allows for the possibility of a third type—the composite form, what Arp calls a concretion. This is contradictory when compared to the objects such simple organic forms bring into conjunction. Or again, in Paul Delvaux's work the contradiction is not of objects but of situations. Bare-breasted women do appear in buildings, but not on the public square, and not tied round with huge silk bows. Visible possibility contradicts conventional impossibility, referring the viewer to the world of dream.[16]

Even in the programmatic Breton and the sometimes formulaic Magritte, contradiction does not function as an absolute. Mostly it enters into solution with normal discourse or with normal representation. Take this poem of René Char:[17]

Le Nu Perdu

Porteront rameaux ceux dont l'endurance sait user la nuit noueuse qui précède et suit l'éclair. Leur parole reçoit existence du fruit intermittent qui la propage en se dilacérant. Ils sont les fils incestueux de l'entaille et du signe, qui élevèrent aux margelles le cercle en fleurs de la jarre du ralliement. La rage des vents les maintient encore dévêtus. Contre eux vole un duvet de nuit noire.

The Lost Nude

They will carry branches whose endurance knows how to use the knotty night which precedes and follows the lightning. Their word receives existence from the intermittent fruit that propagates it in tearing itself apart. They are the incestuous sons of the incision and the sign, who raised to the rims the circle-in-flowers of the jar of rallying. The rage of the winds keeps them still unclothed. Against them flies a down of black night.

This poem generates a host of contradictions: branches-night, night-lightning, night-knots, fruit-intermittence, propagate–tear apart, word-fruit, sons-flowers, jar-rallying, down-night, singular *nude* and plural *they*. At the same time each of the five sentences locates an unnamed *them,* a persistence of attribution that in no way rules out reading *them* as *everyone*. The reference to incest, to rites, and to agriculture, would substantiate such a reading. Night comes up in the first and the last sentence. To anticipate my further discussion, the imagery is mostly "Mediterranean," drawn from the benevolent cycle of nature in a warm climate and the simple structures and utensils associated with life there: branches, knots, light-

ning, fruit, rims of a well or an urn (*margelles*), jar, winds, down—
not to speak of the nude of the title. The form, again to anticipate,
is the "wisdom" utterance, repeated in five cryptic predications. Culture (*parole, porter rameaux, incision, sign, rim, jar*) alternates
with nature. Some of the contradictions conform to the "white-
haired revolver" type: their mystery will not resolve even into antithesis. Such is the case with *down* and *night*, or *jar* and *rallying*.
In a frequent topos of Char's he mentions speech, perhaps the very
speech of the poem. He does so minimally, however, and *parole*
and *signe* cannot especially be singled out to qualify the poem, any
more than *rameaux* and *duvet*. The opennness of these attributions,
their diffusion and their generality,[18] falling beyond and to one side
of the contradictions, creates an air of urgency to a communication
that must be at once so elliptical and so condensed.[19] The images
correspond to another dictum of Breton's:

> Les objets de la réalité n'existent pas seulement en tant que tels: de la
> considération des lignes qui composent le plus usuel d'entre eux surgit—
> sans même qu'il soit nécessaire de cligner des yeux—une remarquable
> *image-devinette* avec laquelle il fait corps et qui nous entretient, sans
> erreur possible, du seul objet *réel* de notre désir. (Italics Breton's)[20]

> The objects of reality do not just exist as such: from the consideration
> of the lines that compose the most ordinary of them, there arises—without
> one's having to bat an eye—a remarkable *image-riddle* with which it makes
> a single body, and which puts us into contact without possible error, with
> the one *real* object of our desire.

3

This statement, like such poems as *Le Nu Perdu*, connects the devices of contradiction—or at least that which is puzzling in an image—with both the source and goal of language, with the desire
that reveals the unconscious.

The connection between contradiction—an abrogation of the
yes-or-no schematized in the digital computer—and the unconscious, can be seen as a mechanical interchange. This connection
gets amplified in the various cyberneticizations of the unconscious
by Lévi-Strauss, whose father was a painter active during the heyday of Surrealism; by Lacan, who was a patron and associate of the

Surrealists at the same time; and by Deleuze and Guattari, who
draw on a post-Surrealist painter, Robert Lindner, for a visual representation of their own systematized "erotic machine."

The contradiction that opens Éluard's poem serves to provide it
with a tuning up to exaltations and raptures of erotic effusion:

> La terre est bleue comme une orange
> Jamais une erreur les mots ne mentent pas
> Ils ne vous donnent plus à chanter
> Au tour des baisers de s'entendre
> Les fous et les amours
> Elle sa bouche d'alliance
> Tous les secrets tous les sourires
> Et quels vêtements d'indulgence
> A la croire toute nue.
>
> Les guêpes fleurissent vert
> L'aube se passe autour du cou
> Un collier de fenêtres
> Des ailes couvrent les feuilles
> Tu as toutes les joies solaires
> Tout le soleil sur la terre
> Sur les chemins de ta beauté
>
> Earth is blue like an orange
> Never an error words do not lie
> They give you no more to sing
> In turn some kisses understand
> The mad and the loves
> She her mouth of alliance
> All the secrets of the smiles
> And what vestments of indulgence
> To believe her wholly nude
>
> The wasps flower green
> Dawn passes round the neck
> A necklace of windows
> Wings cover the leaves

> You have all the solar joys
> All the sun on the earth
> On the roads of your beauty.

This is really quite simple, almost completely anaphoric. The initial contradiction not only elevates it; that enigmatic statement also keys it into the unconscious, endowing these effusions with an air of mystery not entirely alien to Char's more complex and elliptical poem. And the imagery of the two poems, recognizably from the same repertoire, verges easily on the erotic, though less explicitly in Char's particular poem. The nude has the honor of entitling Char's poem, but the nude is "lost."

Once the signified is allowed to float, through the sentence or across the canvas, then it will float often towards that goal of the unconscious, the object of erotic desire. And at the same time the object itself, the figure of a woman bared for love, will float into connection with other signifiers. Among images the desired woman serves as the most imperious, and for Breton the image almost by itself acts to focus and expand the mind (*esprit*), "One could even say that the images appear, in this vertiginous course, as the sole guides for the mind. The mind convinces itself little by little of the supreme reality of its images. At first confining itself to undergoing them, it soon notices that they flatter its reason and correspondingly expand its cognition (*connaissance*)."[21] Breton declares that the elusive woman, Nadja, organizes for him the perception of reality, "Who were we in the presence of reality, that reality that I know now lies at the feet of Nadja like a tricky dog?"[22]

The directness of the images and the indirectness, to the point of multiple contradiction, in the syntax, derive from, and refer to, a common source. As Maurice-Jean Lefebue says, "Archetypes draw their power from being images, not vice versa."[23] Letting images dominate, liberating them somewhat from rational syntax, forces the cognition to open up for connections. The comparison of this process to alchemy is a frequent one,[24] itself somewhat arbitrary and irrational, when alert thinking is compared to a pseudoscience. In turn alchemy is compared to Eros, and by a further free comparison Eros is figured to operate the way a mechanical process does. Contradiction, as it were, surfacing in dream enigmas of words allowed to float free towards each other, traps the unconscious and makes it face the emptiness of automatic response patterns, erotic at their root, under the figure of stalled machines. *Le Grand Verre* of Duchamp glorifies and trivalializes such a process; his own obsession with the process is advertised in the long decades he spent on the work. In *Étant donné le gaz d'éclairage et la chute d'eau*, too, a weathered door with peepholes gives on the juxtaposition of two classic icons, the landscape and the nude, each rendered in three-dimensional superrealism. She is sprawled in the landscape, offered and inaccessible. Her face is just out of view. This juxtaposition goes beyond surrealism: it is neither a match nor a "mismatch," to adopt Hedges' term. But paradoxically the pervasive mismatches in *Le Grand Verre*, in Breton's poems generally, and in such films as Buñuel's *L'Age d'or* and Artaud's *La Coquille et le Clergyman*, generate at once access to the possibility of erotic fulfillment and a skewed definition of an impossibility inherent in the desire for complete fulfillment or complete communication. The more complete the communication, the more incomplete. The more riveted the eye of the desiring person, the more fixed in immobility towards the object. At the same time, such juxtapositions become machines, verbal or wordless, for generating multiplicities of sense. In Max Ernst's collage novel *Une Semaine de bonté*, free visual juxtaposition makes many elements comment on each other—erotic pursuit, the impossibility of erotic fulfillment, the displacements of the unconscious through censorship, and the mimetic realism of nineteenth-century engravings.

Such connections are already made in a much-quoted composite image from the work that Breton copied out by hand from the sole manuscript in the Bibliothèque Nationale, the *Chants de Maldoror* of Lautréamont: "Beau . . . comme la rencontre fortuite sur une table de dissection d'une machine à coudre et d'un parapluie" (Beautiful like the chance encounter on a dissecting table of a sewing machine and an umbrella). Breton would orient this statement just towards "the simplest sexual symbols"; yet its juxtaposition of three different areas of technical instrumentality only initially links through the suggestion of a sexual act at once hallucinatorily obvious and unachievable.

Another remark of Breton, from the same treatise celebrating the perfect intercommunication of the dream life and the waking, could serve to generalize this image as well as others, "The voluntary incorporation of the latent content—arrested in advance—into the manifest content, stands here to weaken the tendency towards dramatization and towards the magnification that, in the contrary case, the censorship imperiously employs."[25]

The Movement enlisted such declared advances in consciousness, such manipulations of the unconscious, in a spectrum of political programs ranging from Communism to Anarchism. Char, however, in effect declares the unassimilability of his more complex image-collocations to such programs. In his letter to Breton bowing out of a collective exhibition in 1947, he advances Eros as his excuse, though his examples, as always, set leapfrogging contradictions into motion that cannot be confined to Eros, while not being separated from it:

> Ma part la plus active est devenue . . . l'absence [ellipses Char's]. Je ne suis plus guère présent que par l'amour, l'insoumission, et le grand toit de la mémoire. Nulle littérature dans cet aveu. Nulle ambiguité. Nulle dandysme. Peux-tu sentir cela? La transvaluation est accomplie. L'agneau "mystique" est un renard, le renard un sanglier, et le sanglier cet enfant à la marelle.[26]

> My most active part has become . . . absence. I am scarcely present but through love, though insubmission, through the great roof of memory. No literature in this avowal. No ambiguity. No dandyism. Can you feel that? The transvaluation is accomplished. The "mystic" lamb is a fox, the fox is a wild boar, and the wild boar this child playing hopscotch.

A glance here at Nietzsche's *transvaluation* saps the term of politics and puts it through a series like Nietzsche's own, ending in the child, perhaps with a further glance at Heraclitus B 52, "Time sporting is a boy playing checkers; the kingdom is a boy's." Putting the mystic lamb into lower case and also into quotation marks strikes a side blow at religious institutionalism—a standard Surrealist gambit. The fox could refer to the Jesuitical side of the Church. But these predications go beyond that, nor does even the first one refer just to the Church; why is not Char himself a lamb turned fox, the docile younger associate who through the war has needed both the cunning of the fox and the boldness of the wild boar? The series is almost circular, since of the three the child most resembles the lamb. It is also deliberately cryptic as well as condensed, the bare sequence of images matched through predication and mismatched through perceived incongruity. The rhetorical frame of saying he will leave Surrealism gracefully gets adorned by this pyrotechnic display of surrealist images, whose condensations of possible allegorical and analogic senses, as typically in Char, both stretch the easy flow of surrealist rhetoric and conform to its canons.

4

Surrealist poetry, in fact, presents a marked variety of textures, aims, and image linkages, not to speak of symbologies. Lorca draws much more heavily than Breton or even Éluard on Romantic stereotypes, and on Iberian icons (when others are relatively free of identifiably nationalistic cues):

> La vaca del viejo mundo
> pasaba su triste lengua
> sobre un hocico de sangres
> derramadas en la arena,
> y los torros de Guisando,
> casi muerte y casi piedra,
> mugieron como dos siglos
> hartos de pisar la tierra
> No.
> ¡Que no quiero verla!
>> (*Llanto por
>> Ignacio Sánchez Mejías*)

> The cow of the old world
> passed its sad tongue
> over a muzzle of blood
> shed in the arena sand,
> and the bulls of Guisando,

half death and half stone,
bellowed like two centuries
sated with trampling the earth.
No.
I don't want to see it!

Elsewhere this lament for a dead bullfighter imports extravagant imagery easily recognizable as Surrealist ("and the oxide scattered crystal and nickel"; "when the sweat of snow was coming"). The unconscious is not much in view, though Lorca rests on its assumptions, rather than wholly floating its signifiers, in other poems. At this point in the *Llanto* he simply gigantizes the bulls, and a cow, who are the species responsible for the death of the bullfighter. In an iconography much like that of Picasso's *Guernica,* the violence of domestic animals is a harbinger of death.

The bulls of Guisando are a pre-Christian stone monument near Avila, a nationalistic icon and an obscure possible precursor of bullfighting, here used as a suggestion of long-elapsed time. The gigantism works, actually, in both space and time: a giant cow (in space or time) passes a sad tongue over a muzzle of blood. Stone bulls do not bellow, nor do they resemble two centuries or trample the earth. But there is a logic underlying all these tropes that is easily retrievable. A surface surrealism performs here the function of validating extravagant statement, and of allowing here not Eros but personal suffering, the long-enduring troubles of a nation, and the general Unamuno-like tragic destiny of man, to blend around the age-old Indo-European image of cattle.

A similar "Spanish" register of surrealism—pastoral and romantic imagery leavened by hyperbole—may be found in Neruda:

El mar obscene rompe y rasga,
desciende montes de trompetas,
Sacude sus barbas de toro.

Las suaves señoras sentadas
como en un barco transparente
miran las olas terroristas. . . .
("Las Viejas del Oceano")

> The obscene sea breaks and slashes,
> descends mountains of trumpets,
> shakes its bull's beard.
>
> The soft seated ladies
> as in a transparent ship
> look at the terrorist waves. . . .

Neruda sets his old women by the sea and then free-associates on them. Hints of political upheaval, of man's fate, and of ancient feminine fragility, move easily through the conventional images (*woman, sea, mountain, trumpet, beard, bull, ship, waves*). There is only a touch of sexuality (*obsceno,* the only such detail in the poem). This is a meditation on a set scene, a verbal picture not entirely foreign to the Renaissance trope of *ekphrasis.* The picture suggests certain canvases of Picasso, of women by the sea, though Picasso's women are robustly involved in pastoral tasks and not seated in inarticulate contemplation.

Breton's women are different, and so is the rapidity of his generation of contradictions along a sentence line that changes the picture too often for ekphrastic focusing:

Dukduk

> Le sang ne fait qu'un tour
> Quand le dukduk se déploie sur la péninsule de la Gazelle
> Et que la jungle s'entrouvre sur cent soleils levants
> Qui s'éparpillent en flamants
> A toutes vapeurs de l'ordalie
> Comme une locomotive de femmes nues
> Au sortir d'un tunnel de sanglots
> Là-haut cône
> Gare

> Blood makes one turn only
> When the dukduk deploys itself on the peninsula of the Gazelle
> And the jungle half-opens on a hundred rising suns
> That scatter flaming
> Full steam of the ordeal

Like a locomotive of nude women
At the issue of a tunnel of sobs
Up there cone
Railroad station

Is the railroad station, conjoined with nude women, borrowed from Paul Delvaux? In any case it forms part of a bird's-eye geography decked out in the exotic imagery recommended and employed by Rimbaud. These signifiers do float, and we cannot be sure that the first line refers to either mortality or sexuality. A post-industrial scene vies with raw nature in this dizzying sequence, and the eroticism need not be especially praised because it is so deeply, almost comfortably, assumed to be a source of imagery. Sobs have nowhere to go.

The less frenetic movement, the quieter tone, of Éluard generally softens the edge of his humor and allows the signifieds to float with seeming effortlessness. The lines are as though spoken by someone content to be where he is, and long acclimated to a place where dream and waking easily interpenetrate. So in the poem quoted above, or in this:

> Ma fenêtre aux belles plumes
> Allume la porte sèche
> Et je verse l'innocence
> Sur la tête de mon chien.
> ("Les Raisons de Rêver")

> My window of beautiful feathers
> Lights the dry door
> and I shed innocence
> On the head of my dog.

Even the still scene described by Neruda is full of exaggerated movement. Here all that moves is the light. Éluard's attributions parcel the world into barely possible connections embellished by a contradictory surface. It could be said that light "feathers," and through a window it could indeed illuminate a door, igniting it in that sense. Doors are usually dry, though not often called so. *Dry* stands in easy contradiction to *shed* since *shed* can imply *liquid*.

Innocence is not a liquid, and indeed in the case of a normal pet dog, he would shed hair on his master, not vice versa. The innocence this master sheds on him could be equally an attributed Romanticization of dumb nature or the harmlessness of the master's automatic unconscious, shed everywhere and therefore also incidentally on the head of the dog. The iconography of the whole has not departed from that of domestic interiors by Bonnard, Vuillard, and Matisse. Yet the connections make the window at once more abstract than those of Baudelaire, Mallarmé, or even Apollinaire, and at the same time more casual. The energy of surrealizing has been digested within and is accessible for image-making on demand.

Long residence in France and Spain and long study of their literatures has made W. S. Merwin the heir of these practices. He distils Éluard and Lorca, say—or many others—into a repertoire of common and neutralized surrealist gestures, a "deep image" practice far less tied to specific significations than the other American poets so labeled:

Full Moonlight in Spring

Night sends this white eye
to her brother the king of the snow

This poem takes a fairy-tale imagery and renders it in sentences that join the smoothness of Éluard to the portentousness of Lorca or Neruda. Or again, each of these five nouns is heavy with "Mediterranean" weight, recalling the normative vocabulary employed by Rafael Alberti. Trivialization is effectually forbidden. The title of this short poem in relation to the text makes it stand to primitive poetry as art song does to folk song: One way to read it is as a sort of riddle, the main way. Moonlight is a white eye. Yet it varies from the riddle form in that *her brother the king of the snow* does not function as a clue. *Spring* is left over, or else *snow* is left over, and the temporal sequence that would resolve the contradiction between them has no anchor in the timeless present of the poem. The white eye is either a welcome gift, like God's creation of sun and moon, or it is a dangerous one, since the snow will melt after many such nights. It is sunlight, though, not moonlight, that melts snow. And the night itself is undone in the presence of its visual opposites, white and snow. An easy coherence still obtains through all this, produced by the parity, simplicity, and primary significance of the nouns, the single verb, the single adjective.

Another derived surrealism widely divergent from this extends the line of Breton, as James Tate:

> Little hands were sprouting
> in the cracks
> of the sidewalk
>
> they have been told nothing
>
> a champion of kisses
> somewhere writing
> my own filthy epitaph
> ("Cycle of Dust")

If the erotic is present here, it has been rendered cosmic, and the gaps between contradictions are further widened. Bill Knott needs recourse to Breton's exoticism to import similar effects into the humdrum and the everyday, as in "Bake-off":

> They wandered thru the hand in hand.
> They found themselves winners of each other's
> Look-alike contests, but weren't surprised?
>
> Other strangers than our own may remember
> Forget to lick the birthmarks off,
> We . . . they joined hands with a wand.

Compared with such developments, Char's conundrums sound positively classic:

> *Lyre*
>
> Lyre sans bornes des poussières
> Surcroît de notre coeur.
>
> Lyre without limits of dusts,
> Surplus of our heart.

In still another direction Frederic Will intensifies predications into a single narrative of portentous slippages between adjective and adjective, agent and object:

> Red stables filled with whole horses.
> A leather window taped to prairie.
> He picks up a rock, holds it
> coldly against the moon.
> Takes a knife, peels off the shell.
> Cuts back into naked
> central rock.
> Starlight, dead in the rock.
> ("Starlight in the American Stable,"
> *Epics of America XII*)

Or again, Philip Levine adds the leaven of occasional surrealizing to the bread of reminiscence. The poem "1933" begins with reflections on the death of his father and ends, "I would be a boy in worn shoes splashing through rain." In between we have been gradually elevated to this:

> In the cities of the world
> the streets darken with flies
> all the dead fathers fall out of heaven
> and begin again
> the angel of creation is a sparrow in the roadway
> a million ducks out of Ecuador with the names of cities
> settle on the wires
> storks rise slowly pulling the houses after them
> butterflies eat away the eyes of the sun
> the last ashes off the fire of the brain
> the last leavening of snow
> grains of dirt torn from under fingernails and eyes
> you drink these

A symbology and a tonality reminiscent of Apollinaire are enlisted in a hyperbole common to Breton and Neruda, Lorca and Vallejo.

In his more abrupt, more condensed conjunctions, Paul Celan may be said to permute the rapid-fire contradictions of Breton and

the wisdom-aphorisms of Char for a poetry that strives below and
beyond philosophical statement.[27] In a surrealism that has enlisted
the later Heidegger's injunctions about the depth-cognition possible
for poetry, Celan's statements verge on philosophical propositions.
At the same time they undermine this possibility through intense
images. A Stevens-like meditation on the nature of poetic speech
goes further than Stevens to illustrate Heidegger's "die Sprache."[28]
A bare predication is never permitted. Repetition is permitted, however, in Celan's staccato version of verse refrain, a practice spectacularly played back upon recursive images in "Todesfuge." Celan,
however, soon leaves behind such specific references to even events
so apocalyptic as the Holocaust which that poem sets into meditation. As Peter Szondi says of recursions in Celan, "The compositional principle that in music is called *stretto* (*Engführung*)
provides on the one hand a resolution over the function of these
repeated verses and over the loose, self-narrowing connection between . . . parts of the poem. On the other hand it proffers [or
represents, *stellt vor*] these parts as so many voices, as voices in the
literal and not only in the musical sense."[29] And in effectually har-
monizing Celan's practice with that of many post-Romantic poets,
surrealist and other, Szondi says, "The ongoing movement [*Vo-
rangehen*] does not image the content of the poem but its progression in itself, and the poem is not a representation of reality but itself
reality."[30] "Schneebett" fuses description, evocation, and definition
in kernels of evasive meaning where the floating of the signified
and its repetition reinforce one another:

Schneebett

Augen, weltblind, im Sterbegeklüft: Ich komm,
Hartwuchs im Herzen.
Ich komm.

Mondspiegel Steilwand. Hinab.
(Atemgeflecktes Geleucht. Strichweise Blut.
Wölkende Seele, noch einmal gestaltnah.
Zehnfingerschatten-verklammert.)

Augen weltblind,

Augen im Sterbegeklüft,
Augen Augen:

Das Schneebett unter uns beiden, das Schneebett.
Kristall um Kristall,
zeittief gegittert, wir fallen,
wir fallen und liegen und fallen.

Und fallen:
Wir waren. Wir sind.
Wir sind ein Fleisch mit der Nacht.
In den Gängen, in den Gängen.

Snow-bed

Eyes, world blind in the cleft of dying: I come,
Tough growth in the heart.
I come.

Moon-mirror steep wall. On down.
(Breath-flecked light. Strandwise blood.
Clouding soul, once again form-nigh
Shadow of ten fingers-clamped.)

Eyes world blind,
Eyes in the cleft of dying,
Eyes eyes:

The snow-bed under us both, the snow-bed.
Crystal on crystal,
time-deep grated, we fall,
we fall and lie and fall.

And fall:
We were. We are.
We are one flesh with the night.
In the passages, in the passages.

The individual "names" are as smooth and general as those in
Char or W. S. Merwin, but their syntactic combinations are roughly
broken off, complete in their condensations almost before the

reader is aware they have reached a terminus. The process allows much latitude for dialectical recombination of the metaphors.

The "snow-bed" of the title is a fundament, "under us both"— dream landscape, winter landscape, a death soporific, a wordless and a colorless base for words. The generality is so severely maintained that in this particular poem the presence or absence of Eros cannot be determined, and the possibility cannot be dismissed that *us* refers to lovers on a bed of pure conjunction or of communicative disjunction.

To fall is equated with having been, "We fall: we were," equated in turn with a present of being, a state at the same time of pure transience, "in the passages," "In den Gängen," "in the goings." The poem has fed on the general current of Existentialist discussion without simply miming it. "We are one flesh with the night" again verges on Eros—but it also verges on the wordlessness of obliteration and the darkness which is the opposite, but also perhaps an ultimate likeness, of snow. The process begun in Rilke's *Sonnets to Orpheus* has been stepped up to the point where it easily assimilates the soft symbolizations of Trakl.

5

There is a narrative substratum to "Schneebett." It sounds as though it is telling a story. At the same time its narrative or nearly narrative moments have the permanence of the exemplary. It is going nowhere, and the situation is always the same. Lacking a verb, "Augen, weltblind, im Sterbegeklüft:" could be taken as a kind of historical present. It could also be the verbal result of taking stock of a situation that impels the response—or the equivalent definition—the other side of the colon: "Ich komm." From this tonic inception all the verbless clauses could be aligned in a temporal sequence—or taken as an aspect of some state, some "snow-bed" of existence, that will never submit to codification in the words that keep getting aimed at it.

The presence of a narrative reference to an event, even incipiently, has the effect of tying floating signifieds to a single occasion. The signifieds, after all, do not float wholly free. Logically as signs they resist standing firmly in place as either the tenor or the vehicle of a metaphoric expression. But temporally the reference to an event holds them in place. Similarly, though less intensely, in Reverdy's poems, menace and discovery, through the constantly maintained obliquity of the narrative, fade into each other. The speaker experiencing events in Reverdy's poems gives no cues that could locate them in a designated outer world. The metaphor pulls against, but also with, the narrative, and the resultant obliquity gains thereby an air of inevitability and imperturbability.

Breton has frequent recourse to narrative, often a blurred version of a conventional love search taking place in a Romantic landscape ("Au regard des divinités," "Silhouette de Paille," "L'aigrette," "Tournesol"—the examples are legion). In "Je Reviens," "le soir tombe" (night falls). And "il est clair que nous allons depuis long-temps à l'aventure" (it is clear we have long been going to adventure).[31] The names of the street or streets refer to personal experience, floating their signifieds by violating the rules for forming French street names: Rue-où-peut être-donné-le-droit-à-la-bonne-chère, Rue-des-chères-bonnes-âmes:

> Nous entrons dans un tabac vermoulu
> Il faut écarter d'épais rideaux de gaze grise
> Commes les bayahondes d'Haiti
> Au comptoir une femme nue ailée
> Verse le sang dans des verres d'éclipse
>
> We enter a worm-eaten tobacco shop
> One must part thick curtains of gray gauze
> Like the bayahonds of Haiti
> At the counter a wingèd nude woman
> Sheds blood in eclipse glasses
> (A bayahond is a large spreading
> tree native to Haiti.)

The narrative holds here to a constant visualization, constantly transposed. In Renaissance painting the work to be done was an *istoria,* in Alberti's term, a represented story. This poetry, in its narrative, reverses that complex frame for artistic procedure: instead of visual materials rendering and freezing a verbal account from the Old or New Testament, words set up an event that comes to a mysterious term in visual representations whose fabulous components, like the winged nude women, hint at allegory but do not compose into it.

It is not that the surrealist poem aspires to painting, the surrealist painting to poetry. Rather, in the painting the presence of contradictory "lexical" elements, of iconography—an enormous apple dominating the sea, a phalanx of strange upthrusting protuberances—throws the viewer not just to piecing these together, as though he were interpreting a dream by Freudian means. Nor does it lead him just to reaffirm the Surrealist manifesto of full access to the dream life in the waking world. Instead the silently juxtaposed objects in Magritte or in such poems as Reverdy's "Galeries," suggest communication while at the same time withdrawing it, thus richly enlisting at once the sense evocations and the impenetrability of the image.

So in the surrealist poem, the blurred but persistent narrative line constantly thrusts through to a communicative act that as constantly arrests itself on the rich and impenetrable image.

6

All poems are ostentatious; they exhibit their language. In a Romantic and post-Romantic mode a poetry incorporates reflections on the nature of poetry: its ostentation is reflexive. Much of Wallace Stevens, of course, is reflexive in this sense. And so, returning more emphatically to Surrealist terrain, is René Char. A large portion of Char's work consists of aphorisms on the nature of poetry.

These for the most part exhibit a certain obliquity, still more than does "Lyre," quoted above. The obliquity of the Surrealist not only implicitly acknowledges the refractoriness and artificiality of his medium, words or paint. It also constitutes a comment on the cryptic nature of the message. Surrealist "humor," fainter and more constant than the irony of, say, Stendhal, melds the self-satisfaction of discovery, the serenity before illogicality, and the disappointment before the partiality of all statements, into a single attitude, communicated by an overriding tone. Such a "humor" can be felt, as the faintest of overtones, even in Reverdy.

Every lover is a clown, Lévi-Strauss says, and the note of the clown is stronger in Éluard's love poetry than, say, in a Renaissance sonnet sequence. Breton edited an anthology, *L'Humour noir*. In his long "Ode à Charles Fourier," an upwelling afflatus of political aspiration is spirited into levity by addresses about cherry girls and strawberry girls (*céristes, fraisistes*) in the occupational cadres of the new society. And Stevens, too, leavens his reflections by a humor that further qualifies them; Professor Eucalyptus enters his house in New Haven and is the occasion for meditations. "Laughter," Breton says, "stands at the edge of nothingness, and gives us nothingness as a security pledge [*nantissement*]."[32] As Marie Louise Gouhier says, "The surreal is always comic: every revery effectually amplifies, every image dilates to become an image of the world"[33]— an image that shimmers with a shrugged self-qualification, self-obliteration, and self-distancing from other images through contradiction. So when Annie Le Brun, emphasizing the drama in Surrealist humor "born from the self's confrontation and the restrictive forces of existence," deduces from it another world view, that view does not and will not stay in place. "Humor is a synthesis of the imitation of nature under its accidental forms and of a humor in so far as it is a paradoxical triumph of the pleasure principle over real conditions."[34] Yet those "conditions réelles" are stable at no instant. They are inflated, sapped, and absorbed by the pleasure principle, itself elevated to the chief instrument of liberation-understanding, just as in Breton's manifestos. The zero degree of this attitude, the work of Duchamp and more simply of the Dadaists generally, arrests the process into a demonstration of absurdity, while retaining the domination of the unconscious and the mechanization of the erotic as principles. Arp, for example, Dadaist or not, never goes so far. Duchamp for the Surrealists is a priest manning the border of their rich terrain. His ultimate solemnity guarantees the significance of their laughter.

7

Surrealist practice in poetry is a counterinstance—some would say an extreme instance—of the philosophical difficulties inherent to relations among the signifier, the signified, and the object of reference. On the one hand the surrealist poem envisions a dream word by erasing, or tending to erase, the distinction between tenor and vehicle, floating both the signifier and the signified far away from an object, single or composite. On the other hand, by according a dream significance to every small object and slight event in the waking world, the erasure of distinction operates in the service of a giant reference, a giant referent. Even Heidegger's distinction between *Rede* (deep speech) and *Gerede* (chitchat) is erased; there becomes no such thing as trivial language.

This is especially the case in the heavy emphasis in surrealist poetry on image nouns, those storehouses of word sense. And particularly so with what could be called Mediterranean words—*olive, sun, light, tree, road, fruit, vine, grape, sea, earth, moon, bird, field, dawn, wheat, water, flower, summer, winter, mountain, grass, stone, lightning,* etc. One might call such words pastoral, but they refer to no set system, or transposition of set systems, that we associate with that literary genre. Mediterranean words are at once preliterary and ultraliterary.[35] Their social reference is to the age-old culture of herding and agriculture, in the Mediterranean basin, as such terms become the inevitable scene for the slow fruitions and easy recurrences of a rockbed human life. Char, for all his wisdom, rarely writes a poem without heavy recourse to this vocabulary. Merwin, for all the subtle turns in his verse, draws very largely on it, as do Lorca, Neruda, and the Spanish Surrealists generally.

Especially noticeable in Reverdy and Merwin is a drive towards wordlessness which is also a drive toward amplification. The Mediterranean images are made to seem to rise effortlessly towards the threshold of consciousness, to lull as they focus. The deep image induces a surrender to primal metaphor, at once supreme and elusive.

When such poetry verges towards the solemnity of wisdom-statement, as it does in Char's hands and Merwin's, the Mediterranean images endow it with an air of reassurance and perennial rightness. Jean-Pierre Richard detects both movements, though he does not allow for the fusion they remarkably carry through in Char's work. "In Georges de la Tour (as Char sees him) every face is an almond whose light 'transposes' . . . towards an essential solitude. Without any sort of negation, without break of closure or

consciousness, the world thereby discovers the virtue of friendship."
That is what I have been calling the Mediterranean element. "From
the Heraclitean side, on the other hand, the landscape builds as an
active antagonism and becomes drama. It governs as project of
tenderness no longer but a pledge of contraction."[36] Yet the persistent contradiction in Char's poems, "on the meditation and resolution of which Char has founded his whole poetics,"[37] does come to
resolution not through logical progression but through the steady
proffering of images in an act of utterance that is at once laconic
and ostentatious.

8

Laconic and ostentatious—these adjectives will well designate what
a painting communicates, and Surrealist poetry often interacts with
painting. Often, indeed, the poet takes a specific painting as his
point of departure or as his object in view. So Char's "Le Requin
et la mouette" (The Shark and the Seagull) departs from a work of
Matisse notable for its sweeping, nearly abstract lines. The lines of
seagull and shark, in the painting, rhyme at points, and the two
taken together, in the air and in the water, can easily be adapted as
icons for the benign and the malevolent aspects of the sea. The sea
itself comprises a "triple harmonie" in Char's poem (sea, shark, seagull). The sea is Mediterranean, but the term is not allowed to lull;
it occasions the recapitulation of a prolonged search; "je vois enfin
la mer dans sa triple harmonie." This is the beginning of the poem,
and Char declares that he sees at the outset, "je vois." The sight
could easily be taken for a sight of Matisse's painting, but Char at
no point mentions Matisse or painting. Rather, he develops a series
of moral and intellectual deductions from the sight. The one time
he names the shark and the seagull they could be taken either as
figures of his principle of contradiction or emblems for the impenetrability of a visual work, "Le requin et la mouette ne com-
muniquaient pas" (The shark and the seagull did not communicate).

   The absence of specific reference to Matisse frees the poem for a
multiple set of relationships to the painting. It may act as though
interpenetrated by the Mediterranean spirit without the interposi-
tion of a work of art, and at the same time it can function as an

oblique series of reflections on the nature of art, or indeed as an *ekphrasis* of this particular work. Its derivation of forces from a sight can extrapolate into the sort of comment that Char often makes on the moral and epistemological energy inherent in poetry or painting. Or taking it the other way around, everything moral and epistemological is referred back to the visual in a large natural cosmos, a Mediterranean resolution. Yet constantly the poem can be read simply as a series of reflections occasioned by Matisse, and its bold, simple sentences as verbal analogues to the sweeping lines of the painting.

It is a plain work, and Char provides not a single color word in this poem. He often has recourse to ordinary color words, though, as Surrealist poets generally do. Color words, taken for themselves, have a Mediterranean flavor too. Green and blue, orange and violet, red and yellow, reduce statement to a simple visual cue, enveloping experience in the delights of an almost immediate apprehension.

To speak of painting, or of the image generally as Char often does, at once highlights and distances the image, mediating it through an alien but analogous form. The painting itself, indeed, crosses the line between dream and waking in a special way: it is an object in the visual field, like a tree or a house or a telephone wire. And at the same time it draws on dream sources to interpret the visual field.

"Art," Char says in a poem/statement about Braque, "is a route that ends in a path, a diving board, yet in a field for us" ("L'art est une route qui finit en sentier, en tremplin, mais dans un champ à nous"). In another about Balthus, speaking of the presence of a robin redbreast (in his work), "The enigma that I call the redbreast is the pilot hidden in the heart of this work in which the situations and the personages husk before us their disquieting will. The decalogue of reality according to which we evolve here undergoes its verification."[38] Char's derivations from and about painting extend all the way back to the art of the caves, about which he has written a sequence with a title abstract enough to move every such reflection first through nature, "La paroi et la prairie" (The wall and the plain). There the bull, the lark, the trout, and the serpent appear under the title, "Les Fascinants," those that bind by fascinating and fascinate by binding. "Le Nu Perdu," again, can be read as the title of a painting, as a painting (*Le Nu*) that has been lost, as a verbal act that finds the painting by losing it, as an indication that the nude is not mentioned in the poem, and as an act prior to either poetry for painting that could occasion either.

The very freedom of relation between poet and painter, and the closeness of the relation in the general surrealist conception, allows for variety in the relation. The surrealist poems about painters differ much from one another. None conform to the *ekphrasis* of the modern formalist type-poem-about-a-painting, though nearly all can be seen to echo the poem about painters by the nineteenth-century precursor poet–art critic Baudelaire, "Les Phares." Éluard has written many poems about painters, but they tend to be in the evocative mode and to stay fairly indolently in the Mediterranean satisfactions. They differ from Char's by being still more distant from "rational" statement about painting. Char and Éluard each differ in turn from Breton, whose poems about paintings, as it happens, are more restrictedly art critical than those of either. Of course Breton's statements about paintings draw on Surrealist image collocations, but these are often fairly easy to see as partial descriptions of an actual painting in view. This is especially the case with *Constellations,* a series of twenty-two poems, one each to accompany twenty-two paintings of Miró that Miró gathered under the same title. A reader can always match some of the statements, and often many, to specific objects in the actual painting under consideration.

Still different from Char, Éluard, and Breton, are many extensions by later poets of Surrealist assumptions in an approach to painting. A notable and distinctive example is the series of poems on painters by Aaron Rosen, who has digested the Surrealist approach and turns it back on itself. His poems aim near-Surrealist statements at a point of reference where the aspiration of the painter intersects with the achievement of the painter and with a consequent apprehension of the human condition (see figure 5).

Giorgio de Chirico

The sky that concludes
Openly these cool lines

FIGURE 5. *The Departure of the Poet,* Giorgio de Chirico (1914).
Oil on canvas, $33\frac{7}{8} \times 25\frac{7}{8}''$.
Private Collection, USA.

Of unemployed
Regret

Will treat each scalp
Of evening
Like a stitch in time

As a dream of justice descends
                    in a stage whisper
Its slant found in the courtesy of repetition

Like a shadow that airs its about-face
Or a platitude, its blindness cleaned,
That puts its breath back
Before it breathes on us[39]

The surrealist adjustment of word and image aims to empower
a human perception for making such connections while remaining
free for others. Its implied principle, as well as the principles
Breton took it upon himself to state, enfranchises the very variety
of its own manipulations.

VI

William Carlos Williams
Ideas and Things

The tension between visual perception and signification remains enigmatic in painting and sculpture through the flat absence of words, which have a capacity to expand, and even to encapsulate, a statement. This tension remains enigmatic through the stubborn disjunction between the declaratively comprehensive (or even archly ironic) title and all one sees, as in Poussin or Klee,[1] or between a bit of newspaper or a phrase included in a painting and the rest of it, as in Picasso's *Ma Jolie.* The tension is playful in Demuth's *I Saw the Figure 5 in Gold* (figure 6), a painting that re-renders or illustrates Williams' prior poem on the same subject, including in itself *Bill* at the top in red, *WCW* at the bottom center also in red, and *Carlo* in yellow dots under the straight top of the *5,* as though registering an almost total fragment of *Carlos* written in lights seen at a distance.

Williams himself came to his characteristic style through painting more exclusively than did any other modern poet, trying his hand as a painter, reading poems at the Armory show, and mingling with Cubists and Futurists and Dadaists, in equal com-

FIGURE 6. *I Saw the Figure 5 in Gold,*
Charles Henry Demuth (1928).
Oil on composition board, 36 × 29¾ ".
The Metropolitan Museum of Art, New York.

pany with their American followers, from 1913 on. Indeed, the triplets of his late style can themselves be found in work arising from the same milieu of artists; the form is used in poems published by Walter Arensberg in 1917, in a journal edited by Marcel Duchamp. In this rich, complex, and prolonged interaction,[2] we may presume that Williams looked deeply at work he also commented on, because when writing about poetry the masters he invoked were certainly not Whitman or any in the English tradition, and not his friends Pound and H.D., or the Imagists either—although he wrote a few poems that may be said to fleetingly resemble theirs: "Imagism was not structural: that was the reason for its disappearance" (*Selected Essays* 283). When Williams invoked a master in his mature but still formative thirties, it tended to be the master of composition, Cézanne. He dedicated Book 5 of *Paterson* to Toulouse-Lautrec. And when he talked of how a poem goes together, he spoke of planes (as though echoing Gaudier-Brzeska through Pound). "I meet in agreement the force that will express its emotional content by an arrangement of appearances [of planes]. . . . I amplify 'planes' to include sounds, smells, colors, touch used as planes in the geometric sense, i.e., without limits, except as intersected by other planes."[3]

Even at his simplest, Williams may be said to aim at reproducing in words the tension between visual presence and signification, or between description and a theory that is either explicit or built into the work by a partial disalignment of planes. His poems work much as the lines that cross Demuth's *Figure 5 in Gold* imitate Cubism, by seeming to start out as parallels but breaking before we see either a full cylinder or an extended parallelogram or a radiating wheel or even lights with a shaft opening more widely (suggested by the four white circles vaguely like spotlights at the top and intersecting the 5).

Now Williams shows a persistent, homey populism, as it found expression in poems like "The Yachts." Much of *Paterson* builds on a recurrent sympathy for the downtrodden and the distressed. This expressed sympathy, together with Williams' insistence on painterlike visual notation, has led some critics to stress the side of notation or visual presence of things and people in his work. And contrariwise he exhibits a declared and variously exemplified emphasis on the structure of the poem as a "machine of words."[4] So other critics have been content with tracing the analogy (at best only partial) between the theory embodied in his work and some version of the common concerns of European philosophers in the tradition of Husserl and Heidegger. Or else they have extrapolated inferences from his practice into self-consistent rich descriptions about the verbal utterance, descriptions that still do not get the hang of what is going on in a particular Williams poem.[5] Either of these procedures would work more comfortably—if not more finally—with Stevens, whose *initial* rhetorical tone-signature involves never straying entirely from a base of something resembling philosophical discourse. But it will not do with Williams, whose simplest poems deploy the sort of tension between the seen and the uttered that a painter more directly exemplifies. Williams' poem about the fire engine he saw on the way to Demuth's studio, which Demuth's title quotes, offers much more processive qualification in its formal presentation than the verbal description of a visual object need offer:

> *The Great Figure*
>
> Among the rain
> and lights
> I saw the figure 5
> in gold
> on a red
> firetruck
> moving
> with weight and urgency
> tense
> unheeded
> to gong clangs
> siren howls
> and wheels rumbling
> through the dark city.

(*Collected Earlier Poems* 230;
line 8 is missing in this edition)

In describing a scene he runs through the visual events of a moment. With an abrupt and abstracted version of a sonnet in this fourteen-line poem, Williams offers not rhyme words but terminal words for each of his lines.[6] The terminal words are made emphatic both by the shortness of the lines and the fact that in nearly every line, perhaps in every one, the terminal word is also the most predominant word in the line.

The quick end of the line means we are pausing nearly as often as we are speaking in reciting this poem, arresting the voice at the point of accounting for the compositional integer. The first seven end words are arguably visual words, and they comprise an even half of the poem (breaking either mold for the sonnet, 8-6 or 4-4-4-2). The next three words are inferences tending towards abstraction: *urgency, tense, unheeded.* Two of these abstractions are the only two given a line to themselves, except the two lines preceding these three, which culminate the visual description in an exact notation, *red/firetruck.* We then switch to a matching three words of sense impression, and they record not sight but hearing, *clangs, howls, rumbling.* We conclude, as neatly as the sonnet would, on a word that frames the entire scene, *city.*

Our procession from sight as the engine whizzes by, to reflection about it, to hearing it after it disappears, has been schematically recorded. It has reached near emblemization in "the great figure" 5. But also the elements of that procession, leveled to a sort of simplicity, at the same time enter into a combination whose angles do not quite meet: sight is interrupted by thought before it is complemented by hearing. The abstractness of Demuth's painting, the absence of the fire engine, and the mirroring-deepening of his three gradually diminishing 5's, may be taken to try to catch some of this quality from the poem it illustrates, as his inclusion of Williams' initials in simultaneous homage and casualness catches something of the crisp naturalness and structured urgency of the voice in the poem.

The tension between what is seen and what is thought persists at the most minimal point; the poem about the red wheelbarrow begins with the phrase *so much depends.* If we compare Williams' Imagist poems with those of Pound or H.D., they will always be seen to incorporate more reflective qualification than those poets do, as well as often a larger proportion of stated inference:

El Hombre

It's a strange courage
you give me, ancient star:

Shine alone in the sunrise
toward which you lend no part!
                    (*CEP* 140)

The poem seems to report a visual event—a star known to be present (because it was seen the night before) but not at the moment visible in what is seen as wholly outshining it, the sunrise. In doing this the sunrise seems to present a sort of puzzle: the star is still shining. The sun itself is a star, and the poem may also be said to include it logically in *ancient star*. Part of the puzzle may be the fact that the light is absent not only to the eye; taken at its point of origin, the star would be always absent, since the light we see from a star was actually emitted as long as thousands or millions of years ago, and even the sun's light was emitted eight minutes ago. An act of analogy from the actual visual sight to the thought about the chain of connection through the human race produces "courage." And the whole is attached to a title angled by being put in a language that suggests both the tragic bravery of the bullfighter and the sly laissez-faire of the Latin humble idler, *El Hombre*. (We are not far in time from Pershing's expedition against Pancho Villa, and Williams was devoted to his own Puerto Rican mother—herself a cultivated painter.) Far more abstract, this poem, than H.D.'s *Oread* or Pound's *In a Station of the Metro*. But compare it to the poem that Stevens took it as an epigraph for:

Nuances of a Theme by Williams

It's a strange courage
You give me, ancient star:

Shine alone in the sunrise
toward which you lend no part!

I

Shine alone, shine nakedly, shine like bronze,
that reflects neither my face nor any inner part
of my being, shine like fire, that mirrors nothing.

II

Lend no part to any humanity that suffuses
you in its own light.
Be not chimera of morning.
Half-man, half-star.
Be not an intelligence,
Like a widow's bird
Or an old horse.

As Stevens' dropping the archly skewed *El Hombre* from Williams' title may be taken to imply, this poem is far more homogeneous in tone, and far less structured than its seemingly simpler counterpart, however elaborate its philosophical invocations and deductions may be. In this established sequence, the powerful and far-reaching near surrealism of the two terminal similes are still included in the even tone of speculation, and the humor of "Like a widow's bird / Or an old horse" is only an undertone. The *or* refers any deductions we might make about the tenor and the vehicle of these two similes back to the fully established, if subtle, process of deduction. Stevens offers us more abstraction than Williams does, but his shifts are fewer and less marked. The visual for Stevens is digested into the deductive, where for Williams, as for the painter, the visual and the deductive remain in persistent tension.[7]

2

Williams both emphasizes and disjoins his particulars, the objects of his careful naming, a naming that is at once economical and exuberantly forward thrusting. Free verse in his hands, as with the terminal words of "The Great Figure" above, works to underscore this process, to insist on the isolation of the particulars while disjoining them by not submerging them in an ongoing flow or subordinating them to a perceptible overall design.

The effect of this double procedure is to touch on the figurative character of the object while at the same time wrenching the object away from figuration. The focus of the photographer, so to speak, is overlaid with the focus of the painter.[8]

For the painter cannot help some sort of iconographic context for what he chooses to depict; that act of presenting a painting in itself declares the creation of a brand-new iconographic reference, a figure. And at the same time the painter's act commits him to attention and representation of what in theory at least are purely visual properties; he aims at this kind of mimesis. The proportion of mimesis to figuration may differ between Giotto and Chardin, between Cézanne and Pollock. But in all these mimesis and figuration remain copresent. *Emblem* harmonizes with *expression*.[9]

The wordlessness of painting allows for various kinds of easy harmony between the figuration of objects and their bare delineation. The words of the poem, however, implicitly set such harmonies at odds. The act of naming *saxifrage* easily designates the object, without the painter's difficult process of recapturing it through stroke after stroke of the brush. And at the same time, as recent critics have insisted, the relations between the signifier and the signified in any word are complex enough and remote enough from their presumed referent to make the act of naming problematic. The name *saxifrage* not only describes but carries its own figuration. Further, "every word is a prejudice," as Nietzsche reminds us, and there operates in every word a strong bias of interpretation; the name *saxifrage* views the flower from the process by which it comes into the light, and not by any properties of appearance: the flower, soft as it is, can break a rock.

Now with Williams we cannot pause at any aspect of these harmonies and gestures. The figuration and the delineation of the object are offered together, but in a sort of subdued bristling of interaction between figuration and delineation. Notable in Williams is the sharp focus, the occasional dwelling on the description of a single object like a rotten apple or "the reddish / purplish, forked, upstanding, twiggy / stuff of brushes" ("Spring and All," *CEP* 241). This focus makes a point of delineation without committing itself to the theorist's abjuration of figure, as in Stevens' "without evasion by a single metaphor."

Williams offers us, as Blackmur says, "the Imagism of 1912 self-transcended."[10] The poet may aspire to the asymptotic limit of the painter's seemingly pure object, in Williams' view. It is that quality he praises in the work of Marianne Moore, comparing her to Ingres; "Ingres realized the essentiality of drawing and each perfect part seemed to float free from his work by itself. There is much in this that applies beautifully to Miss Moore."[11] Yet he also refers to "the inevitable flux of the seeing eye toward measuring itself by the word it inhabits,"[12] and to an "inclusiveness without redundancy." Thereby he overlooks figuration in favor of the process that precedes, and may always be taken to qualify, any figuration. " 'Beauty,' " he says, "is related not to 'loveliness' but to a state in which reality plays a part."[13]

The very phrasing of the key aphorism "no ideas but in things" contains elements that lead to possible qualifications. He does not say only the thing, or the thing first and last, or even the idea rests on the thing. The pluralization of both *ideas* and *things* releases them to swarm with signification, and to multiply possibilities: the phrasing permits us to infer that many ideas may cluster about a single thing, that a single idea may be composed of many things, and that the process of conjoining thing to thing may produce one idea or many.[14]

And then the negative form of the utterance has the effect of pointing it toward "things," "washed clean" of ideas in Stevens' phrase. Stevens theorizes, however, and Williams goes through verbal motions that do not stop for long at theory, as he imbeds such utterances as these in a poem, where the utterance, even taken by itself, has the further qualification of parentheses:

> *A Sort of a Song*
>
> Let the snake wait under
> his weed
> and the writing
> be of words, slow and quick, sharp

to strike, quiet to wait,
sleepless.
—through metaphor to reconcile
the people and the stones.
Compose. (No ideas
but in things) Invent!
Saxifrage is my flower that splits
the rocks.
                    (*Collected Later Poems* 7)

Compose, invent, metaphor, and *words* pull the declaration of
the poem away from delineation and towards figuration, though
the nearly climactic and subversively parenthetical statement we
have been examining urges nothing if not delination. *Snake, weed,
stone,* and finally *flower,* are the things mentioned, and all of them
have properties that seem to be of the most pronouncedly figurative
sort. The snake and the flower are allegorical, and simply so; they
are also traditional: the hidden reptile can be found in a fragment
of Sophocles. *Stones* in this context has the abstract sense not far
from "all inanimate objects," since it opposes *people.* But the *rocks*
of the last word are certainly concrete, since they stand to be broken
by the flower. "My flower" is at once motto or emblem and an actually growing "thing" whose activity is suggested in the enjambe-
ment on *splits.* Yet at the same time we are back with mere words
in the lexicon, since *that splits the rocks* merely translates *saxifrage*
from the Latin name given it for this property. We may visualize
leaves massed at the base of a plant for saxifrage or rockfoil, but no
particular color, since the plant produces flowers of various color.
The process of the poem finds a rather large simple "idea" in one
thing or in many. At the same time it associates that idea somewhat
with the difficulty of coming to expression, to finding terms for one
thing and another that will bring their disparity into some sort of
harmony, "through metaphor to reconcile / the people and the
stones." While we cannot rest on any term, like *metaphor, ideas*
or *things,* the significance of the poem lies in affirmation: it is "a
sort of a song." It harnesses but does not depict an intellectual rest-
lessness; still less does it offer a consistent theory of such. It asserts

the power of the poem as a simple gesture that comes through in spite of difficulties that would seem insuperably recalcitrant. The flower splits rocks.

In *Paterson* this same key utterance is given the prominence of an initial explanation after the opening description of the waterfall and its effect, and it picks up on the very first words of the poem. "To make a start, / out of particulars":

> —Say it, no ideas but in things—
> nothing but the blank faces of the houses
> and cylindrical trees
> bent, forked by preconception and accident—
> split, furrowed, creased, mottled, stained—
> secret—into the body of the light!

Here the key utterance is assimilated to its expression, *say it*. It is put between dashes. And as we read to the end of this verse paragraph, of which I have quoted the whole, we move towards delineation, the gesture, frequent in Williams, of pausing to try to catch a visual effect by heaping up the verbal brush-strokes of descriptive adjectives. This time we are, as it were, powerfully drawn to the "things" end of the utterance, whereas in the short poem above the movement is strongly towards "ideas."

Later, in book 3, the expression *beautiful thing,* a persistent and disjunct refrain, redirects the principle of "no ideas but in things" by offering a single "thing" of which there is a single idea, it is "beautiful."

Williams' separate assertions oscillate between figuration and delineation, but of course they gravitate towards delineation. In one case a poem entitled "The Unknown" ends with the typical assertion, "detail is all" (*CEP* 423), and it is soon followed by four poems each entitled "detail" (*CEP* 427–28). It is, he says, "the poem that lifts the dish / of fruit" (*CLP* 91). By a rule that can also be seen to operate in painting—in, say, Velasquez or Vermeer or Georges de la Tour—sharpness of focus seems to carry with it intimations of ideality. And this is very much the effect of Williams' short "object" poems, like "The Red Wheelbarrow," or:

Nantucket

Flowers through the window
    lavender and yellow

changed by white curtains—
    Smell of cleanliness—

Sunshine of late afternoon—
    On the glass tray

a glass pitcher, the tumbler
    turned down, by which

a key is lying—And the
    immaculate white bed
        (*CEP* 348)

This is a "take," much like a photograph of the Stieglitz whom Williams knew and wrote about. It is a take of an island known for Puritan whaling expeditions. Something of the austerity of the island life, of the freshness and openness of a resort by the sea, and of the entered leisure of the present seaside resort, is conveyed in the description of a room that must be that of a hotel or rooming house, or we would not have the key and the pitcher and tumbler on a tray. The group of details is composed through such minimal stylistic gestures as an impressionistic variance between capital and small letters, a gathering tendency to enjamb, and the framing of the couplets. White prevails, on the curtain and the bed, accompanied by its cousins yellow (flowers, sunshine) and transparency (glass, window). An aesthetic point is made: the colors of the flowers are "changed" by the white curtains. This is the tonic note. The bed hangs grammatically in the air—or else it is coordinated with the series of initial verbless noun phrases, *flowers, smell, sunshine*. White, of course, also suggests cleanliness, and the picture composes towards maximum redundancy which is also maximum simplicity. The sharpness of focus for the very suspension of the last line insists on the figuration that lurks in such resolute delineation. The sea is not mentioned, the island is not mentioned, the Puritans are

not mentioned; all are felt, and the leap to them is provided only
by the act of composition.

Williams is, in Kenneth Burke's words, "the master of the
glimpse";[15] he achieves "rubbings of reality," as Stevens says.[16]

In a later poem, the I, the writer, painting, and a general if traditional definition of maleness and femaleness, all enlarge the evocations around a single miniaturist detail:

Raindrops on a Briar

I, a writer, at one time hipped on
painting, did not consider
the effects, painting
for that reason, static, on

the contrary the stillness of
the objects—the flowers, the gloves—
freed them precisely by that
from a necessity merely to move

in space as if they had been—
not children! but the thinking male
or the charged and deliver-
ing female frantic with ecstasies;

served rather to present, for me,
a more pregnant motion: a
series of varying leaves
clinging still, let us say, to

the cat-briar after last night's
storm, its waterdrops
ranged upon the arching stems
irregularly as an accompaniment.

                                    (*CLP* 99)

As may mean "in the function of an accompaniment," and it may
also mean "like an accompaniment." This ambiguity picks up the
one questioned in the poem, as between motion and stillness, resumes it in the last line, and reapplies it improvisationally to the

raindrops of the title. It then turns out that all the ruminations of earlier stanzas have been a prelude to this one. The dynamic poem comes around behind the specially choice visual impression to go the "static" painting one better on its own terrain.

We cannot say we have a doctrine here. Williams' observation may be applied, "each thing is secure in its own perfections."[17] (*Perfection* is a favorite word of Willams'.) The ideas, finally, come to rest on things. To tighten the theory, either in speaking about the poem or in deducing the process within it, would run the risk of losing the gradualness of the process by which this comes to be the case, unless that too were built into the theory. The raindrops are only delineated by the way, and at the end. It is their figurative function to lend themselves to this process; only arbitrarily and momentarily, as in "A Sort of a Song" above, does Williams lend his procedures to any schematic use of "metaphor."

Stones and people, separate in conception, may be seen to interact when the proper objects are brought into view. The red stone grasshopper of Chapultepec, adduced in *Paterson,* was a metaphor and something more to those who created it. Mentioning it touches on an exemplum fusing nature and culture without schematizing their relationship, or that of the artifact to the poem. So later the Paterson fire of 1902 provides an occasion for at once celebrating and losing the books that are at once mainstays and hindrances to perception. The poet can turn to an object transmuted by the fire and by meditating on its visual properties imply the relevance of its other connections and the possibility of transcending them—by the primacy of just such a visual act:

> An old bottle, mauled by the fire
> gets a new glaze, the glass warped
> to a new distinction, reclaiming the
> undefined. A hot stone, reached
> by the tide, crackled over by fine
> lines, the glaze unspoiled . . .
>
>   The glass
> splotched with concentric rainbows

> of cold fire that the fire has bequeathed
> there as it cools, its flame
> defied.
>
>   (*P* 118)

Metaphor is here grazed but at the same time held off in the very ease with which a momentary allegorical application comes into the picture.

The special oscillation between delineation and figure permits Williams a sharp ambivalence between neutrality and sympathy when he comes to include in his poems the persons of the deprived and insulted, or the scene they are forced to inhabit.[18] It is a persistent motif in *Paterson,* and throughout his poetry, as in this passage from an early one:

> Where a
> waste of cinders
> slopes down to
>
> the railroad and
> the lake
> stand three children
>
> beside the weed-grown
> chassis
> of a wrecked car
>
> immobile in a line
> facing the water
> To the left a boy
>
> in falling off
> blue overalls
> Next to him a girl
>
> in a grimy frock
> And another boy
> They are intent
> ("View of a Lake," *CEP* 96)

The resource of words, lines, and stanza divisions empowers the poet to cross the line between the highly abstract painter, say the Juan Gris of Williams' praise, and the painter of social concern from the Ashcan School to the thirties, or the photographer who chooses to place himself in the iconographic line of strong "industrial landscape" that Williams has taken up. Each of the triplets above is either a segment or a picture in itself, and each changes a partiality of syntactic shape made still more predominant by the absence of punctuation. That absence is in the service of structured visualization, and not of flow, as it is in Apollinaire and others. The visualization is in the service of sympathy, but only tentatively; we have not reached the marvelously stark flatness of Charles Reznikoff's *Testimony*. The sympathy is qualified by a neutrality that the painter who chooses such subjects almost always loses, since the sympathy leaks through the wordlessness of the presented sight, and Williams has words that he structures so as to prevent such leakage. Sympathy remains even when neutrality is asserted and persons are emptied out "beyond all feeling" in the escalation of inferences over a detail from such a landscape.

3

One of Williams' persistent devices is the recourse to the naming of color. The painter simply applies his color, and we see it immediately as attached to its object, as initially concrete. Or else the painter makes it abstract by offering it in patches that designate no object, or by attaching it to an object that would never have such a color in nature, a purple body or a red sky.

The word releases the poet from having to choose these alternatives. The word in itself comprises abstraction, and Williams handles that abstraction in a way that enlists a natural concreteness as well:

The Red Wheelbarrow

so much depends
upon

a red wheel
barrow

> glazed with rain
> water
>
> beside the white
> chickens
>   (*CEP* 277)

The opening couplet casts a shadow of abstraction over the remaining three. Each of these presents a separate color sense, though the middle one names no color and just depicts a visual impression that is close to transparency, "glazed with rain / water." Only in the last couplet is the color word given the terminal prominence that rings again and again in the color words of "The Great Figure." *Red,* the first color word, is positioned differently in a sort of verbal trompe l'oeil, since in its line we incorrectly infer that the wheel is painted red (as it may also be) and not the more prominent body of the barrow. Some doctrine akin to "no ideas but in things" has here been expressed through a scene where color juxtaposition is pronounced, and indeed crucial,[19] though of course there are other interactions in the poem.

Naming the colors in "Nantucket" states the enigmas that that poem also releases through its willed taciturnity.

"One has to keep looking for poetry as Renoir looked for colors in old walls, woodwork, and so on."[20] Williams chooses to quote, and obviously to obey, this injunction that Stevens lays upon him. So for him the search for poetry would, at the simplest of moments, arrest itself in the evocation of some primary colors, the red fire engine or the red wheelbarrow.

At a further minimal point, color is still retained:

> *The Locust Trees in Flower*
>
> Among
> of
> green
>
> stiff
> old
> bright

```
broken
branch
come

white
sweet
May

again
(CEP 93)
```

The lineation insists on the blocklike character of the individual words. In the pared sequence, even and yet syntactically broken, the color words match and yet stand out in distinctly different function: The *green* that ends the first triplet is an adjective (as well as a noun) breaking the normal English order for adjectives, dependent and momentarily final. The *white* of the last triplet comes pristinely first, though at the same time it is winding down towards the last isolated word. And the entire poem is matched with another of the same title (*CEP* 94). A further approach of the elements of the palette to one another, and the colors will run together; this is a "Love Song," and the colors are correspondingly harmonized into homogeneity in a perceptual transition from spiritual to physical:

```
        I lie here thinking of you:—

        the stain of love
        is upon the world!
        Yellow, yellow, yellow
        it eats into the leaves,
        smears with saffron
        the horned branches that lean
        heavily
        against a smooth purple sky!
        There is no light
        only a honey-thick stain
        that drips from leaf to leaf
        from limb to limb
```

> spoiling the colors
> of the whole world—
>
> you far off there under
> the wine-red selvage of the west!
>
> (*CEP* 174)

The top and the extreme edge are impervious to the yellow stain, but the "smooth purple sky" and the "wine-red selvage" still wear a single tone of warm color that associates to passion, royalty, and intoxication.

We are on our way, in this extreme of practice but not in declared doctrine, to the late Stevens' theory of resemblances, a theory Williams himself casually propounded at a much earlier point: "There is no thing that with a twist of the imagination cannot be something else. Porpoises risen in a green sea, the wind at nightfall bending the rose-red grasses."[21] But he goes on to a woman chasing her son. The naming of color reassures; but taken by itself it also arrests.

4

The quickness of emblemizing in Williams, and the penchant for visual depiction, are both deceptive. They ride a current of steady attention, and it is of that process that they are surface manifestations. The figure varies, the ground stays the same.

"Poetry," Williams says, is "the emplacement of knowledge into a living current."[22] The current of the poem, so to speak, is made to bend sharply around the arresting colors, the spare but sharply angled locutions. The laconic *so much depends* has generated abundant comment, as has "This Is Just to Say":

> *This Is Just to Say*
>
> I have eaten
> the plums
> that were in
> the icebox
>
> and which
> you were probably

saving
for breakfast

Forgive me
they were delicious
so sweet
and so cold
(*CEP* 354)

The title itself, an ambiguous lead-in to the poem, advertises its own minimalism. But the minimalism of the speech act residing in apology sets a flow going that spills into another kind of attention, channeled by the short and varied lines.

Williams uses plums as well as apples to illustrate the proper object of the painter.[23] Collocating the plums and the icebox, with the emphasis of making each word terminal for its couplet in the first quatrain, identifies a nascent quasi-Futurist or even Cubist painting at the outset of the poem. The last quatrain underlines three physical properties and trails off in the act of savoring the objects named, the word *delicious* exhibiting in context the prominence of its length. The middle quatrain, however, firmly carries along the note of apology.

For the speech act itself, Altieri is able to extend its complexity and use it for theoretical leverage:

The implicit authorial act in the poem is likewise an act of measuring; it too calls attention to the qualities exhibited in its production of a discourse. Now, however, the measure is more abstract, for the implicit poet does not simply measure a specific situation but makes the speaker's art a sample expressing his artistic ability to render his complex grasp of the nature of apology and forgiveness through the structural patterns he creates . . . if the speaker were to say much more . . . he would introduce rhetoric . . . if he were to say less he would completely sacrifice his humanity to natural desires.[24]

The gracefulness of this complex act of requesting forgiveness works to frame, to launch, to economize, and to move along, the disjoined attention to the objects under consideration. Action itself moves to the center, aided by image. The carefully blocked-out lines at once obstruct and emphasize the "simple" speaking voice, which is made to betray its own persistently narcissistic delectation in the

act of excusing it. At the same time the voice is building a firmly
anchored structure around a single series of sense perceptions, apparent only after the fact of utterance but at that point more apparent than the act of apology.

The flow lends itself to the long look, to the complex gesture, to
the randomized and unmetaphorical particular that still advertises a
special significance by the way it is made to enter the flow. It may
slow to the fixity of a visual impression or quicken in the flutter of
a conversational exchange. "January Morning," a "suite" of fifteen
sections (*CEP* 162–66), begins with church domes in Weehawken
and ends with the poet's stated response to young girls who "run
giggling / on Park Avenue after dark." "The Clouds," another
longish poem, ends in a bravura series of quick, alternative visual
characterizations (*CLP* 124–28). Transient incidents that fleetingly
reflect mysteriously significant psychological dispositions occupy
"The Young Housewife" (*CEP* 136), "Good Night" (*CEP* 145),
and "Danse Russe" (*CEP* 148), to list but three further examples.

Theory about the flow is only one of the forms the flow can
take—a moment in the flow and not its source, as in Stevens. Thus
The Red Wheelbarrow, or "A Sort of a Song," or the theoretical runs
in *Paterson,* or "The Pause" (*CLP* 179), the sense of whose title we
must deduce from the poem that in fact describes no particular
pause. "The mind's a queer sponge," Williams says, to begin a
poem whose title is "May 1st Tomorrow" (*CLP* 195), a spring
poem that takes only a brief look at the spring, and then only from
the viewpoint of the mind which is said to produce its effects,
"squeeze it and out come bird songs / small leaves highly enameled / and moments of good reading."

5

The object in Williams' poetry, taken by itself, has an enigmatic
capacity to engage the attention. Sometimes he will have it do so
for an entire poem, as in "Simplex Sigillum Veri" (*CEP* 463),
which applies this Latin designation to a close description of an
ordinary pencil. The pencil is simple, if a seal of the truth. Other
objects are rich with association, like the waterfall that opens *Paterson* and at once echoes a Wordsworthian theme and mutes it, through

the particular phrasing and because this particular Passaic Falls has undergone massive pollution. We may also say that when Williams puts the falls in the place where the invocation would go in an epic poem, he both refers to European tradition and undercuts it in favor of painting. The waterfall and its psychological effects for Wordsworth, Hölderlin, and others are a topos in European Romantic poetry—but not so pronouncedly in European Romantic painting. It is the American painters, from Cole on, who erect the waterfall into an important icon for the Romantic landscape. This rich past is present, all of it, in Williams' choice of icon.

The object, as we have been saying, is drawn into a focus, either by itself or in its relation to other objects; and its focal character predominates over its figural significance, expression over emblem. For "The Rose" (*CEP* 249), "It ends— / But if it ends / the start is begun / so that to engage roses / becomes a geometry—"

Roses are plural, identical, and easily emblematic. More usually they stand in "jagged" relationship to each other. As Williams early says, in criticizing a sort of failed imagination, "the attention has been held rigid on the one plane instead of following a more flexible, jagged resort."[25] This jaggedness, a primary characteristic of his best work, renders the term *metonymy* an unfortunate one, for all its current utility, to be applied to the poetry of Williams.[26] Metonymy suggests a sort of even contiguity, and an avoidance of its presumed opposite, metaphor. Not only does Williams not avoid metaphor. His objects almost always stand in a deliberately jagged relationship to each other, as well as exhibiting the generality and diffusion I have in an earlier book described as governing his style.[27] Yet there is a sense of a simple current running in Williams, a rhythm so "shallowly" concurrent with a speaking voice that current and undercurrent become one. And this is something like a metonymic effect in his rhythms, if not his statements—though the jaggedness consistently obtrudes on this current like rocks breaking up a stream. Indeed, to pursue this metaphor, a waterfall is a splendid example of extreme current produced by extreme jaggedness. And throughout his career Williams deliberated how he might put a waterfall, the falls at Paterson, at the head of his longest poem. He offers, as Riddel says, "a weave of disparate loci."[28] The poems of Williams possess themselves not only a "stark dignity of entrance," to adapt one of their phrases ("Spring and All," *CEP* 241–42). They offer "myriads of counter-processions" (*CEP* 183). "A Celebration" (*CEP* 188) runs through seasons and events and colors and sights. "Young Love" condenses its terms into a nearly Cubistic form: "Wrigley's, appendicitis, John Marin: / skyscraper soup" (*CEP* 253). In a more usual painterlike juxtaposition, he celebrates a "Nude in a Machine Shop" (*CEP* 107). And the verbalization of "The Hermaphroditic Telephone" (*CEP* 286) takes us to a point where Cubism merges with Surrealism—where all the theory we may deduce from those pictorial procedures may be brought to bear on the poetic juxtapositions.

Even a moderately coherent description, as in "Trees" (*CEP* 142) or "Spring Strains" (*CEP* 159) may offer a markedly contrapuntal effect. Naming Cubism in "This Florida: 1924" (*CEP* 329–31) becomes the occasion for an especially jagged series:

> And we thought to escape rime
> by imitation of the senseless
> unarrangement of wild things—
>
> the stupidest rime of all—
> Rather, Hibiscus,
> let me examine
>
> those varying shades
> of orange, clear as an electric
> bulb on fire
>
> or powdery with sediment—
> matt, the shades and textures
> of a Cubist picture
>
> the charm
> of fish by Hartley, orange
> of ale and lilies
>
> orange of topaz, orange of red hair
> orange of curaçao

orange of the Tiber turbid, orange of the bottom
rocks in Maine rivers
orange of mushrooms

of Cêpes that Marshall loved
to cook in copper
pans, orange of the sun—

I shall do my pees, instead—
boiling them in test tubes
holding them to the light

dropping in the acid—
Peggy has a little albumen
in hers—

The unarrangement of wild things is senseless; and yet "let confusion be the design" (*CLP* 87). The oranges here, perhaps fourteen of them, exhibit a startling jaggedness as he moves from the rich iconic power invested in each.

In *Paterson,* on its greater scale, we have a greater jaggedness. The women who recur are now giants, now a plaintive poet who wishes to have her femininity acknowledged, now the dour oldest or youngest wife of an African chieftain, now the hapless prostitutes-become-mothers of a backwater, now one of their descendants pulled into the fictions of an elegant lesbian. The "beautiful thing" of *Paterson,* as also of the separate poem "Paterson: Episode 17" (*CEP* 438), is at once an interruption, a summary, and an undertone to the flow of the poem. "The pure products of America / go crazy" ("To Elsie," *CEP* 270–72). And yet the poem may also be surveyed under the orderly archetypes of Williams' "Author's Note" and the slightly different ones of his epigraph.

Within its orders the jaggedness veers to the extremity of long quotations from personal letters to a full page of the core sample analyses from digging for an artesian well (*P* 139). Or to statements that on one face are bold metaphors and on the other absolutely literal statements at a certain time of year, "The rose is green" (*P* 30).

The varying tension between figuration and delineation always reins in the "things," while keeping them jagged in facets of sense, a literary proto-Cubism that may serve also, through the qualities of words themselves, as a literary post-Impressionism, Cézanne merged into Braque.

Maximizing Minimalism

The Construct of Image in Olson and Creeley

The Figure of Outward—this phrase attached to Robert Creeley by Charles Olson in the dedication of *The Maximus Poems*—exemplifies what it recommends, a purification of image through an evacuation of image. The phrase came to Olson in a dream at Black Mountain, and he teases it out as late as 1969, in lines still addressed to Creeley.[1] It comprises what is almost an oxymoron: *outward* is too open-ended and abstract to be a figure. Thus it implicitly enacts the objectism of Olson,[2] and very differently the comparable process for Creeley, who can be thought of as realigning the practice of Williams through complications—and simplifications—induced by Olson. Creeley is to Williams as Mallarmé is to Baudelaire.[3]

Another contradiction is entailed by this practice. Not only does "The Science of Image"—to quote Olson's lecture title from a series at Black Mountain[4]—realize the image by flattening it. The persona of the poet becomes magnified through an "ego-less" proprioception. For Olson the person comes into focus through being coordinated with a combination of accurate, resurrected facts of history or myth and notations of small-scale momentary actions. Creeley drops the history and adapts the notations to an enlargement that generalizes the speaker without allegorizing him. He is frozen as an image of himself. As in Olson, depersonalization becomes repersonalization—or "proprioception"—through the exact alignment of the image along lines that rest on a confidence in the force of this process. Such a confidence parallels, and in time must be taken as somehow following, the Surrealist confidence in the automatic force of the unconsciously selected image. Still, the difference, in both Creeley and Olson, does not lie in this (shared) axiom of the incorporability of depth meaning into the poem.

The difference between them and the Surrealists—or the lesser San Francisco poets of the fifties who made the "discovery" that one detail set randomly by another could realize the poem—lies in the theoretical mounting that can be taken to precede the poem:

> of rhythm is image
> of image is knowing
> of knowing there is
> a construct[5]

Olson takes a locus, the city of Gloucester, and reconstructs it through the juxtaposition of historical and personal detail, remaining effectually faithful to Pound's definition of the image as "that which presents an intellectual and emotional complex in an instant of time." But where Pound realized his "Vorticism" by a close attention to the work of the painter Wyndham Lewis and the sculptor Gaudier, Olson stayed "inward." In Pound's terms, he startlingly derived *phanopoeia* from *melopoeia,* "of rhythm is image." The formula works for Creeley too, and the greater modulation of his verse from line to line, by comparison with Olson's, entails a closer attention to a single image-complex, rather than to a series.

Olson gradually and, for a poet, belatedly, worked out such an approach in an atmosphere of painting, as an associate of Ben Shahn during World War Two, then in the ambience of the Institute of Contemporary Art in Washington, D.C., then in a Black Mountain

heavily centered on painters and painting. Yet the focus on Gloucester stays resolutely free of the pictorial aspects of the town, whose
most predominant images, rendered a thousand times, had been
those of the visual artists who worked and summered there for
nearly a hundred years. All through Olson's childhood and youth,
when he summered there from Worcester, the most pronounced
group of fellow visitors was that of the artists. These artists find
almost no mention in *The Maximus Poems*. Of course in this he
may be said to follow their principle: they mostly did not paint each
other. Marsden Hartley's eyes (Letter 7) are paralleled to those of
someone in Olson's personal circle, and to those of fishermen. This
section praises Hartley for the persistent effort of painting, in so far
as it resembles the other persistent efforts which keep coming up in
Olson's narratives here. Hartley is not praised for the results of his
painting, and by the end of the letter the focus is on his hands,
which visibly show the wear of effort, like the hands of the mate on
a gill netter, to which Olson compares them.

Olson, in a sense, follows the painters by letting their subject—
the look of the town, the aspects of the fishing industry—become
his. At the same time "of image is *knowing*," and the picturesque is
left aside. The *Maximus* poem on Ten Pound Island mimes none of
the shimmer to be found in Childe Hassam's beautiful painting of
that island. Nor does the poem try for any analogue to the Luminism of Fitz Hugh Lane, who painted the same island many times.
Olson's access is by aligning detail from historical records, "of
knowing there is / a construct."

While Olson does not give much attention to artists who were his
contemporaries, the great painter of the previous century, Fitz Hugh
Lane, is referred to nine times by Butterick's count (see figure 7).
Lane's historicity admits Olson's angle of proprioceptive purchase:

> Lane's eye-view of Gloucester
> Phoenician eye-view
> 1833 14 October 443 Vessels at anchor in the harbor besides
> what Lay at wharfs.

In this complete poem, the poet's persona assumes full presence
by electing for total absence. He achieves psychic depth by abjuring

FIGURE 7. *Gloucester Harbor*, Fitz Hugh Lane (1852).
Oil on canvas, 27¼ × 47½".
Cape Ann Historical Association, Gloucester, Massachusetts.

all but the surface, down to a mere numbering, the date and the 443 vessels. In this context the details of the poet's mother's death, or his *cris de coeur,* are aligned to "objectism." His largeness (*maximus*) becomes strictly a dimension of his philosopher's stance (Maximus of Tyre).

The means has been found to turn a principled approach to directness toward a more thoroughgoing indirectness, to make the conscious verge on the preconscious. On the evidence of Creeley's voluminous exchange of letters with Olson during years formative for both, Olson also found example and stimulus for his own achievement of the same ends, by different means.

Creeley remained fairly classical in principle: form as an extension of content was already a maxim of Valéry's before Williams took it over.[6] Creeley's poems usually eschew juxtaposition of image in favor of keenly syncopated rythmic juxtaposition, "of rhythm is image." Taken as rhetorical statements, Creeley's poems exhibit a coherence that would have pleased John Crowe Ransom (who in fact was the first major editor to publish Creeley). It is in what the angles of the lines reveal of the stance and ratiocinative energies of the speaker that the purification of image, the "construct," lies. Creeley has leaped a step in Olson's definition series; he exemplifies "of rhythm . . . is knowing":

> *Blue Skies Motel*
>
> Look at
> that mother-fucking smoke-stack
>
> pointing
> straight up.
>
> See those clouds
> old time fleecy pillows,
>
> like they say, whites and greys,
> float by.
>
> There's cars
> on the street,

> there's a swimming pool
> out front—
>
> and the trees
> go yellow
>
> now
> it's the fall.[7]

Written at a time in the late seventies when Photographic Realists dominated a whole sector of painting, this poem could be taken as an ekphrastic description of such a painting. Certainly the subject is one that has no parallel in Creeley's earlier work. While following Williams' lead in the acceptance of what the eye takes in, Creeley allows his speaker reactions of a greater miscellany. He also keeps them below the threshold of Williams' often very philosophical reflections.

The speaker begins in the first two lines to register the familiar reaction of the vacationer: he has not left the industrial city behind. The priority of what is noticed, and the single tired colloquial compound taking up half the line (*mother-fucking*), assimilate his reaction to a Freudian undertone that slows into obsession in the more deliberate lines three and four. In the next lines the speaker turns away, still confined to tired comparison (*pillows*) and tired qualification (*like they say*), along with the visual catalogue (*whites and greys*) that relaxes still further into the last four couplets of the poem, ending in a perfectly routine memory of why it is the leaves would be yellow. The only feature not routine in this poem is the rhythmic disposition of its three sentences evenly into eight couplets arranged 2-2-4, while unevenly into varied line-lengths and into modulations that the relative shortness of the lines tends to magnify. Between the evenness and the unevenness, the sound of the poem comes into being. This is true of all poetry, but Creeley has purified the principle and made it serve delineation. "Of rhythm is image." A single process of visual perception distributes its elements in a structure that rises to an abstractness allowing, without allegory, an assimilation to the more than visual. Mondrian is, so to speak, re-rendered as a Photo-Realist. The post-Surrealism of Marisol, which

Creeley approaches in a gingerly prose, has been bypassed through further depersonalization.

In another poem from the same collection, the visual remains the focus, and the play of three simple colors reminds one of Williams' practice in this regard. But the occasion has abjured Williams' intellectual content; it is a "shaggy dog" image, an image that presents itself as lacking point:

> *Morning*
>
> Light's bright glimmer
> through green bottle
>
> on shelf
> above. Light's white
>
> fair air,
> shimmer,
>
> blue summer's
> come.
>
> (*Later* 67)

The modulation increases as the intellectual energy declines. The whole poem confines itself to the process of inferring from two visual details of light, connected to green and to white respectively, that something else is present of a third color, *blue summer*. "Of knowing there is a construct." Turning this realization, which would usually be subliminal, of how summer light may be identified, into a sequence of common, modulated words, abstracts a relation between the visual and the subliminal.

The goal of the painter has been brought over into words. Proprioception has taken place, through means very different from Olson's. "Of image is knowing."

2

Setting an image in a poem by itself makes the image accrue metaphoric properties. Just as the "found object," by a kind of perceptual contradiction, evokes the sensibility of the sculptor who has set it before us, so the "emptied image" of Fitz Hugh Lane's Gloucester harbor, in the little section of *Maximus* quoted above, links with the sensibility of the speaker.[8] The connections with the "epic" salients of the poem gives it another dimension. There are two time-dimensions in the Fitz Hugh Lane poem anyway, since his paintings continue a generation later than 1833 and this one is a normative date, more for the ships than for his painting. On the long view, Lane is coordinated with the Phoenicians. Olson's sensibility advertises that it does not advertise itself; it maximizes its minimalism by constructing a relation, virtual (metaphoric) rather than actual (literal), with the times of the city and the time of the poet. The "symbolist" metaphor, by contrast—the swan of Mallarmé or the palm of Valéry or even the somewhat livelier eel of Montale—offers a special near allegory of congruence between the sensibility of the poet and the object of his perception. The poem consummates this act of identifying the two and offers them to us clean and whole. The Surrealist does not proceed by any different assumption; but he dialectizes the process by calling attention to it in the course of the poem, and by shifting images constantly.

Stevens represents himself as following a similar course for the poem.[9] In his work—most explicitly, perhaps, in "Thirteen Ways of Looking at a Blackbird"—perspectivism and the momentary Gestalt are subjected to a process of mutual qualification. Imagination and reality are never permitted to fix into a formulable philosophical doctrine, however complex. Sometimes the constructed speaker in Stevens' poems is a sort of philosopher-poet, as in "An Ordinary Evening in New Haven," and a play with imagination and reality takes predominance. Sometimes, notably in "Esthétique du Mal" and "Le Monocle de Mon Oncle," high questions of love and death strongly direct the flow of discourse, and the images are inspected for primacies of feeling as well as for aspects of perceptual validation. In either case "Poetry is the cry of its occasion," and the imagistic yield comes from angling the poem so that other questions than aesthetic and epistemological ones are seen from the corner of the eye. Arch titles, and such figures as Professor Eucalyptus and Madame Papadopoulos, emphasize the improvisatory and ironizing nature of the discourse. The professor is imagined to teach at a Yale never named, but he takes his name from a tree, a name concealed behind a Greek expression that itself means "well-concealed" (*eu-kalyptos*)—the tree itself named for a property of its own seed. And the poem keeps seeding itself, from a well-concealed source—into trees that offer a grove it invites us to enter. Metaphor and metaphoricity qualify each other, and Stevens stands always at one remove from the "absolute metaphor" of such as Reverdy and Merwin. Olson, however, maximizes a prior doctrine that places the fact of his own existence squarely before us at every point. Qualifications have been ironed out beforehand, obviating the speculative amplification of Stevens as well as the humor of either Stevens or the Surrealists. The poem is "equal, that is, to the real itself."[10] The metaphoric properties of the image are fully buried in the "found objects" of the speaker's perception, and their metaphoricity arises from their constructed relation to the speaker. A set is predicated which relativizes this construct and renders absolute metaphor, by implication, too simplifying an act.

Olson's actual subject matter in some ways resembles that of Robert Lowell. In both poets the personal and the New England regional-historical are mingled. They even share a posited special angle on events, and a kind of overriding gloomy stoicism.

What differentiates them is the approach to figuration, and that becomes nearly everything. Lowell, except in *Life Studies,* starts from a randomized Renaissance-cum-nineteenth-century prose rhetoric. At best his figures approach the near allegories of Montale and Valéry. More often they are mere instantiations, as in a prose essay or in eighteenth-century satire. *History* presents a purely sequenced series of moments from the past, millennial but random, where the honorific does duty for the imagined. Its conception, as well as its execution, is recognizably in the same register as a similar nineteenth-century work, *La Légende des Siècles* of Victor Hugo. Without figural clarity, Lowell's poem perpetually strains after and out of attitudes. The personal and the historical fuse in pyrotechnic effects without any structure of interdefinition.

The psyche's confrontation with the singular detail in *The Maximus Poems* constructs "synecdochally" along the lines of Namier's studies, work valued in the graduate schools of the thirties when Olson was a graduate student of history as well as of literature. Just as Namier's microscopic studies, man by man, of the makeup of a British Parliament represent the constituents of policy, so Olson's tiny incidents from the chronicles of Gloucester operate synchronically, and synecdochally, to epiphanize the city; and then, expanding the synecdoche, to epiphanize America, or any country. They also operate diachronically. Contemporary with the Braudel of *la longue durée,* though perhaps not aware of him, Olson simultaneously makes the "space" in which the city is situated—its contours between sea and land, its geological formations, its relation to other terrain—function as a long-term determinant of the psychological and social actions foregrounded by his poem. *Space* is a major term in his critical vocabulary, where it is always coordinated with or defined through terms like *millennium, history,* and *process.* Olson takes the geographer Carl O. Sauer to substantiate this long view, as he takes Jung to substantiate his coordinated notion of the psyche's extension into archetypes.

In Olson's critical writings the historical-microscopic, the geographical-millennial, and the archetypal, are reasoned into interdependence over and over again. He angles these interdependences into *The Maximus Poems* in such a way that the images, though "flat" and in a seemingly linear sequence, transcend the found objects or actions with which they begin. The gestures of rhythm, and such rhetorical devices as the open-ended parenthesis (where the distinction between coordination and subordination is subverted), lend them a complexity beyond such visual analogues as the photograph or such literary analogues as Michel Butor's linear matching of found objects, *Mobile.*

Take "Stevens Song," from *Maximus Three.*[11] This Stevens is not Wallace Stevens, as the "song" might suggest, but a Gloucester carpenter of the seventeenth century who resembles Olson's father, and Olson himself, in combining professional skill with personal fecklessness and truculence. The psychoanalytic here converges with the archetypal by the imaging convergence of short view with long view.

> out of the fire out of the mouth
> of his Father

eating him

Stevens ran off,

    having called Charles the Second

a king he could not give allegiance to

Stevens was then

63 years old and did he ever

return? when was the chief shipbuilder

of England and

the maritime world of the day (1683?)
in Gloucester first doing
running off, where? . . .

. . . .
Stevens ran off
My father

stayed
& was ground down. . . .

. . . .
On the side
of the King the Father

there sits a wolf
which is not his own will

which comes from outside

. . . .
when
I was

a dog when Tyr
put his hand

in Fenris
mouth

—it was not a test,

it was to *end*

that matter, Fenris
simply bit it

off Thereby
there awaits

a Reason: the Quest
is a Reason

               Stevens
went across Cut Bridge

my father
lost his

life the son
of the King of the Sea walked

away from the filthy wolf
eating the dropped body, the

scavenger

Here the mythological references, though culture-specific, become archetypal through their function, "psychologically," in a recorded history, that of Stevens and Olson's father and the speaker Olson-Maximus himself. The Greco-Roman Saturn who eats his children, the Norse wolf, and a long meditation on an Egyptian death ship (omitted in one of the ellipses of the quotation above) define, by simple imagistic coordination, the act of Stevens, who is both coordinated and subordinated to Charles the Second. Here the British king of America is both an actual figure of power and, by dim mythological possibility, a sort of Saturn in the psyche of Stevens, as Olson's father's supervisors in the post office were, as well as the congressmen to whom he appealed for redress. The common locus for Stevens and the Olsons coordinates-subordinates them to these archetypes, and generates the underlying abstracting possibilities in their imaged montage-isolation, the abstractions of *test, end, Reason,* and *Quest.* The single archetypalized action enters a powerful orbit of definition by virtue of the coordination accorded it. And this concentrating process is associatively brought to bear even on the poem's points of especially flat and succinct utterance, like the Fitz Hugh Lane section quoted above.

3

Creeley is to Williams as Mallarmé is to Baudelaire. His abstractness, too, develops increasingly the big jump between early (*For Love*, 1962) and middle (*Words*, 1967). Intellection is triggered by an abruptness in the conjunction of word and line.

The adolescent Creeley announced himself publicly as a prospective Latin teacher—and subsequently spent a spell as one. This fact finds its embodiment in the hard-bitten words lodged into place over a fleeting sentiment or, indifferently, a minimally characterized image (as the vague poetic purpose was concealed under the intention to teach a dead language). The dead words take on new life by being treated as inert; their overtones are released for double play by being arrested into an ordonnance that the opted "natural" voice is made to seem easily to govern. Qualification of image becomes implicit in rhythm. One near analogy for the rhythms of Creeley may thus be the *Odes* of Horace, except Horace's poems are far more bound than Creeley's, and his consistent abstractness pares down his poems. Williams releases Creeley from Horace, and releases him to use that for which Horace stands while bypassing entirely the Mallarmean tradition he recapitulates roundabout.

Creeley's phrasal suspension, his near hyperbaton, also may be taken as a version of Mallarmé's—it can be found so markedly in neither Williams nor Olson. It takes the visual for granted as only the work of a successor to Mallarmé and Williams could. The movement is mild enough not to rise to stern abstraction, its strategy for self-possession being the sound of a hesitant, nascently apologetic voice, which directs visual perceptions to psychological use.

These are preconscious poems in which all the functions of the *I* and the *it* take place. Under a Diogenes self-light. Their shadow includes conscious and precludes unconscious, by the act of eschewing special structures while concentrating on the sort of urban feature highlighted in photographs like those of Aaron Siskind and paintings like those of Dubuffet:

The Cracks

Don't step
so lightly, Break
your back, missed
the step. Don't go

away mad, lady in
the nightmare. You
are central,
even necessary.

I will attempt to describe you.
I will be completely without
face, a lost
chance, nothing at all left.

"Well," he said
as he was leaving,
"blood
tells."

But you remembered quickly
other times, other faces
and I slipped between the good
intentions, breathlessly.

What a good boy am I who
want to. Will you,
mother, come quickly,
won't you. Why not

go quietly, be left
with a memory
of an insinuation or two
of cracks in a pavement.[12]

The movement here operates under the aegis of a Freudian interpretation of crack. But it does not close the gap with such an interpretation. Like someone hopping the cracks in the pavement, it at

once avoids and evokes such associations, minimizing and gliding past, while focusing on, the child's superstition as it shades into a common area with the "lady" traditionally addressed in poems from Dante to the T. S. Eliot and the Robert Graves of Creeley's youth. The poem remains focused, from beginning to end, on the cracks. They at once permit it to stray far and haunt an act of straying with psychic significance. The voice hesitates before the largeness of experience that it will bring off an act of suggesting. "Attention a whip of surmise."[13]

In such poems the "something evermore about to be" of Wordsworth is flattened out into visual traces. His rhythmic modulation gives Creeley, deservedly, a classic air. "It is all a rhythm" ("The Rhythm," *Words* 19); and this is often put to visual use:

> no sun
> but sun
> (*Pieces* 5)

This is an entire strophe, two words repeated and one like pattern repeated, arguably four pitch levels and even four stress levels, paradox caught and transcended in the exactness and delicate modulation of the voice. A central doctrine of Wallace Stevens' is pared even below the Williams threshold for conversational use. It is minimalist. The style achieves a balance between the fluid and the sculpturesque—almost a visual impression as the reader assimilates the lightly freighted short lines and slips through the frequent enjambements on to the next. Creeley is poised, so to speak, between the soft fluency of late Merwin and the "powerful frozen moments" of Gary Snyder.[14]

There is another minimalism, of Ponge, say, fixed on an inspected object; or of "deep image," given over to feelings of mystery aroused by object. Creeley is also cryptically an anti-Surrealist, coming around behind post-Surrealism in the prolonged meditation on Marisol. He does not dwell on images, much as he hinges on presenting them. In "The Flower" the particularity of the arbitrary image, repeated, escapes into deadly anecdote. "Pain is a flower like that one, / like that one, / like this one" (*For Love* 96).

> My voice is
> a foot. My
> head is
>
> a foot. I
> club
> people in
>
> my mind, I
> push them this
> way, that
>
> way . . .[15]

Here what begins as something like Magritte's Surrealist lexicon of arbitrary significations quickly moves itself, in its elementary economy, back into the stream of simple personal interchange, "the damn function of simile always a displacement of what *is* happening" (*Pieces* 49). The soft equivalences are not meant to cancel each other out. They would, if the earnestness of this voice is fully credited. Hence the hesitancy.

On the farm, we imagine, Creeley acted out, and acted beyond, as a chicken farmer, "the white chickens" of Williams' famous *so much depends.* Clucking and pecking, ducking to pick up grain by grain, *singulatim,* the singularity of the chickens escapes their fixed image.

She Went to Stay

Trying to chop mother down is like
hunting deer inside Russia
with phalangists for hat-pins.
I couldn't.

(*For Love* 75)

This is the overblown, arbitrary simile and image complex as a final hesitancy. The mind going through the poem is made to move around such possibilities. To joke about them in necessary transit.

A displaced and self-displacing pseudoepigrammatic shot at "defining" an intangible moral stance makes it so elusive as to be revelatory—so elusive no image will do, only the fragment of a tale.

The image of Williams is redone and abstracted as an action of small actions in process:

> *The Rocks*
>
> Trying to think of
> some way out, the
> rocks of thought
>
> which displace,
> dropped in
> the water,
>
> much else.
>
> (*Words* 2)

The convolutions of an inexplicably folding world stand also ready, increasingly so in Creeley's prose. In his prose work of most commanding presence, *Presences,* the hesitancies expand their habitat and relax before small humiliations and the shadow of horrors, taking their distant cue from visual artifacts, the sculptures of Marisol. Even such an entity as the Rockefeller villa at Bellagio dissolves into vignettes of a mordant hesitancy. At the same time the voice counts on acceptance. In *Presences* real people from a remembered past do not suffer the dimness of *The Island* or the paleness of *The Gold Diggers.*

The intermultiplying numbers of these sections do not shrink to the somewhat willed definitions of *Numbers:* they play off against each other as distantly as Creeley's vignettes play off against Marisol's sculptures.

We are gradually made aware that he touches these artifacts with a mobile ten-foot pole. The distance between Marisol's sculptured objects and the random personal associations of the poet's prose is maintained adroitly, and the terms of possible connection are adroitly varied at the same time. This distance may be equaled to that between her ikons, slapped into place with terrible jauntiness, and the laminations in the unconscious that they evidence; or to the distance between the deep subject of a Creeley poem and its offered *momenta* of intermittent, resolutely abstract, and minimal visualization:

Go forth, go forth
saith the grandmother, the fire
of that old form, and turns
away from the form.

And the forest is dark,
mist hides it, trees
are dim, but I turn
to my father in the dark.

(*For Love* 70)

Creeley's father is persistent but absent; Olson's is present but intricately struggling with history. Constructing the image helps both poets to say so.

VIII

Expressionism Not Wholly Abstract
Ashbery and O'Hara

Their attention constantly preoccupied by the art world in which John Ashbery is an art critic and Frank O'Hara was a curator,[1] these poets continue and extend Breton's definition of himself as manipulating the same material as the visual artist does. Yet to take the measure of either American poet, with reference to art, requires a fair amount of definition at this late and complex stage of modernism.

To take Ashbery first, he fuses the openness to unconscious experience of the Surrealist program with the antiart self-obfuscation and unresolvable contradiction of Marcel Duchamp. Either of these techniques resists formulation in terms of the other, since the Surrealist proffers enigmas in the service of revelation and Duchamp mounts his enigmas, or his single enigma, as a defiance against the possibility of revelation. If Ashbery's poems are aligned at either of these poles, they assert their affinity for the other. So the "Duchamp" pole enters his work, it would seem, through his prolonged study of Raymond Roussel, and yet no poem of Ashbery's adheres

167

fully to the method of lateral free-association that constantly modi-
fies Roussel's narrative line:

> La Colonne qui, léchée jusqu'à ce
> que la langue saigne,
> guérit la jaunisse
> > (MOSQUE ABOU'L MA'AIEH—
> > Environs de Damiette)

> Traitement héroique! user avec la langue
> Sans en rien rengainer qu'elle ne soit exsangue,
> Après mille autres fous, les flancs de ce pilier!
> Mais vers quoi ne courir, à quoi ne se plier,
> Fasciné par l'espoir, palpable ou chimérique
> (Espoir! roi des leviers! tout oncle d'Amérique
> ((Ce pays jeune encore, inépuisé,
> > > béni . . .
> Pour ces champs infinis, où gaillards, le nez frais
> (((Un jour d'un chien souffrant fait un chien hydrophobe;
> ((((pendant notre hiver notre tignasse essaime[2]

> The Column Which, Licked Till the
> Tongue Bleeds, Cures Jaundice.
> > (MOSQUE ABOU'L MA'AIEH—
> > Outskirts of Damietta)

> Heroic management! to use with the tongue
> Without sheathing anything till it lack blood,
> After a thousand other fools, the flanks of this pillar!
> But towards what not to run, under what not to bend,
> Fascinated by hope, palpable or chimerical
> (Hope! king of levers! every uncle from America
> ((That country still young, unexhausted, blest . . .
> (((those infinite fields, where gallant, the nose fresh
> ((((One day a sick dog is a rabid dog;
> ((((while our winter our shock of hair swarms

At the rate of this ever-immobilized Zeno's arrow of discourse,
no action will take place, and we will never hear about Napoleon's
campaign in Egypt. It is all warm-up, verbal association, lateral

Surrealist commentary. Ashbery has ingested the Breton-like contradictions of the Surrealists and moved to the level of a supple syntax, in which improvisation does not lose the air of intellectual control. It can assume the Surrealist unconscious as a resource to draw on.

Ashbery dwells on the image in a single line more than Roussel does. His association is usually from image to image, rather than from an irrational connection in the lexicon of phonetic resources of the word that lead it to another. *Billard* and *pillard* (Billiard table and plunderer) is Roussel's own example; through such associations, phonetic in this case, the narrative line jumps the track to a new line and goes on till it jumps that track for still another.[3] Ashbery seldom if ever adopts this method, letting two disparate images, instead, reveal their mutual strangeness. That is, the Surrealist pole asserts itself the moment we try to define him in terms of the Duchamp pole. Yet, contrariwise, he rarely offers the celebration of Éluard, the narrative brio through simple contradiction of Breton,[4] the wisdom of Char or Celan, the seamless "Mediterranean" iconography of Merwin or Neruda.

The painters he moved among, of course, were the Abstract Expressionists, painters who themselves modify prior practice. The biomorphic forms of Gorky are more personal and tragic than those of the glib Tanguy or the polymorphous Matta. Gorky's intense and blurring iconography harks back to the starving haunted figures of the blue period of the Picasso he had earlier imitated. Yet he subjects such figures to psychic as well as visual redefinition. So too, without regard to how the pictures were painted, Pollock subjects the biomorphic forms of Masson to the crucible of still further abstraction. The large field permits a calligraphic intensification of every inch: it grows exponentially more complicated as it grows more abstract, from the still Masson-like *The She-Wolf* to such fully mature works as *Blue Poles* and *Yellow Islands*. Such works are closer to the abstractness of the late Kandinsky than to Masson, and they may be said to adopt Kandinsky's color mystique. Yet they synthesize and centralize the visual field more than the kaleidoscopic Kandinsky ever did.

Ashbery's work offers analogues to all these changes. So his bringing Daffy Duck into the field of Amadis de Gaul and the Italian grand opera built on that figure recalls the iconographic congeries of de Kooning's women paintings. Such paintings retain the tragic Expressionist iconography, the "sloppy" brushwork, sexuality, and even the palette, of Schmidt-Rottluff, while organizing the canvas in ways not wholly unassociated with the handlings of women in Braque's post-Cubist paintings of the twenties and thirties. In addition, de Kooning presents these women with the neo-primitive crudeness of graffiti, like a latter-day Dubuffet. The society portrait, the attractive nude, the child's terrified image of Mother, and the primitive idol, have been brought into a fierce coherence well beyond that of the figures in Picasso's *Demoiselles d'Avignon* of forty and more years before. Semi-abstraction has subverted and conflated all Kenneth Clark's separate spiritual spheres for presented woman in *The Nude*. Semi-abstraction, in Ashbery too, erases the coordinates by which the playful is distinguished from the serious, or revelation from obfuscation. Deconstruction and superconstruction in such work become versions of each other.[5]

2

In one sense for these poems the absolute metaphor of Surrealism is redefined by being assigned not to the object named but to the connections between object and object. For the single object, referentiality is firm, well-nigh univocal, and by itself resistant to participation in the logic of figural expression; as in the beginning of this poem significantly entitled "Collective Dawns":

You can have whatever you want.
Own it, I mean. In the sense
Of twisting it to you, through long, spiralling afternoons.
It has a sense beyond that meaning that was dropped there
And left to rot. The glacier seems

Impervious but is all shot through
With amethyst and the loud, distraught notes of the cuckoo.
They say the town is coming apart.
And people go around with a fragment of a smile
Missing from their faces. Life is getting cheaper

In some senses. Over the tops of old hills
The sunset jabs down, angled in a way it couldn't have
Been before. The bird-sellers walk back into it.
"We needn't fire their kilns; tonight is the epic
Night of the world. Grettir is coming back to us.
His severed hand has grabbed the short sword
And jumped back onto his wrist. The whole man is waking up.
The island is becoming a sun.

                                                            (*HD* 5)[6]

Here the strophic spacings do not occur at points of logical shift, as usually in poetry, but rather at points of tight syntactic connection, on enjambements. Nothing marks the lapse from one sentence to another, and so they implicitly refer their sense back to a connection in the consciousness that obligingly presents a rumination, running as well as disconnected. A metalinguistic drift begins this particular rumination, twice using the word *sense* in slightly different senses. *Meaning that was dropped there and left to rot* is a metaphor, angled against the predominant referentiality and nonfiguration of the next sentences. There are glaciers, and they are well known for a bluish cast that in a certain light could look amethyst, as that stone has a look of color prismed in ice. The description of the smiles, too, is referential in the art-interpretive sense. It is a way of saying the people are never fully smiling. This sentence could be taken as imitating the depth-*ekphrasis* characteristic of Rilke, a description attempting to get beneath an actual look by interpreting it as though it were an art object. The next sentence, about the sunset, is still more severely confined to reference. It accurately describes the facts of changing light.

Such attentive description, in fact, is frequently found in Ashbery, and is a recurrent constituent of his compositional repertoire, a sort of visual and painterly anchor of reference:

The houses doze and seem to wonder why through the
Pacific haze, and the dreams alternately glow and grow dull.

                              ("Pyrography," *HD* 8)

This combines a description of an effect of light in an actual city of the Pacific, once called "the poetry capital of the USA," with a characterization of life there.

> His eyes are empty rectangles, shaped
> Like slightly curved sticks of chewing gum.
>
> ("The Explanation," *HD* 14)

In these lines a sentence of accurate visual description makes the person into a picture reminiscent of effects, again, in de Kooning or Dubuffet.

> And songs climb out of the flames of the near campfires,
> Pale, pastel things exquisite in their frailness
> With a note or two to indicate it isn't lost,
> On them at least.
>
> ("Business Personals," *HD* 18)

Songs is a metaphor, but one initially enlisted to describe a particular effect of disappearing light above a campfire. Melody and song frame this sentence in the poem. The visual moment is picked up and aligned to the incongruent. So further in the same poem, the Rilkean description of depth effects is encased in a metaphor (*dripping*) that skews it enough to involve the lute, too, in metaphor:

> The idea of great distance
> Is permitted, even implicit in the slow dripping
> Of a lute.

Further on description is coordinated within the sentences of the very song referred to, "Only danger deflects / The arrow from the center of the persimmon disc, / Its final resting place." This unserious danger signifies simply the risk that the arrow will not hit the bull's-eye of a target, where it can be left for a "final resting place." As the stronger sense of the word *danger* for arrows—lost backwards in time to a world where arrows were serious military weapons—is itself deflected by the predicate reference to the bull's-eye of the target, the sentence itself comes to rest on a visual effect. *Persimmon* here is a color, one that accurately describes the red bull's-eye of a target in certain lights.

"Melodic Trains" (*HB* 24), a poem about time, opens with a moment of complex visual description:

> A little girl with scarlet enameled fingernails
> Asks me what time it is—evidently that's a toy wristwatch
> She's wearing, for fun. And it is fun to wear other
> Odd things, like this briar pipe and tweed coat.
>
> Like date-colored sierras with the lines of seams
> Sketched in and plunging now and then into unfathomable
> Valleys that can't be deduced by the shape of the person
> Sitting inside it—me, and just as our way is flat across
> Dales and gulches, as though our train were a pencil

One kind of Pop style, the combination of high-gloss fingernails with something like a Mickey Mouse wristwatch, is described as equivalent in spirit ("fun") to another, the sporting of British icons, a pipe and tweeds. The elaborate description of the tweeds after the strophe break stays visually accurate: there *is* a kind of tweed that has in it the color of dates seen through a haze, and this *is* in turn the color of mountains. Tweeds do tend not to follow the contours of the body. But the resemblance, purely visual through the simile, opens away from the purely visual when the reference to the train in which the speaker moves takes the visual vehicle and transposes it to a possible visual tenor, mountains seen outside the window of the train.

"On the Towpath" (*HD* 22–23) speaks with visual accuracy and firm reference about "violet cabbages" and says correctly, "The sun fades like the spreading / Of a peacock's tail." This simile, while visually based, contains within itself a contradiction referred to the visual realm, since *fading* stands as a kind of opposite to *spreading.* Later in "Melodic Trains," a reference, *The child opposite me / With currant fingernails,* changes the visual notation of the *scarlet enameled fingernails* of the first line, and the skewed drift of the sentences framing these references permits us to read into them the possibility of metaphysical deductions from physical changes of the sort offered by Stevens' "Sea-Surface Full of Clouds."

Ashbery offers no such deductions. He implies them as he aims his designations away for other, discordant targets.

The trueness of the visual comparison can be elaborate and far-fetched, as in Marianne Moore:

> Just now a magnetic storm hung in the swatch of sky
> Over the Fudds' garage, reducing it—drastically—
> To the aura of a plumbago-blue log cabin on
> A Gadsden Purchase commemorative cover.
>
> ("Daffy Duck in Hollywood," *HD* 31)

A purpling storm will, at moments, appear visually less menacing, and odd blues do decorate the first-day covers sold by stamp dealers. The effect here approaches collage: the connection is visual, but the farfetchedness of the two elements in the visual conjunction enforces attention to the Surrealist, or even Dadaist, logic of their visual similarity.

Or, as one of a variety of such transitory effects of significance-transposition anchored in the visual, an elaborate icon of Pop architecture is drawn into a hyperbole of praise, perhaps love-praise, as in Éluard and Apollinaire, but for the moment only:

> The name of the castle is you,
> *El Rey.* It is an all-night truck-stop
> Offering the best coffee and hamburgers in Utah.
> It is most beautiful and nocturnal by daylight.
> Seven layers: moss-agate, coral, aventurine,
> Carnelian, Swiss lapis, obsidian—maybe others.
>
> ("Valentine," *HD* 62)

Here there is blurring of reference at the beginning and end of clear reference. The truck stop is clear and the seven layers are clear, but it is not clear where to lodge the two *its* of introduced predication in the series *name: castle: you: El Rey: it: truck-stop: it: seven layers.*

3

By withdrawing the work from sequenced argument, from detach-
able wisdom, and from the Surrealist's programmatic adherence to
a celebration of the communications between unconscious and conscious, Ashbery effectually foregrounds the mood or tone of the
poem. That it manages an openness to varied experience comes to
seem incidental to the fluidity and yet consistency of its mood. This
resembles, to continue, the effect of Duchamp, a whole that cannot
be the sum of parts. At the same time the parts, like the coffee mill
as against the malic moulds of Duchamp's *Le Grand Verre,* are prevented by the creative fluidity of the whole from unambiguous referential, or figurative, status on their own:

> *Variant*
>
> Sometimes a word will start it, like
> Hands and feet, sun and gloves. The way
> Is fraught with danger, you say, and I
> Notice the word "fraught" as you are telling
> Me about huge secret valleys some distance from
> The mired fighting—"but always, lightly wooded
> As they are, more deeply involved with the outcome
> That will someday paste a black, bleeding label
> In the sky, but until then
> The echo, flowing freely in corridors, alleys,
> And tame, surprised places far from anywhere,
> Will be automatically locked out—*vox*
> *Clamans*—do you see? End of tomorrow.
> Don't try to start the car or look deeper
> Into the eternal wimpling of the sky: luster
> On luster, transparency floated onto the topmost layer
> Until the whole thing overflows like a silver
> Wedding cake or Christmas tree, in a cascade of tears."
>
> (*HD* 4)

Deconstructive and metalinguistic analyses become apposite here,
given the title, one version (or variant) of which designates a tex-
tual alternative. Yet they, too, become subverted in the mood gen-

erated by the voice that holds its disparate particulars so evenly in its flow. The word *fraught,* the fact of being fraught with danger, the valleys, the sky, and tomorrow verge towards what might have been an ordered statement, if it had moved towards convergence. Or it might have been a prophecy,[7] given the quotation from St. John the Baptist. This quotation—"a voice crying in the desert"—is curtailed, and it is cited in one of many variants of a much-varied official text, the St. Jerome translation of the Bible which until recently was authoritative, beyond even the Greek text, for the Roman Catholic church. Instead of converging order, there is a much-qualified and subtly distinguished description of the sky, which itself collapses into progressively less visual attributions, until it ends in the naming of tears—within the quotation marks that at once distance them and assimilate them to another primacy, that of the quoting voice.

This voice resembles the voice of Reverdy, except that the particulars named are far more diverse than any in the absolute metaphors of Reverdy's moderately coherent poems. And Ashbery can be far more pyrotechnically incoherent than this, as in the opening of "Daffy Duck in Hollywood." The Pop, and seemingly camp, subject matter of that poem points up the fusion of attitudes in Ashbery, comprising all at once the satirical or ironic, the neutral, and the accepting-celebratory. Camp itself offers an endless regress of irony, and even self-acceptance or scene celebration are immediately ironized. Duchamp—or Rauschenberg or Rivers—neutralizes, but at the same time preserves, that irony. Ashbery, though, submerges it, and his poems borrow tone from camp without being campy, even so much so as O'Hara's. Irony only floats in strange solution; the refusal to focus into coherence becomes a verbal gesture of ineluctable acceptance. It is not only, as again with Surrealists, that coordinates have been lost to distinguish the trivial from the momentous. Hence irony only shadows the discrepancy between the small everyday gesture of starting a car and the attitude of trying to probe the sky—for prophetic wisdom or for visual sharpening? The possibilities of language here converge with the impossibility not so much of communication as of full constation and a fixed ordering of particulars. The poem insists on letting ultimates

into its utterance while qualifying the utterance into randomness—
a "variant," "sometimes a word will start it." Something like free
association is identified with something like the primary inception
of any act of verbal accounting. Or of self-expression, or of philosophizing.

We can almost firmly identify the speaker at the beginning of
"Daffy Duck in Hollywood." It is Daffy Duck himself, referring to
the cartoonist who invented him:

> He promised he'd get me out of this one,
> That mean old cartoonist, but just look what he's
> Done to me now! I scarce dare approach me mug's attenuated
> Reflection in yon hubcap, so jaundiced, so *déconfit*
> Are its lineaments—fun, no doubt, for some quack phrenologist's
> Fern-clogged waiting room, but hardly what you'd call
> Companionable.

Now Daffy Duck in Disney's cartoons, like Donald, produces utterances that come out as quacks and the word *quack* itself comes
through to serve as an adjective. When Daffy Duck's quacks are
listened to carefully, they are decipherable as statements. And those
statements are usually complaints of being put upon—the running
note of Ashbery's poem. The indeterminacy of voice admits so
many varied particulars, however, that it threatens to drown out
and mollify the strident note of complaint. The duck's voice is a
cultured one, as Ashbery ventriloquizes it, with references to grand
opera and to medieval and Renaissance literature. Its complaints
about Hollywood are those that might be delivered by any cultured
visitor to that city. The complaint would be stepped up if the visitor
were trapped in that city, as Daffy Duck effectually is, a fictive creation of its media. He is trapped, too, as the dead end of a whole
tradition of Western art, a figure at once evocative and one dimensional. (Disney was listed as an analogue to Surrealism in the 1936
Museum of Modern Art Surrealist Show.)

The fiction of mechanically repetitive animal noises, quacks,
emerging into speech, enables all the statements in this poem to
glory in their splendid articulateness while suggesting a fundamen-
tally inarticulate core. This is the procedure of *Finnegans Wake,*

with the relations between articulate and inarticulate differently calibrated. There the unconscious deforms every word into a slag of multiple sense that is at the same time near nonsense. Ashbery recasts the solemnity of Joyce into Pop absurdity. In Ashbery's poem, of course, the dizzying possibility of nonsense affects only the syntax ("me mug's attenuated"), which happens only rarely, and often as not the syntax teeters back into balance ("reflection"). The act of matching word and word is not arrested and not especially intensified; instead it is diluted, and tonally diluted, into the simultaneous alternative of mixing word and word. We take on trust the remote coherence, and its very remoteness.

Looking more closely at the speaker's attitude to Hollywood, we find that incoherent segment of a giant noncity providing the coherence of reference for every single statement. The poem is a litany of complaint-description, and its high incidence of literary references can always be taken, always obliquely, as the complaint that Hollywood turns classics into trash:

> Amadis
> Is cozening the Princesse de Clèves into a midnight micturition
>   spree
> On the Tamigi with the Wallets (Walt, Blossom, and little
> Skeezix) on a lamé barge "borrowed" from Ollie
> Of the Movies' dread mistress of the robes. Wait!

Heroes like Amadis de Gaul from the Grail legends have undergone many mutations from their untraceable origins in the Dark Ages through high and then popular culture. Daffy Duck, a Quixote-turned-his-own-windmill, can be conceived of as the final reduction of such archetypes, as Hollywood remoulds and exploits them. It does so indifferently also to protagonists of profound love moralizations in high cultural novels like *The Princesse de Clèves*. Hollywood throws the whole courtly love ethic into its Pop grist and does not mind violating the purposive chastity of a Grail knight or traducing the mature, deep scruples of a poised woman. It simply has the one make the infantile proposal of a urination contest to the other, locating the "spree" on the banks of a river sacred to Hollywood Anglophiles, the Thames. The name, though, has been assimilated to the opera mentioned at the beginning of the poem, *Amadigi di Gaula,* and it is named gratuitously in Italian, the Tamigi. This complex of "cultured" references does not prevent the unceremonious lumping together in miscellaneous orgy of these traditional figures with the invented family of a Pop cartoon.[8] The sentence trails off into near nonsense: a "lamé barge" makes sense only as a sort of visual effect, distantly recalling Shakespeare's Cleopatra (grist for another Hollywood epic). "The barge she sat on like a burnished throne / Glowed on the water."

We may detect, too, an underlay of "intertextual" reference to T. S. Eliot. He not only adopts this quotation from *Antony and Cleopatra* into *The Waste Land.* That poem too combines the Grail legend, the Thames, sexuality, love by water, and social degeneration. But "Daffy Duck" is not a parody of *The Waste Land,* and neither is it an affirmation of Eliot's themes. If Hollywood's dream mills coin sexual myths into indistinguishable pap where chastity, devotion, and perversity all coexist in a world of mingled depravity and innocence, Ashbery's voice seems to be accepting all this as part of the "change" he dwells on at the end of the poem. In preterition he ends on a visual effect, since as his italics indicate, the sky is indeed green, more specifically parrot green, at twilight over Los Angeles:

> We don't mind
> Or notice any more that the sky *is* green, a parrot
> One, but have our earnest where it chances on us,
> Disingenuous, intrigued, inviting more,
> Always invoking the echo, a summer's day.

The coherence of the poem invites a metaphorizing of its referents, but statements like the last, the generalizing fluid voice, undercut that possibility. The signified is not figurative. The signifier does not float either, as often in Surrealist poems. The referent remains fixed each time. In Ashbery, as in Pollock and de Kooning, the choice to simplify or absent the act of figuration drives the surrealizing deeper. In "always invoking the echo" the voice is freed for a greater range than simple celebration. Its disjunctions advertise the self-limiting that allows for self-extensions in its self-questioning.

4

In his occasional recourse to figuration, Ashbery does not allow the parts named to move towards larger *Gestalten,* and so ground does not alternate with figure.

Thus he adopts for the title of one poem a powerful phrase from Emily Dickinson's "Because I Could Not Stop for Death"—"The Gazing Grain." In Emily Dickinson's eschatology the strange elisions of visual registering when her speaker travels through the afterlife forbid our univocal assignment of metaphor to *gazing* or to *grain.*[9] The phrase could simply describe the visual effect of spikes of wheat—and in that case *gazing* would be a metaphor; the spikes of wheat resemble a looking eye with respect to flashing. In another possibility, though, in Dickinson's afterlife the grain could be people already ripe for God's harvest. In that case *grain* would be the metaphor and *gazing* would be literal. If visual, metaphorical; if psychological-spiritual, then literal. These conditions reverse the usual ones, when we think of the visual as implying literal description.

Ashbery, however, if he refers further to Dickinson's poem, does so only to contradict it in his conclusion:

We come back to ourselves
Through the rubbish of cloud and tree-spattered pavement.
These days stand like vapor under the trees.

(HD 11)

This only touches on figuration. The simile *like vapor* is either visual-physical or psychological. *Rubbish of cloud* and *tree-spattered pavement* repeat the figurative shifts of *gazing grain* on a diminished scale, since the first is either a visual analogue (the clouds look like rubbish) or a rudimentarily figurative description of bits of cloud left from larger ones. *Tree-spattered pavement* offers two possibilities, both visual: either a pavement that has seeds or leaves on it shed from trees, or a registering in two-dimensional perspective of the trees as a tapestrylike splash on a pavement. All this withdraws from Dickinson's phrase, and from her poem, which Ashbery "qualifies" from the very beginning:

> The tires slowly came to a rubbery stop.
> Alliterative festoons in the sky noted
>
> That this branchy birthplace of presidents was also
> The big frigidaire-cum-cowbarn where mendicant
>
> And margrave alike waited out the results
> Of the natural elections.

The circumlocution of the second sentence also circumvents or skirts full figuration. It is nearly literal if we read it that campaign slogans trailed from airplanes in an America abundant of trees forces beggar and nobleman to wait out the democratic results in a country equally given to industry and agriculture. Yet even in this reading metaphors crop up. *Frigidaire* opens into generality if it be taken as a synecdoche for all mechanized products or a metonymy of the product standing for the means and paraphernalia of production. If it be taken as a straight metaphor, then America, in a common attribution, is "the air-conditioned nightmare" of Henry Miller's phrase, a place that systematically lowers everybody's temperature. And it is at the same time a country of hicks, a "cowbarn." Such readings, and the metaphoricity of *cowbarn* and *margrave,* are local and topical anglings of this sentence. More deeply, the entire sentence suspends its area of reference from the physical-political to the psychological-personal. The terminal phrase *natural elections* is not metaphorical but simply ambiguous, between a collective plebescite and an individual choice. As a theological term, it may also touch on Dickinson's, and America's, Calvinist background. The speaker of the poem is as perplexed as Emily Dickinson's speaker, and he lacks her theological resources. Language instead must do duty for them, and it will betray him if he yields to the constant pressure to succumb to straight metaphor.

The calm and assuredness-in-questioning of this voice manages the figural shifts of its references in a way reminiscent of de Kooning's post-Cubist practice: words, like segments of line and color, are simultaneously mimetic and abstract, without allowing for a convergence of the abstract and the mimetic. Consequently, they do not fully enfranchise even such comprehensive readings of individual passages as Keith Cohen's suggestive assignment of attack against bourgeois society via a comparison of its "investments" with those of the Freudian psyche:

> Seeking in occasions new sources of memories, for memory is profit
> Until the day it spreads out all its accumulation, delta-like, on the plain
> For that day no good can come of remembering, and the anomalies cancel each other out.
>
> (*DD* 31–32)

Underlying these ominous lines is the implicit comparison between the capitalist's financial investments and our everyday libidinal investments, staked largely in the past. Profit margins are thus measured by the number and density of one's memories, as though by remembering one eluded the present.[10]

The lines are protreptic as well as ominous; they are subprophetic. And in being so, an underlying comparison of memory to a river ("delta-like") suspends assignment of figuration to either the psyche or the physical terrain: Is *memory* a metaphor, or is *plain?* In this alternation, *profit margin,* too, can be metaphoric, and the *cancel each other out* in the last line could imply an annihilation or a fulfillment, both of them beyond psychic history or economic organization.

As characteristically in Ashbery, such detail hovers into and out of metaphoric possibility, all the while retaining a firmness of signification. The images, almost always milder than in Surrealists like Breton and Péret, still do not succumb to the uniform mildness of Reverdy. Ashbery's images, even when ostentatiously surrealistic, are assimilated not to the stark mystery of narrative, but to reminiscence, anecdote, recapitulation, confession, boast, all flowing into one another, as in the naturalistic last line of "Night" (*TCO* 24), "The kids came and we all went the briars." In the even more extravagant "Leaving the Atocha Station" (*TCO* 33–34), the title locates all metaphors, in one dimension, as aspects of a real journey from Madrid. "Night" entertains explicitly Surrealistic turns while managing to avoid the implied final repetitions of Breton or Neruda:

> Ordeal a horse and
> My lake and sat down
> We must the gin came faster in cups
> Under the scissors mill just like you was sixteen
> In the orange flowers a pale narcissus hung
> You was saying the alligators the grove
> And a plied a rodolite of the gray
> Fishing manure . . . the gray roses the best
> And the bed hung with violets
>
> (*TCO* 23)

These attributions enter figuration not so much through the forcing of contradiction as through the elision of one domain into another. Breton's *white-haired revolver* is a supreme contradiction, since revolvers have no kind of hair and in any case are not an opposite to hair. *Scissors mill* elides the domain of paired cutting objects into the domain of grain-grinding mechanisms, but either could be a metaphor for the other, and both together could be a metaphor for some other possibility, including the possibility of ineffectuality. (You can't mill scissors. In that sense a scissors mill would be like a sky pump or a blank writing.) The title "Houseboat Days" submerges an oxymoron, since a house and a boat are in principle contradictory terms: a house stays in one place, on land, while a boat moves on water. In the complications of culture, however, the hybrid *houseboat* does exist, usually moored in a stationary situation so as to become more house than boat, except for the water underneath. Houseboats can move, though, and movement is suggested in the figural trompe l'oeil transpositions of the conclusion to "Houseboat Days":

> A little simple arithmetic tells you that to be with you
> In this passage, this movement, is what the instance costs:
> A sail out of some afternoon, like the clear dark blue
> Eyes of Harold in Italy, beyond amazement, astonished,

Apparently not tampered with. As the rain gathers and protects
Its own darkness, the place in the slipcover is noticed
For the first and last time, fading like the spine
Of an adventure novel behind glass, behind the teacups.

(*HD* 40)

Motion or rest? Is rest inside ("behind glass, behind the teacups") a figure for motion outside, or vice versa? The "simple
arithmetic" of logical calculation "tells you" that the figural sums
do not themselves jibe, though at a given point what seems a contradiction—*clear* and *dark* both applied to a single color, blue—does
in fact designate a recognizable color of sky. Not sky but the "eyes
of Harold in Italy," a hero who figures not in sight but in the sound
of a composition by Berlioz. That whole phrase is a simile, appended ambiguously to *afternoon* or to *A sail out of some afternoon.* Moving ahead, the figural *cache-cache* continues by the indeterminacy about what the three last adjectival phrases of the
sentence modify. They could be applied cumulatively, and alternately, to all five nouns, *sail, afternoon, eyes, Harold,* and *Italy.* A
different "arithmetic" of figural construction would organize each
of these syntactic possibilities, but the principle allowing for the
differences, once established, is indeed "simple." It is a sort of expo-
nential metaphor, or algebra of metaphor, in which the evasiveness
of ultimate overall sense permutes and abstracts the figural relations of the individual references.

Starting from such a base of utterance, extravagances of figural
possibility are reined in, including metalinguistic references to the
pictorial dimension of the language. "And *Ut Pictura Poesis* Is her
Name" (*HB* 45), illustrates, demonstrates, and evades the wrenching allegorical metaphor of the title, itself a near-Surrealistic viola-
tion of traditional lexical classes, since a phrase cannot serve as
nomenclature in an English lexicon (even if it can in an Indian
one, "He who tames the thunderbird," etc.). And this phrase itself
embeds a comparison, *Like painting is poetry.* Comparison heaps on
comparison, and they topple on their own, without consideration
for the uniform obliquity of their application to the sequent sentences of the poem. In it a humdrum small "fact," *She approached
me / About buying her desk* may be followed at once by a pyrotech-

nics of locutions in which figuration is still only a possibility, *Suddenly the street was / Bananas and the clangor of Japanese instruments*. This is a possible description of an actual metropolitan scene, where fruit vendors and a group of exotic instrumentalists would enter into random juxtaposition. Or some equivalent for them, as reading *effects of oblong yellow light* for *bananas* and *exotic claxonings and other street noises* for *the clangor of Japanese instruments*. But the whole sentence can also be taken for a Surrealistic figural characterization of a moment in the life of the street, expressionistically rendered. Nor is *street*, firm in its reference, unambiguous in its figural possibility. For *street* we could read, metaphorically, *avenue of conjunction for the approach of poetry to painting*, a reading reinforced by a visual datum (*bananas*) and an auditory one (*clangor*). All these structures of tenor, with or without vehicle, permute against an alternate syntactic reading for the sentence: *Bananas* is a slang term for *insanely frenetic*, a state that would turn *the clangor of Japanese instruments* into a redundant, equivalent predicate, both expressions signifying *insanely frenetic*. Yet there is the fainter possibility of a third syntactic construction. In this third, permutable reading, *the street was bananas* would be a complete clause, and coordinate with it *and there was the clangor of Japanese instruments* would be a second clause, omitting the main verb of predication so as to elide the linguistic designations in the direction of wordless art, *ut pictura poesis*.

These readings do not reinforce or enrich one another particularly or along the lines of Empson's ambiguities, the generality and diffusion of Mallarmé and Montale.[11] They are discontinuous enough, and random enough, to return the auditor to the mysterious voice emitting them.

5

A much-remarked feature of Ashbery's poetry is the deployment of various "shifters" in the poem, the personal pronouns that in the theory of Jakobson and Benveniste permit one to "shift" into utterance. *I* does not refer the way nouns and pronouns usually do. It serves merely to shift a locution from thought into utterance. Ashbery inconsistently moves from one shifter to another—from *I* to *you* to *he* to *we* without the usual corresponding indicators of transformation in the sentence sequence. This feature itself is random in the poems. There are many that do not change their pronouns, and the randomness would legitimate our assimilating this feature neutrally to the random figural shifts as a corresponding and enabling device for them.

The tentative identification of the speaker raises the question of what modality of existence he might by implication be positing. John Koethe defines the self of the Ashbery's speaker by reference to the view of Kant, distinguishing this self from the usual one of Descartes and the emptier one of Hume:

> The reification of the self as the psychological ego represents what might be called a Cartesian concept of the self. According to this conception the self *is* an object in the world among other objects. . . . Hume's critique of the Cartesian conception boils down to the idea that experience simply fails to acquaint us with any single persisting thing we might mean by "I," but rather discloses only the various sensations and passions we mistakenly ascribe to a persisting "self" whose experiences we take them to be. . . . Kant [says] "We do not have, and cannot have, any knowledge whatsoever of any such [Cartesian] subject. Consciousness is, indeed, that which alone makes all representations to be thoughts, and in it, therefore, as the *transcendental subject,* all our perceptions must be found. (Italics added)[12]

Now the Freudian unconscious presents not so much a fourth conception of the self to add to those of Descartes, Hume, and Kant. Rather, the unconscious acts as a powerful, and indeed capital, modifier of such organizations. The emphasis on the Freudian unconscious by the Surrealists, and by the psychoanalyzed Pollock, imports into the work of art an omnipresent determinant that is by definition uncontrollable, though it can be partly managed, according to the Freudian formula "Where Id was let Ego be."

Staying with Koethe's helpful triad, though altering it somewhat, we may say that Ashbery's shifts of voice result not in an equivalent for the transcendental ego but an ego aware of the unconscious and resolutely undisturbed by the surface appearances of the Humean empty ego. The possibility of the unconscious permits the voice to admit randomness and to accept, in a kind of cheerful resignation often close to Ashbery's tone, the impossibility by definition of fully establishing a transcendental ego. Breton and Péret and Éluard, much more directly cheerful, have, so to speak, solved such questions for themselves before starting the poem by simply backing the unconscious. Char, in a sense more classical, withdraws the self into the mystery of a fully surrealized utterance. The self of Char is a construct seen the more powerfully because it is seen obliquely.[13]

Pollock's actual painting is not just the record of unconscious processes: all paintings are that in some sense. More distinctly it is a representation of perceptions where inner and outer cannot be distinguished, as the Surrealists (Breton's *Les Vases Communicants*) and Wittgenstein had maintained all along. So Ashbery's nearly Abstract Expressionism is expressionistic for displaying the variegations of a self calling for, and escaping, high philosophical definition. It is abstract—or almost abstract—because it both employs abstractions and suggests by its organization an abstracting process undertaken so as to allow the unconscious to center statements without overwhelming them. As Harold Bloom has said, Ashbery starts from Stevens.[14] And it is all of Stevens he starts from: the initial determinant of rhetorical philosophizing, the deep emphasis on the image and the meaning of the image, the ironization of the self in a way that evades a radical ironization of the utterance.

Used as a sort of catalyst for art, Ashbery's poetry provides a measure that allows us to move from de Kooning and Pollock, to the persons or groups of Pistoletto mounted on mirrors to allow space for the observer's reflections, or the low-keyed large canvases of the British duo Gilbert and Richard, who document a personal life that conceptualizes by splitting the consciousness into two marginally differentiated personages largely prominent in each work.

The title poem of *The Tennis Court Oath* provides an example that foregrounds the interrelations among persons perceived and perceiving. Across it moves the possible story of shared perceptions and amorous gestures in which *I* could be subordinated to *he*, and both in turn to *the doctor* and *Philip*. The shifts of egos, the removal of coordinates, would not prevent our reading either of these pairs as versions of the other. *The mulatress approached in the hall,* assuming her presence to be episodic and only perceived (rather than perceiving), instantiates the capacities for the partially transcendent, shuffled ego, to engage with persons momentarily characterized as less complexly transmutable. (Of course the mulatress could be conceived of as a reader of the poem and in that sense as complex as anyone—though not so represented in the poem.) A shadow of logic is always present, Breton turned in the direction of Roussel to validate the surrealized connections. The instances of image-names, *blood* and *wall* and *wind* and *earth,* serve as terms in an argument that by definition would not move from possibility to actuality:

> the blood shifted you know those walls
> wind off the earth had made him shrink
> undeniably an oboe now the young
> were there was candy
> to decide the sharp edge of the garment
> like a particular cry not intervening called tin dog "he's
> coming! he's coming" with an emotion felt it sink into peace.
>
> (*TCO* 11)

"The Tennis Court Oath" defines a specific moment in the French Revolution. It is political and interpersonal by lexical definition, involving a great many more persons than are mentioned in Ashbery's poem. Here, taken globally, the signifiers of the poem do float: the text of the poem can be read as an account of that historical event, an account that the persistence of the unconscious keeps obliquely away from references obviously corresponding to the event. Simultaneously, though, the title can be read not literally, as a reference to that historical event, but metaphorically, as a hyperbolic characterization of transitory relations among the designated persons in the poem. Their transitory events in their personal lives are as momentously important to them as the French Revolution to the public. Further, the emergence of the unconscious as a reflexive factor in personal life is in some senses due to the French Revolution. And beside such permutations, there is the simpler, copresent possibility, that the persons in the poem have been engaging in a game of tennis, declare an oath in a language obliquely different from such performative speech acts, and as an issue of the élan arising from their spontaneous interpersonal concord they decide to label it the Tennis Court Oath. Something like this last possibility would harmonize with the spirit and the language of Ashbery's collaborative novel, *A Nest of Ninnies.* But in any case the title is obliquely disjoined from the flow of the poem. It applies to the poem, indeed, only in that both the Tennis Court Oath and the poem deal with interpersonal relations.

In this poem almost schematically, as generally in Ashbery's work, the possible shifts in one locution from literal to metaphorical, accompany and permute the possible shifts within the roles of a person or from person to person.

The deflection of such whole poems from a univocal designative sense makes their rhetoric seem a sort of obligato or excursus from a preexistent, unfurnished text. In "Self-Portrait in a Convex Mirror" the "text" is the painting of that title by Parmigianino. In that poem, as increasingly in his later poetry, Ashbery adheres generally to the rhetoric of critical discourse, and endless regress is provided by the relation between the poem and an object labeled as itself a reflection and a distortion. In this poem, as elsewhere, Ashbery achieves what he quotes Sydney Freedberg as attributing to Parmigianino, an aspectualized conjunction of bizarrerie and harmony. In an early poem, "The Picture Little J.A. in a Prospect of Flowers" (*ST*), Ashbery revises a title of Andrew Marvell's by ironizing it and rendering it reflexive through substituting his own initials for those of Marvell's subject (not himself, but one "T.C."). As modern painters from Picasso to Rauschenberg, not forgetting the arch Duchamp, will include parts of earlier paintings in their work or large references to them, so Ashbery often incorporates references to prior works. "Daffy Duck" is a figure at once visual and literary, an animated figure in a recursive series of cartoon plots. "Loving Mad Tom" (*HB* 16–17) refers to a character in *King Lear.* In the long "As We Know" (*AWK*), the text is the matching doubled run of verses in the other column. Each text can be conceived of as prior to the other, and the permutation of speakers is expressed in, and contributes to, the permutation of utterances that could not possibly be read simultaneously and assimilated. Such an impossible reading has to be imagined, in a destruction-of-sequence through the pairing of sequences. An analogue here would be the vanishing perspective of Pollock, whose paintings are neither two dimensional nor three dimensional but both simultaneously, as some earlier modernist paintings are too.

In "Fantasia on 'the Nut Brown Maid'" Ashbery has taken a prior poem, a long anonymous dialogue from the turn of the sixteenth century. He has matched its speeches, assigned to He and She, with corresponding speeches of his own, again doubling the matching of texts with the permutation of persons. In such a perspective every speech of Ashbery's poem can be read as a surrealized and metaphoric version of the original rhymed poem, especially as he touches base now and then on its topics, and at points of closure on its very words. The phrase *a banished man* ends his first speech, as it does the first speech of "The Nut Brown Maid." And Ashbery's last words, *I sing alway,* are those of the earlier poem. At the same time he allows his poem midway through to dissolve into prose, and by the end of the poem he is solidly in prose, diverging from his rhymed original except in the archaic last words, which must be read to quote and catch up the original rhythm. Closure is firm, in sound and sense, but the firmness in context only incidentally mimes the order of the earlier poem. Its relation to Ashbery's poem remains expressive and abstract.

II

1

Frank O'Hara, the author of the "Lunch Poems" typed on an open-air demonstration typewriter during his lunch hours, is more explicitly an action poet than Ashbery, though recognizably performing in the same atmosphere of action painting. The contrasts and similarities between the two, in fact, furnish a sharpening of perspective, as with other literary pairs like Racine and Corneille or Jonson and Shakespeare or Eliot and Pound—or Picasso and Matisse, de Kooning and Pollock. One could amplify such a discussion by adding Kenneth Koch as a third, a comparison which would add an especial richness to the extension of Surrealist sexual preoccupation (*Sleeping with Women*) and the metaphoric structure of "intertextuality" (*Ko*).

An initially simpler celebratory posture allows O'Hara to invest his named particulars with full, if fleeting, emotional support, as well as with metaphorical possibilities. He unabashedly welcomes the fleeting, processed Hollywood movie, with none of Ashbery's glum qualification. As O'Hara says, "The cinema is cruel / Like a miracle" ("An Image of Leda" 13).[15]

O'Hara is serious about the movies. The "star system" of his unabashed praise seriously constellates feelings for which the stars are a name, silent until the vein of Parker Tyler's interpretations (*Magic and Myth of the Movies*) can yield such ore as this:

> Marilyn Monroe in her little spike heels reeling through
>   Niagara Falls,
> Joseph Cotten puzzling and Orson Welles puzzled and
>   Dolores del Rio
> eating orchids for lunch and breaking mirrors, Gloria
>   Swanson reclining,
> and Jean Harlow reclining and wiggling, and Alice Faye
>   reclining
> and wiggling and singing, Myrna Loy being calm and
>   wise, William Powell
> in his stunning urbanity, Elizabeth Taylor blossoming,
>   yes, to you. . . .
>   ("To the Film Industry in Crisis," 100)

The syntax here is endemically French enough to recall both Claudel and Éluard, but O'Hara's feeling is strong enough not to get swamped, here at least, in the French-fertility source retapped by his friends Koch and Ashbery. But the splendid naming here! Those names given not by parents but by publicity agents are redeemed from what looked like an unredeemable vocabulary, the vocabulary of publicity.

These depth deductions of visual apprehension are well-nigh Rilkean, as with some of Ashbery's. But Rilke himself is subjected by O'Hara to gaily ironic distancing. Here is Rilke's *Aus einem April:*

> Wieder duftet der Wald.
> Es heben die schwebenden Lerchen
> mit sich den Himmel empor, der unseren Schultern schwer
>   war,—

> The woods smell sweet again.
> The soaring larks lift up with them
> Aloft the heaven that was heavy for our shoulders—

O'Hara dares to make his feeling casual, and his own, by "de-poeticizing" the language: *wieder duftet* gives way to *of course;* by abandoning a classic austerity and letting the romantic tears start forth unabashedly:

> We dust the walls.
>   And of course we are weeping larks
>   falling all over the heavens with our shoulders clasped
> in someone's armpits, so tightly! and our throats are full.
>   (80)

O'Hara retains of the austerity only Rilke's form, kept on meticulously like a frock coat in which he cuts capers and pours out his "heart." He does not refurbish the sonnet anew in his four-teen-line poem; instead he takes the stance of contenting himself with Rilke's refurbishing. His *Aus einem April* is a commentary of Rilke so full-throated that all the chaste ironies of Pound's com-mentaries on Propertius and Gautier, Waller or Homer, get lost in the Saturnalian shuffle, which includes Surrealist translation-parody (*We dust the walls* for *Wieder duftet der Wald*). In what is per-haps his only comparable passing reference to Rilke, the exalted *O reine Übersteigung!* of the *Sonnets to Orpheus,* is mocked, deflated, and honored in one swift effusion:

> so ecstatic like churchbells against the flanks of horsetails,
> sleight of hand, "O reine Überschreigung" of an old lavatory.
>   ("Second Avenue" 65)

There is no German word *schreigung,* and O'Hara was attentive enough to the accuracy of foreign locutions that we must assume that he here clowningly pretends to invent a nonexistent portmanteau German word that illustrates, by excess, Rilke's own term, as well as the overshrieking he seems to mean, *Überschreiung* (itself a coinage). Since sound is in question, the Rilkean phrase may be taken to suggest flushing a toilet in the old lavatory appended to it. The appendix, though, is a Dadaist gesture of defacement carrying with it an un-Dadaist rush of combinatory glee.

O'Hara's rhythms, too, even in the long lines of "Second Avenue" and other poems, are tauter and more rapid than Ashbery's, and they are more precise:

> Peace! to be true to a city
> of rats and to love the envy
> of the dreary, smudged mouthers
> of an arcane dejection
> smoldering quietly in the perception
> of hopelessness and scandal
> at unnatural vigor. Their dreams
> are their own, as are the toilets
> of a great railway terminal
> and the sequins of a very small,
> very fat eyelid.
>   I take this
> for myself, and you take up
> the thread of my life between your teeth,
> tin thread and tarnished with abuse.
>   ("For James Dean" 97)

Those alternate similes give six dimensions to the *dreams,* and are heard to do so. Part of the modulation works in the shift, at this point, from predominant feminine endings (six out of seven, if you count *dreams* at the beginning). There is a nervous assimilation of word to loaded word in a line, "of *rats* and to *love* with *envy* of the *dreary, smudged mouthers* of an *arcane dejection.*" These words blast windows in each other, blast them clean, as *smouldering* does in *quietly in the perception; hopelessness* in *scandal;* all within the sovereign single line; the carry-over from line to line is only rhythmic—and how this word isolation keeps the rhythms on their toes!

O'Hara early describes his procedures in terms of a Duchamp-like deflation of the history of modern painting:

> Picasso made me tough and quick, and the world;
> just as in a minute plane trees are knocked down
> outside my window by a crew of creators.
> Once he got his axe going everyone was upset
> enough to fight for the last ditch and heap
> of rubbish.
> > Through all that surgery I thought
> I had a lot to say, and named several last things
> Gertrude Stein hadn't had time for; but then
> the war was over, those things had survived
> and even when you're scared art is no dictionary.
> Max Ernst told us that.
> > How many trees and frying pans
> I loved and lost! Guernica hollered look out!
> but we were all busy hoping our eyes were talking
> to Paul Klee.
> > ("Memorial Day 1950" 7)

The title licenses both the tone of recollection and the references to the war in which O'Hara served. Literal designations elide a large process ("Picasso made me tough and quick, and the world"). They also elide the distinction between past modern art and present life, between Picasso and the tree-removal experts, as between art and the cataclysmic duresses of ontogeny and phylogeny. Outside and inside—trees and frying pans—are also elided. The speaker takes stock at a fairly high level of generality. Generality here is coded into the nouns and proper names, while metaphoring is largely confined to verbs and verb phrases (*got his axe going, fight for, loved and lost, hollered, eyes were talking*).

The poem "Why I Am Not a Painter," instead of metaphorizing its particulars, recounts the matched experiences of writing a poem over a time while visiting a friend who is working on a painting. In both the poem and the painting the key subject is absent by its presences, and it is the title that serves as the evasive sign, rather than the metaphor, of that subject:

Where's SARDINES?
All that's left is just
letters, "It was too much," Mike says
        . . . . My poem
is finished and I haven't mentioned
orange yet. It's twelve poems, I call
it ORANGES. And one day in a gallery
I see Mike's painting, called SARDINES.

(112)

The switch away from naming to entitling happens in both poetry and painting, and the processes are so parallel that they contradict the title. The anecdote does not explain why O'Hara is not a painter, performing upon the relationship between title and this poem the same switch away from naming and into entitling that he has recounted for ORANGES and SARDINES.

Closer to Ashbery's practice, a variant of O'Hara's style plays frenetic Breton to Ashbery's calm Reverdy:

Grappling with images of toothpaste falling on guitar strings,
your lips are indeed a disaster of alienated star-knots
as I deign to load the hips of the swimming pool, lumber!
with the clattering caporal of destiny's breast-full,
such exhalations and filthiness falling upon the vegetables!

("Second Avenue" 58)

The signifieds float here in Surrealist fashion, too loosely to function as metaphors. They exhibit an almost Roussel-like linearity, but their central action remains personal in a way analogous to the Expressionist Ashbery but alien to the objective Roussel and Breton.

The disjunction between title and particulars even in O'Hara's more normal syntactic poems operates to suspend the speaker between literal and metaphoric, unconscious and conscious, as between momentary and permanent. All these suspensions work for the Abstract Expressionist painter who is at once freed and bound from working in a material like words that of necessity have a mimetic component:

Music

> If I rest for a moment near the Equestrian
> pausing for a liver sausage sandwich at the Mayflower Shoppe,
> that angel seems to be leading the horse into Bergdorf's
> and I am naked as a table cloth, my nerves humming.
> Close to the fear of war and the stars which have disappeared.
> I have in my hands only 35c, it's so meaningless to eat!
> and gusts of water spray over the basins of leaves
> like the hammers of a glass pianoforte. If I seem to you
> to have lavender lips under the leaves of the world,
>   I must tighten my belt.
> It's like a locomotive on the march, the season of distress and
>   clarity
> and my door is open to the evenings of midwinter's
> lightly falling snow over the newspapers.
> Clasp me in your handkerchief like a tear, trumpet
> of early afternoon! in the foggy autumn.
> As they're putting up the Christmas trees on Park Avenue
> I shall see my daydreams walking by with dogs in blankets,
> put to some use before all those coloured lights come on!
>   But no more fountains and no more rain,
>   and the stores stay open terribly late.
>   (91)

An unconscious component, the city as a surrealist constellation of dreams, is suggested by the visible presence of the first three capitalized nouns in the poem, their conjunction from different semantic domains emphasized by their terminal line position. The common factual, visible presence of the equestrian statue, the small restaurant Mayflower Shoppe, and the department store Bergdorf's subverts the origin of their names in different lexical domains. This being the case, the liver sausage sandwich of the speaker's first act, itself visible as well as edible, enters the same mysterious more-than-literal order. We ask, as the psychoanalyst might, what is the significance of liver sausage. Moreover the name of the sandwich shop enters a dream orbit as it belies its menu. *Mayflower* is an honorific name for an American establishment, reinforced by the pseudoarchaism, the dreamed and vulgarized history of *Shoppe*. Yet in the Mayflower of the Pilgrims there were no liver sausages, and in the subtle but definite class distinctions of the speaker's America, liver sausage is an ethnic rather than a WASP dish. The name of the shoppe and its menu also imply, and oneirically elide, different domains. Metonymy verges on metaphor, without being able to become structured into metaphor. The liver sausage sandwich in a Mayflower Shoppe is worthy of the Duchamp of *La Belle Haleine* or *La Bagarre d'Austerlitz*. The effects condense more dizzingly in the endless camping transvestism of "Irene Dunne Foreskin" ("Biotherm") and other such locutions.

The visual effects are not dwelt on for Ashbery-like interpretive description. Instead they are taken and collocated for their capacity to generate marvels, like the conjunction of decorator's angel and statue-horse in line three. The simile comparing the gusts of water spray to the hammers of a glass pianoforte (an actual musical instrument) enlists either the auditory or the visual powers of the registering speaker. Every item named possesses first the experiential role of filling his time sequences with significant patterns, "Music." The excitation expands to permit more extravagant metaphors, a season "like a locomotive," running quickly backward from winter to autumn. The climactic one compares the speaker to a tear in a handkerchief. The *dogs in blankets* of the next sentence oscillate between literal and metaphorical. In the city of the scene depicted elegant residents do clothe dogs in tiny blankets, literally; in that aspect the "daydreams" walking by are metonymically the beautiful women who own the dogs—the thing real (women) designated by the thing imagined (daydreams). But the whole sentence allows the different reading, where the dogs would be dreamt and not seen, "I shall see my daydreams walking by with dogs in blankets / put to some use before all those coloured lights come on!" Not more than hinted at is a dish sometimes available where liver sausage sandwiches are served, tiny wieners encased in tiny buns, called "dogs in blankets."

The last sentence of the poem gives a stark turn to the scene: in a literal, specific reading (though it could also be read as a general wish), rain happens to stop at a time when the fountains are turned off, but the stores, after the lights have come on, stay open for the dark, into the active winter of the Christmas season. *Terribly* means "very," but in the impulses of this verse progression it does not lose its overtone of terror. Indeterminacies of language register the exciting perilousness of the world.

2

Metaphors in O'Hara serve to heighten and substantiate the alertness of the speaker:

> And curls
> tumble languorously towards
> the yawning rubber band, tan,
> your hand pressing all that
>
> riotous black sleep into
> the quiet form of daylight
> and its sunny disregard for
> the luminous volutions, oh!
>
> ("Jane Awake" 32)

A hyperbole betraying admiration calls the hair of the waking woman "riotous black sleep" and then "the quiet form of daylight." This differs from Renaissance hyperbolic compliment as the women of de Kooning differ from the nudes of Rubens: it attends to a momentary change so rapid it could be taken for illusory: now Jane's hair is disorderly black, and now it catches the light so as to seem luminous. Returned to the visual, it deeroticizes the celebration. The *oh* melts aesthetic admiration into a simply uttered surprise.

Nor can a real point or subject of comparison be elicited from the alternate similes quoted above for the dreams in "For James Dean": "Their dreams / are their own, as are the toilets / of a great railway terminal / and the sequins of a very small, / very fat eyelid." Sparkles and sequins can sometimes be caught on the eyelid—especially the eyelid that has been made up for erotic invitation. That, scandalously, might also be the domain of the toilets. Dreams, too, are erotic, and a common domain for the tenor and its two vehicles supersedes the possibility of a logical hinge in the comparison.

An erotic, or an admiring, attention—a narcissistic one for "In Memory of My Feelings"—is signaled by, and seems to trigger, runs of metaphor:

> Smiling through my own memories of painful excitement
> > your wide eyes stare
> and narrow like a lost forest and childhood stolen from gypsies
> two eyes that are the sunset of
> > > two knees
> > > > two wrists
> > > > > two minds
> > and the extended philosophical column
> > > > > > ("Ode to Tanaquil LeClercq" 176)

This begins a poem to a great ballet dancer stricken by polio. Or again, with the tempo of metaphor-alternation stepped up:

> > Behind New York there's a face
> > and it's not Sibelius's with a cigar
> > it was red it was strange and hateful
> > and then I became a child again
> > like a nadir or a zenith or a nudnik
> > ("For the Chinese New Year and for Bill Berkson" 183)

3

As for the person of the speaker, instead of skewing his shifters, like Ashbery, O'Hara addresses the fragmentation of roles directly if metaphorically.[16]

He presents a multiple person, who always keeps several steps ahead of himself in the successful tightrope act of never letting multiple turn into less than single. Comic bubbles are always let into the drink he will serve us; the drink is heady, and reminds of headiness:

In Memory of My Feelings

> My quietness has a man in it, he is transparent
> and he carries me quietly, like a gondola, through the streets.

He has several likenesses, like stars and years, like
      numerals.

My quietness has a number of naked selves,
so many pistols I have borrowed to protect myselves . . .
            At times, withdrawn,
I rise into the cool skies
and gaze on at the imponderable world with the simple
      identification
of my colleagues, the mountains. Manfred climbs to my
      nape,
speaks, but I do not hear him, . . .
            One of me rushes
to window 13 and one of me raises his whip and one of me
flutters up from the center of the track admist the
            pink flamingoes, . . .
      So many of my transparencies could not resist
            the race!

                                        (105)

In the much-discussed "The Day Lady Died," randomly encoun-
tered particulars do the whole job of displacing, and at the same
time as standing for, the grief of the registering speaker. "And I
stopped breathing" he concludes (146)—a metaphoric hyperbole
that casts him as the vehicle of the whole mourning. Up to this conclusion his mourning has been bracketed in an *Aufhebung* of a
rhetorical cadenza of mere listing. This cadenza is the opposite of
preterition: instead of mentioning what he says he will not mention, the speaker does not mention the grief and loss that is his central topic. The effect places the speaker, and his grave emotion, beyond both the fragmentation of the poem's listed particulars and
the ego-coherence of a firmly uttered formal expression of mourning. This ego is not empty à la Hume, and at the same time it only
verges on transcendence, though it does so climactically, and not
with the tentative intermittence of Ashbery.

Such reflexivity as comes up along the line of the poem is a by-
product of the preening self-concern and self-conscious verbal dex-

terity of the speaker. The other persons mentioned are not Ashbery's ambiguously transmuted presences. O'Hara's equivalent for these are his extravagant metaphoric transpositions, especially evident in late poems like "Biotherm." Instead, the persons in his poems are the real persons from his daily life. Yet they take the glare and highlights of his locutions, passing abruptly in and out of the poems in a way that differentiates them from the real persons concealed under allegorical names in the poems of Pope or his Latin originals.

The very process of time here seems to step up when O'Hara is uncharacteristically alone while at the same time a guest:

> I will wait
> and the house wakes up and goes
> to get the dog in Sag Harbor I make
> myself a bourbon and commence
> to write one of my "I do this I do that"
> poems in a sketch pad
>   it is tomorrow
> though only six hours have gone by
> each day's light has more significance these days
>   ("Getting Up Ahead of Someone (Sun)" 163)

By referring within this poem to the act of writing "one of my 'I do this, I do that' poems," O'Hara provides, simply and smoothly, an endless regress. This poem itself is an instance of what he does, of "I do this, I do that." But it is only an instance. The poem stands as a whole in itself, "this," while at the same time it is here named as only a part of a series of actions subsumed under "this/that." The randomized person collects himself to take account of, and thereby to reduce or redefine randomization. So, correspondingly, what might be metaphors in the poem get caught up and reduced, their logic opened up and prevented from the tenor-vehicle stasis. The trip to Sag Harbor for the dog is both trivial and emblematic, itself an instance in the flow while momentarily characterizing the absent hostess and linking her absence to the enabling circumstances for writing *this*. In such a context O'Hara's more extravagant metaphors (*I am a Hittite in love with a horse*, from "In

Memory of My Feelings") advertise their own extravagance. They become flares signifying the élan of the speaker "doing this and that" as much as they are surrealized hieroglyphs. These poems do not absolutize metaphor so much as they transform it to serve at once as élan and hieroglyph—the immemorial double act of image in both poetry and visual art.[17]

Afterword

Visual Aspects of the Homeric Simile in Indo-European Context

Language conditions thought. Deep presuppositions are built into the diction and syntax of the Indo-European languages. These are also built into their public uses, including the poetic ones. As Émile Benveniste has shown,[1] the presuppositions from people to Indo-European people, and specifically from Indian to Greek, exhibit similarities in social institutions as well as in language—similarities in economic organization, kinship and social structures, authority, law, and religion. Georges Dumézil has expounded still further aspects of these assumptions common to Indo-European cultures. However, the visual practice within a single culture goes so deep that I shall argue a marked difference between the Greek and the Indic modes with respect to this deep integral procedure, however far ranging the Indo-European similarities among them may be. The sharpness, what may be called the dialectic of vision from Mycenean engravers of gems down through Pompeian painters, and in poets from Homer on, differs markedly from the early Indic tradition. The Greek and Roman acuity conditions the heritage that all the poets I have been discussing have effectually drawn on. And in looking at Homer's use of images in his similes, I shall try to bring this whole integral procedure into relief by comparing it to the other chief early Indo-European use, the Rig Veda, matching each tradition with its visual art.

Most early epics are sparing indeed of image and metaphor, even the elaborate Gilgamesh in the long time—more than a millennium—of the various recensions we have. Moreover, putting images into words in the first place for some function other than mere inventory constitutes an advanced mode of expression. Turning to the high art of Homer, we will notice that there is often an intricate visual or explanatory impetus discernible in the Homeric simile, especially when it is somewhat expanded.

As I have pointed out before in discussing the looseness for Homer of subsidiary elements in a comparison,[2] no special similarity exists between arrows and beans or chickpeas in the following simile:

> As when from a broad blade along a great threshing floor
> Beans with black skins or chickpeas are bouncing high
> Under the shrill blast and sweep of the winnower,
>> So from the breastplate of glorious Menelaus
>> The bitter arrow often rebounding away flew afar.
>> (*Iliad* 13.588–92)

A particular kind of motion is discerned, in a way that a modern painter might admire, a "found" motion underlying the bounce of peas on a winnowing fan and the rebound of an arrow from a breastplate. The visual impulse is not so different, I mean, from that of modern "found" sculpture, when Picasso calls a bicycle seat and handlebars a goat's head. The motion Homer describes requires a strain of attention for the auditor, since *beans* is plural but *arrow* is seen singly—it is in the singular—many times (*pollon*).

Along with this visual acuteness the focus dwells on the scene. It constitutes a kind of framing. Details are got into language that poetry does not pick up until it is quite advanced. In English poetry, for example, one would have to wait till the seventeenth century for so concrete an epithet as *black-skinned*. That this is not merely a classificatory term for beans may be deduced from its other use in the Homeric poems, *Odyssey* 19.246, where it is used to heighten the visual appearance, and so the credibility, of a fictional Eurybates whom Odysseus in his wiles is inventing.

The visualization, pushed to this point, amounts to an extreme precision, demarcating a scene where we have the shape of the blade, the extent of the threshing floor, and the color of the beans, as well as the alternate chickpeas whose motion would be the same— a particularized sound and motion for the winnower himself. All this in addition to the firmly named four constituents of the scene: floor, blade, beans, and winnower.

The oddness of a comparison, this or another, may be resolved if its visual base is fully allowed. Both Lee and Fränkel find inappropriate the simile that compares Hector to a boar or a lion pressed by a pack of dogs and huntsman (*Il.* 12.41–49).[3] They are bothered by the fact that Hector is not at bay but mounting an attack. The difficulty is minimized, and really resolved, if we see the comparison as mainly a visual one—a single valiant figure surrounded by hosts of enemies, without regard to the success or failure of the outcome. Or again Edward M. Bradley points out in the comparison of Hector to a snowy mountain (*Il.* 13.754–55), "the quality of snow deemed most relevant is that of incessant movement," where an attention to visual cues, as indicated by other mentions of snow in Homer, solves an even more puzzling simile.[4]

Yet the implied contrast between such windows on a world of peace and the world of war that preoccupies the poem is already present in the difference between this attention to subsidiary visual elements and the contrasting attention to psychological effects in the military action.[5] The two epithets in the tenor of the chickpea simile are *glorious* (*kudalimos*) and *bitter* (*pikros*), these words belonging for us, if less definitely for Homer, to a more inward realm than *broad, great, black-skinned,* and *shrill.*

Further, there is the question as to why we are given the simile at this particular time in the narrative, and we notice that the battle at hand engages this important warrior for the next sixty lines. This simile is more expanded than the two that precede it, the comparison of Adamas' spear stuck in a shield to a "fire-burned stake" (13.564), and the reaction to his death wound, "he gasped as an ox does that oxherd men in the mountains / Have by force bound with ropes unwillingly and drag along" (571–72). What slows the narrative indicates its importance, and we tend to get similes at points of gathering action, as many commentators have pointed out.

These warriors have no time to harvest chickpeas or drag oxen. The Homeric simile, for its very looseness of subsidiary details in the comparison—by drawing on activities unrelated to the main narrative line of the poem—coordinates peace and war in a vast, balanced perspective. Thus war itself gets a still more profound connection, and the image gets by such contrast an anchorage in a coordinated view of life.

The simile is an important vehicle for this whole perceptual process. Thereby it expands as well as interrupts the narrative.

2

The civilized subtlety, and the particular global character, of figurative language in the Homeric poems falls into relief—and raises questions beyond those of rhetorical organization—if we compare metaphor and simile in Homer to the use of these figures in the other great body of early Indo-European poetry that we possess, the Rig Veda. While Greece, as Indo-Europeanists tell us, strangely scants the full repertoire of Indo-European mythology, there are common gods—Zeus and Indra, the Dioscuri and the Ashvins. There are also common folkways and common staples of image the cow, the horse, the sun, the eye, the chariot.[6] Yet, as Hirzel says, in the very assertion of similarity between the two Indo-European domains: "Direkte Parallelen aus unseren griechischen Dichtern lassen sich natürlich nicht geben" (Direct parallels from our Greek poets naturally do not occur) (18).

Similes are very common in the Rig Veda, and in one sense metaphors are too, if one allows as a metaphor an identification so fused as to permit no real separation between tenor and vehicle. Yet these similes are never as expanded as those of Homer, and they rarely contain a visual element. When they are visual, they do not focus in anything like the Homeric precision: on the contrary they offer a vagueness of flash and blur, as in these lines from a hymn to the Usas, the Dawns:

ásthur u citrà Ushásaḥ purástan
mitá iva sváravo adhvaréshu
(4.51-52)

In the East the brilliant dawns have stood
Like posts set up at sacrifices

The point of comparison is the flash or shining, probably, since the word for sacrificial posts, as Macdonnell notes, may derive from the root *svar,* to shine. Yet these visual effects of brightness, *citra* and *svar,* are only potentially assimilable to one another. And the play of light across an ointment spread on a post has no other visual similarity than brightness to the more diffuse and more encompassing light of dawn in the sky. The subsidiary details of the comparison, in this light, cannot be ruled out: a general religious aura—these are hymns—takes in worshipped dawns and sacrificial acts of worship.

We are far from the sharp outlines of Homer, far enough to distrust any assimilation of his narrative epic to some tradition of common origin with the hymns of the Rig Veda. Moreover, the difference between Homer and the Rig Veda cannot be ascribed to some even progression that would place the Rig Veda at an earlier stage because of its earlier date. Homer has no general term for color; *chroma* is first used by Herodotus and Gorgias. The Vedas, however, easy in the interfusion of visual elements under comparison, are comparably easy in abstracting the term. Indra "gives color to the colorless," as Geldner renders *peca,* "ornament, form" in 1.6.2.[7] And a more complex combination of color with form is offered in the more regular word, *varṇa,* as it occurs in a hymn to the Son of Waters: "He, the Son of Waters, of unfaded color" [*anabhimláta-varṇo*] / Works here with a body as of another" (2.35.13). Here we perceive the un-Homeric interfusion of the Vedas among the abstractions, and the casual equivocation of the regular comparative, *iva* (like, as), when the identification with some abstract "other" is made. Still another term, *rupa,* in the sense of "shape, form, beautiful color" is used in a dialogue hymn of the late tenth book. "The seer with his seership fastens color on heaven"

(10.24.7). The term *varṇa* is often applied, with some qualification, as a superlative to the ritual beverage Soma.

The tendency away from visual representation, and concurrently also away from the sharp distinctness of categories, may be seen in a typical run from a hymn to the Maruts, gods of the thunderstorm:

Who as great warriors shine forth with their spears
Overthrowing even what has not been overthrown
with their might
When, Maruts, you thought-swift, to the cars,
Have yoked the spotted mares, strong in hosts,
When to the cars you have yoked the spotted mares,
Speeding, O Maruts, the stone in the conflict,
They discharge the streams of the ruddy steed
And moisten the earth like a skin with waters . . .
Self-strong they grew by their greatness;
They have mounted to the vault, have made them
a wide seat.
When Vishnu helped the bull reeling with intoxication
Like birds they sat down on their dear sacrificial grass.
Like heroes, speeding like warriors, like fame-seekers,
They have arrayed themselves in battles.
All creatures fear the Maruts.
Like kings of terrible aspect are the men.

(1.85.4–8; Macdonnell, somewhat revised)

The comparisons here are as momentary as the reminiscence of related stories about Vishnu and others. In the last line both a metaphor and a simile subvert what we would expect to be a firm distinction between men and gods; the Maruts are "men [*narah*] kings" (though *narah = aner*, in the sense "hero," does suggest a godlike superlative). *Thought-swift* is either a live metaphor or a dead one functioning as a conventional superlative. We can hardly disentangle animist elements from metaphors in the ruddy steed who pours forth the waters of the storm in Vedic mythology—nor is the color meant for sharp visualization; rather it is meant as another superlative. *Adrim* can mean a stone, a pressing stone, a mountain, or a cloud. All these senses are relevant here, almost blurring together.

Adrim further suggests lightning, according to Macdonnell,[8] and for that reason it would assimilate easily to Indra, who is often associated with the Maruts as the bearer of the thunderbolt (*vajra*).

In this culture, actually, the gods easily assimilate to each other in ways that would seem to contradict the extrapolability of underlying rules for myth systems, when distinctions are carefully maintained among the gods in the cultures studied by Lévi-Strauss. He characterizes the myths of South and North America as dominated by a fundamental conflict between fire and water. And yet Agni, the omnipresent fire god associated with the sun and given the major rituals of this culture, is said to be born of water (1.23.20–23). In this tradition the gods sometimes slide into one another, and into natural phenomena. In a later phase they "descend" into disguised shapes or *avatars,*—likeness can be casual or obscure but never extended on a base of firm logical distinction. As Gonda points out, metaphor in the Veda tends towards riddle.[9] Brhaspati is identified with Indra and with Agni, who in turn is declared to be Varuna, Mitra, and Vivasvat, all these gods having their seemingly distinct spheres. And instead of being associated with a single totemic animal, the Greek practice, Agni is compared to an eagle, a buffalo, a bull, a cow, a horse, a steer, a swan, a serpent, and a bird.[10] The lightning of the Maruts is compared to a mooing cow and their rain to a mother with a calf (1.38.8). In another hymn they are compared in swift succession to a buffalo, to mountains, to elephants, to lions, to a deer, and to serpents (1.64.7–8).

The cow, in fact, functions here as a further gathering of attributes and source of mythical associations. The Maruts are said to be born of cows, and their clouds or mountains are also conceived of as cows whose udders will burst with waters, as the "steed" also does. *Cows* without explanation in a hymn to Vishnu (1.154.6) means simply rays of sunshine, though the rapt language of the hymn forbids our taking this simply as a metaphor, "We desire to go to those abodes of you two / Where there are the many-horned nimble cattle." Agni himself, in a seeming contradiction of his existence as fire, is "like the udders of a cow" (1.69.5–6). Indra is compared to a milk-cow at least six times. Narrative elements, even when they are the center of a hymn, are referred to only resumptively and glancingly. Homer, too, assumes his auditors know something of his story, but he achieves a discreteness of presentation that can be at once interrelated and linear.

With all this, the Rig Veda verges on an abstractness about the gods that the Greeks had to subvert Homer to achieve:

> The other Agnis are only branches of you, Agni.
> All the immortals feast with you, universal one [*vaísvānara*:
>   "belonging to all men"]
> You are the navel of the lands, you uphold
> The peoples like a supporting pillar.

(1.59.1)

We move quickly through these moments, so much so that the metaphors are not mixed. The navel and the pillar are both echoed in Greek mythology, but never together, never as nonce terms. And do not try to visualize the architecture!

3

Being often firm in the visual base of items brought into comparison, and always so in the implied clarity of visible elements it names, the Homeric simile can proceed assuredly and expansively towards enriching its complications.

Sometimes the visual base is odd, as in the above comparison of deflected spears to bouncing chickpeas (*Il.* 13.588–92) or of old men to grasshoppers (*Il.* 3.166), Odysseus to a ram (*Il.* 3.195), horses to birds (*Il.* 2.764), a helmet-weighted head to a garden poppy leaning under spring rains (*Il.* 8.306–8), a wave scattering timber to wind scattering husks (*Od.* 5.368–70), persistent fighters to bees or wasps in the hive (*Il.* 12.167–72), a speared warrior Patroclos drags to a hooked fish pulled out of water (*Il.* 16.406–10), bloodstains on Menelaus' thighs to coloring on an ivory cheek piece (*Il.* 4.141–47), the fight over Sarpedon's corpse to flies in the spring (*Il.* 16.640), Menelaus circling Hector to a cow tending a calf (*Il.* 17.4), the river pursuing Achilles to a spring runnel guided by a man with a mattock (*Il.* 21.257–63), snakes of dark-blue enamel to rainbows (*Il.* 11.24), bonds to spiderwebs (*Od.*

8.279), Odysseus and Ajax grasping each other to the rafters of a building (*Il.* 23.712–13), the curing of Ares' wound to milk curdling under added fig sap (*Il.* 11.902–4). Once we have verified the likeness visually, we are left, surely, with something like a sense of discovery—as the original audience may have been to the comparison of waves to mountains (*Od.* 3.290), a comparison by now conventional for our poetry. Still, the oddness seems unanalyzable beyond our noting that domains at some distance from one another have been linked through an underlying visual similarity.

Similes that are preponderantly visual can be very rich, as some of these are.

> As when an octopus is pulled out of its den,
> Numerous pebbles are caught in its suckers,
> So against the rocks the skin from his stout hands
> Was stripped off.
>
> (*Od.* 5.432–35)

The octopus figures prominently in Minoan and Mycenean decoration, and it is here seen so sharply that a sort of close-up effect has been achieved. The hand is magnified so as to seem an octopus. For the pebbles against the suckers of the octopus, and also for the tears along the joined fingers of the hand, a random pattern—of pebbles or tears—has been superimposed on an ordered pattern, of tentacles with suckers or fingers. Moreover, the *polypus* is seen as having many tentacles rather than a specific number, which brings it more easily into line with the gripping and then flailing hand. That motion prior to the tearing must also be precisely in view, the gripping and then flailing of both hand and octopus. Odysseus like the octopus has been immersed in water, but water is short of being his native element. Moreover, his whole person is not compared to the octopus; just his hand. In the complications of this simile the visual element is predominant, as it is in this one from the *Iliad* (21.12–16):

> As at the blast of a fire locusts flutter
> Fleeing to a river, and the untiring fire flames,
> Having started up suddenly, and they huddle at the water;

So at Achilles for the deep-whirling Xanthus
Was the sounding stream filled pell-mell with horses and men.

Achilles is not exactly compared to a fire here, as he is elsewhere
and quite recently in the narrative (*Il.* 20.490–94). Nor is he compared to the swollen river that responds to him, though Hector is
compared to a wave (17.262) and Ajax is compared to a rain-
swollen river uprooting trees in its course down a mountain (11.
492–96).

Yet in light of these other comparisons we cannot wholly dissociate Achilles from either the fire of the vehicle or the river of the
tenor. The visual element is reinforced by the fact that the river
appears in both the tenor and the vehicle (though *potamon* suggests body of water and *roos* a rushing stream). Once again, too,
the visual sharpness permits a shift of scale: the overall visual effect of locusts huddling against water, and men and horses whirled
pell-mell in water, focuses in each case without regard for the fact
that the men and the horses are considerably bigger than the locusts. The horses are also slightly bigger than the men, but in the
swirl of the river their whole bodies would not show for the difference in size to figure in the visualization.

For these particular similes the visual richness keeps the details
of both tenor and vehicle in some relation with the comparison.
This would also be the case with similes that draw on some other
sense than sight, as the comparison of an army's uproar to the noise
of the sea (*Il.* 2.208–10), of Poseidon's shout to that of ten thousand men in battle (*Il.* 14.148–49), of a shout to the sound of a
trumpet (*Il.* 18.219–21), of a wound's pain to birth pangs (*Il.*
11.269–72), of the squeaking of the suitors' souls to the squeaking
of bats in a cave (*Od.* 24.5–9), of Penelope's melting flesh and ensuing tears to the melting and running of snow on a mountain (*Od.*
19.204–9).

For the last comparison the physiological effect begins to involve
psychological attributes as well—and for that reason the comparison
may seem less odd. The poet's command of his world, so apparent
in other ways, permits the similes often to enlist a psychological

situation, anchored as it may be in the physical. Take this simile, another moment in the rich play of Penelope's responses:

The sharp anxieties plague me as I lament.
As when the daughter of Pandareus, the nightingale
        of the green,
Sings beautifully when spring has freshly risen,
Seated amid the thick foliage of the trees,
And often modulating pours out her loud-sounding song,
Lamenting her dear son Itylos, child of lord Zethos,
Whom one day she killed with a sword unwittingly;
So my heart is aroused, divided this way and that,
Whether I should wait with my son and steadfastly guard . . .
Or by this time should follow the best of the Achaeans
                                    (*Od.* 19.518–28)

The comparison is of a song to a feeling, but the song is in three aspects, each having a psychological correlative—(1) *sings* (*aeidesin*), (2) *often modulating* (*thama troposa*), and (3) *pours out* (*cheei*). The feeling is designated as an "arousal" (*ororetai*). Given the visual or other sensual base to the Homeric simile generally, what goes on internally may be seen to resemble what the ear takes in—or what a singer produces. There is a steady issue within (1), which is aroused to a pitch (3), and is involved in being "divided this way and that" (*dicha entha kai entha*), something that may be coordinated with *often modulating* (2).

The details of the story in the vehicle cannot be brought into this complex physical-psychological comparison, but they may compare well with other features of Penelope's situation even if we do not allow this earliest version of the Procne story to suggest the marital infidelity of Tereus (or Zethos) to a Penelope who is, as she says, on the brink of entertaining what she considers might be infidelity. The family in the vehicle's myth has the same constituents as the one in the main tenor of the story itself: a father, a mother, and an only son. As with the speaker, the mother is the center of the story. Penelope is certainly concerned about Telemachus; she is concerned about him for himself and for the fact that he is Odysseus' son.

Moreover the prosperity of the scene in which Penelope finds herself perplexed might be likened to the freshness of the foliage which
she "unrelatedly" mentions. The details of the comparison play tan-
talizingly between the gratuitous and the analogous.[11]

Psychological as well as visual effects may come into the picture
when the rise and motion of a ship's stern is compared to four
yoked stallions on a plain (*Od.* 13.81–85), or when Agamemnon's
weeping is compared to a dark-watered spring (*Il.* 9.13–15), or
when Paris is said to move like a horse fresh from the crib (*Il.*
6.506), or when Agamemnon is said to be killed like an ox in a
crib and his men like boars (*Od.* 11.411–14), or when Diomede is
compared to an autumn star or to a full river (*Il.* 4.5; 4.85), or
when the proceeding army is likened to fire or to large flocks of
geese, cranes, and swans (*Il.* 2.455–65), or even when a warrior
is felled like a poplar (*Il.* 4.482–88), and the suddenness and overwhelming totality of the action are suggested as well as the plunge
of a vertical dead weight to horizontal position.

So the white dust that covers the Achaians under the stir of their
horses, as it is compared to the white chaff that piles up under
Demeter's winnowing (*Il.* 5.499–503), in addition to the likeness
of two powdery substances, may associate this late, decisive moment in the war with a moment of harvest, as well as contrasting
the world of peace with the world of war. There is confidence in
the ranks like the mowing of the prosperous, as well as movement
that looks like that of mowers (*Il.* 11.67–69). A simile striking in
its psychological reach is the comparison of the abatement of
Antilochus' anger to the sotfening of ears of grain by dew "in a
shuddering field." And the visual sharpness remains, though the
psychology is explicit (*Il.* 23.597–98).

The multiplicity of items in a simile allows for this play of association over possible analogies, without at the same time ruling
out contrasts. The comparison of the interior of a house to the
gleam of the sun or the moon (*Od.* 4.45; 7.84) offers alternative
visual intensities but a common superlative of reference to the very
cosmos itself, suggesting not only a physical look—a play of light
from moony softness to solar dazzle—but also the assuredness and
delight of an extraordinary prosperity crowned by *architectural*

achievement: the source is a visual creation in addition to enlisting a visual effect. An exultation, heightened feeling as well as a visual expanse, may be felt to accompany the driving of the deep clouds into the sky of the simile quoted below, or similar ones as in *Il.* 5.770–72:

> As far into the murk as a man may see with his eyes
> Seated on a cliff gazing onto the wine-faced sea,
> So far did the high-sounding horses of the gods spring on.

While we cannot assign exact proportions to physical and psychological elements, the psychological can predominate, as in the comparison of Ajax's withdrawal to a lion whom dogs and men stay up all night to fend off, so that at daylight he slinks away (*Il.* 11.548–56). This offers the usual complex of elements, and its psychological angle is reversed in the immediately ensuing simile: Ajax's withdrawal is alternately compared to that of a donkey persistently beaten in a field with sticks but not leaving until he is sated (11.556–64). Elements of dissatisfaction dominate the first simile, of satisfaction the second. Yet both center on the long difficulty of dislodging the hero, and on the psychological set of both attacker and defenders. In this simile from the *Odyssey,* an almost wholly psychological one, a connection cannot be excluded between his weak but growing force and the "feeble puppies":

> As when a bitch standing over her feeble puppies,
> Not recognizing a man, growls and is eager to fight,
> So his heart growled within him, indignant at their evil deeds.
>   (20.14–16)

Nestor's steadiness amid perplexities is compared to the steadiness of an agitated sea (*Il.* 14.16–22), thereby characterizing two levels of the mind, a surface one and something deeper. Finally the verbal resources of the Homeric simile, even when it does not depart from some visual reference, and with or without a visual comparison, is powerful enough to accede directly to a large conceptual act, as when the turmoil of battle is compared to the whole earth being on fire (*Il.* 2.780), words are said to be like snowflakes (*Il.* 2.222), men to be like generations of leaves, (*Il.* 6.146–49), ideas

tossed about like intestines tossed over a fire (*Od.* 19.25). It is a
concept of military order, not a view of marshaling troops (though
that may be residually present) when the arming is compared to a
mason's fitting stones into a wall (*Il.* 16.212–14). So when Nau-
sikaa is compared to Artemis dancing (*Od.* 6.102), or Apollo's
havoc in war to a boy's kicking down the structure he has built in
the sand (*Il.* 15.362–66), or Achilles looking at Priam as thick
Ate at a murderer, and wonder strikes the onlookers (*Il.* 24.480–
83), or when the grace shed on a man is likened to a craftsman's
work in gold or silver (*Od.* 6.232; 23.159). Odysseus' psychological reactions also enter a conceptual frame through the simile,
when he is glad to see land as a father is glad to see his children
(*Od.* 5.394), or when he weeps like a woman who has lost her
husband (8.525), or when he is glad to see the setting sun as a
ploughman is (13.31), or when he is glad to see his wife as a
swimmer is to see the shore (*Od.* 23.233–39). He has himself been
such a swimmer, but the displacing verbal form of the simile at
once suggests the closing of the circle and keeps it from being
closed. The visual, the psychological, and the conceptual are provided with a firm tissue of connection without having to undergo
full coordination.

4

Homer's special emphasis on the visual in his more expanded similes allows him a firmness that can afford complexity, for all the
looseness of the fit in details of the comparison. It also allows him
a perspectival wholeness, for all the sketchiness of the vocabulary
at his disposal, as Snell and others have pointed out, where one
word, *chros*, stands for both the skin and the flesh under it, and
where general words tend to be lacking. It is not simply, as Auerbach shows, that Homer offers details;[12] he could have done so pell-
mell or blurringly.

  The famous simile of the watch fires across the plain compares
them to the stars in the heaven (8.554–65), and the simile does
not have to say that the stars will be shining above the fires for us
to round them together in an imagined cosmic depth from hills to

sky. A visual description of clouds adds physical depth to the ordinary momentousness of Zeus' action in starting a storm:

> As when a cloud goes inside the sky from Olympus
> From the bright upper air when Zeus stretches a tempest,
> So from the ships arose the shout and the panic.
>
> (16.364–66)

Lattimore spells out the three-dimensionality by rendering *eiso* (inside, within) as "deep into." The dimension of extent is also present in the word *teino, to stretch*. Both dimensions are present in the resulting quasi-aerial view of the panic among the ships, where the word I have rendered "panic," *phobos,* is both physical and psychological, the former getting an emphasis by being paired with the word for shout, *iache.*

A comparable visual expanse is evoked to explain the movement of Hera's horses "between earth and starry heaven" (*Il.* 5.770–72):

> As far as into hazing distance a man can see with his eyes,
> Who sits gazing on the wine-faced ocean on a headland
> So leap forward the gods' high-sounding horses.[13]
>
> (Lattimore, revised)

As for complexity, we see it in the long description (18.483–607) of that imagined visual artifact that has no parallel in the visual arts of Greece until a much later time, the shield of Achilles.[14] This elaborate image is neither simile nor metaphor, though its description does serve, like the similes, to displace, delay, and emphasize the narrative at a key point. It offers nothing less than a view of the whole world on an ordered plane, with everything in place while everything is visually distinct: the cosmos with the girdling river Oceanus, earth, sun, moon, sky, sea, and constellations; two cities of men, one at peace and the other at war; ploughing, harvesting, herding, dancing. The traditional Near Eastern icon of a lion attacking a domestic animal, frequent in the Homeric similes, is here coordinated with all the other scenes (18.587–89).

In this large image the visual distinctness of details permits the structural anchorage that holds the complexity in place. Even when Homer describes a motion of dancing on the actually stationary object, the contradiction does not obtrude, because of a kind of analogy to the sharpness of the other images, the sharpness of his images generally.

Or take the short simile adduced when Athene brushes Pandaros' arrows away from Menelaos:

> She kept it from his kin the same way as when a mother
> Keeps a fly from her child when he is bound in sweet sleep.
>
> (4.130–31)

The comparison is of a physical motion that results in constraint, *eergo*, the verb in both instances meaning "check, press in," though to our eye the arrow or the fly is being brushed away. "The same way," *toson*, might also be translated "to the same degree." No more force is needed from Athene to deflect an arrow than is needed from a mother to brush away a fly. Two kinds of motion, a heavenly and an earthly, are placed into equivalence—and something of the imperturbability of the gods, residual as it may be when they quarrel among themselves, rubs off on the warrior Menelaus. He is wronged by Helen, and he is also destined in the legend to survive the war. This plot that holds him may be said to be embodied in Athene, and to take precise visual form in the gesture of restraining the arrow. But, again, he is not compared to the infant, any more than there is anything other than a precise, panoramic view of the many tribes of Achaeans when their marshaling against the Trojans is compared to the swarming of flies around milk pails in the spring (2.469–73).

This extensibility of the visual in Homer's practice amounts to an act of steady affirmation, and Stanford contrasts Homer's "use of metaphor, in its always positive thrust," with the occasionally privative use in the Rig Veda, "the torrent is roaring but not like a bull," "fire eats up the forest but not like a lion," etc.[15] When "the soul flew away like a dream" in one of the Odyssey's short similes (11.222), an act of perception that still retains a visual element has been extended to the night life and the afterlife all at once. Homer recurrently compares man to the gods, in the epithets *dios* and *isotheos* and in the simile-phrase *theo eikelos,* all meaning "godlike." The affirmation allows a transition onto such an exalted plane.

The Rig Veda, by contrast, never does this,[16] though it does call gods men in the metaphor cited above, as easily as it calls them bulls or lions or even cows.[17]

The similes, as Vivante has penetratingly noticed of the epithets,[18] work at once to expand the narrative at very serious points and to delay it when it is not at a point of quick linear movement ahead. And all Vivante says of the epithets may be applied to the similes in their relation to the action: "The epithets generally belong to a [representational moment]; they tend to be dropped out when [a relational one] prevails." "The poetic quality of this verse mainly consists in the fact that the epithets have no connection with the narrative context." "They are used most often in dialogue when speaking of distant things." "What prompts their recurrence is a sense of recurrence in life itself."

5

The wonder surrounding the similes derives from a comparable sense of recurrence that takes form as it takes linguistic expression. In this sense the mere fact that the similes exist on such an elaborate plan at all is of more moment than the particular logical structure connecting their component parts. A possible measure for the power of visualization at a moment in the history of a culture is to be sought in the visual arts obtaining at that particular moment. This would not be in the aim of comparing poetry to painting and other arts, *ut pictura poesis,* as Horace's phrase has been falsely applied in modern discourse.[19] Rather, the aim would be to supplement the independent achievement of expression, as it issues in visualization, separately in the verbal and the visual modes. It cannot be an accident, surely, that almost no visual artifacts have survived from the culture of the Rig Veda, when we have figurines and seals and pottery and even a mirror from the Harapa and the Kulli cultures immediately preceding it and in a geographical area adjacent or overlapping. All we have of these early Aryans who produced the Rig Veda are some copper hoards of weapons, and a copper figure that may or may not be the outline of a cult figure, and also some examples of simple gray pottery ware.

The visual resources become more complex in India, of course, well after the time of the Rig Veda, and especially after contact with the Greeks on Alexander's invasion, not to speak of persistent contact with the Near Eastern cultures that had already interacted with the Greeks. We may say—tentatively to be sure—that the culture of the Veda invested whatever visual perceptions it had in the great array of hymns, and yet the failure to expand those perceptions into visual artifacts has its counterpart in the facile blurrings and confusions of figurative language in the hymns, a blurring and confusion that is not merely visual but may be taken to characterize, not just negatively, a whole style of thinking and feeling.

Now Homer wrote about a time before his own, and the chronology in his poems involves more than just a present and a past. So if we are uncertain as to how we might locate the lion gate at Mycenae, or the Vaphio cups, or Myceanean reliefs—to mention just a few signal objects—with respect to the Homeric poems, there are two arts that certainly flourished at the time we now believe the poems to have been composed (about 740 B.C.). Both of these arts suggestively incorporate features of the visual elements in the similes. The elaborately ordered funerary urns of "geometric" pottery certainly do parallel the persistent ordering in the poems, even if we do not go as far as Cedric Whitman does in pressing the parallel.[20] And if we look for sharp visual precision in an artifact, we find it strikingly in the miniature art of the seals which had flourished in Minoan and Mycenean times and again in Homer's own. If we take Homer's separate words, as Snell has done, the terms for body (*guia, melea,* etc.) accord well with the stick figures found on geometric vases and Archaic gems.[21] But if we move from diction to syntax, into the elaborate world of the simile itself, the visual analogues are strikingly not to pottery but to the sort of fuller art we find in Mycenean gems—an art that may not have died out wholly, from the evidence of island gems of the tenth century, as well as the fairly speedy resumption of full sculptural representation in later archaic gems.[22] Artifacts like the shield of Achilles or the gold and silver inlay work of a simile that refers to the body of Odysseus (*Od.* 6.232–33), or the gold and silver dogs and the gold lampadophore–*kouroi* of Alcinoos' palace (*Od.* 7.91–102), also suggest a fuller sense of the body, a richer visual sense, than the stick figures of eighth-century vases can represent.

The art work of the eighth century, taken in itself, does not offer a visual world full enough to parallel the visual fullness and acuteness of the Homeric similes, though certain parallels of iconographic subject can be drawn, as Roland Hampe has shown of shipwreck scenes on vases, myths in eighth-century friezes, the two lions attacking a deer in an eighth-century bracelet, and others.[23] The simile of a statue or a grave stele is used for motionlessness in *Il.* 13.437 and 17.434, as Bernard Fenik points out by way of indicating the typicality of the similes generally, especially where battles and journeys of the gods are in question.[24] But allowing for the fairly free distribution of works, and especially durable ones like gems, in the space and time of the early Mediterranean,[25] we may confidently look to Mycenean gems, where we do indeed find visualizations that correspond to the fullness and precision of the Homeric similes.

Several seals from Pylos, indeed, a site that Telemachus is said to have visited and that the legendary Nestor ruled, though they come from Mycenean times, have a visual sharpness scarcely inferior to that of the classical period. Further, they occasionally incorporate iconographic motifs that much later found their way into those poems about their Mycenean civilization, the *Iliad* and the *Odyssey*. One such seal shows a man in a conical hat spearing a wild boar at which his large dog is barking (294; figure 8),[26] recalling the scene of Odysseus' boar hunt (*Od.* 19.437–49). Boldly utilizing the round form of the seal, the early but not primitive jeweler has bent each of his figures into a form that arranges the three of them in a running circle, a way that may be taken as analogous to the "ring composition" of passages in Homer. At the same time there are slight differences of scale and angle that reinforce the distinctnesses of dog, boar, and man from each other; and the most prominent visual binder is the crucial instrument of action, the man's spear. An agate of a lion killing a calf (278; figure 9) recalls the numerous descriptions, usually in similes, of the beast-of-prey slaughter to be found in seals and other artifacts throughout the Near

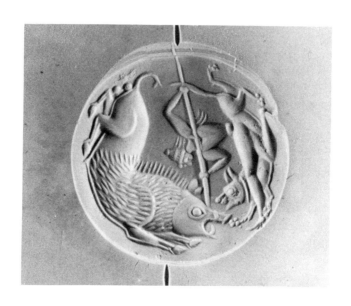

FIGURE 8. Mycenean Seal, *Boar Hunt.*
National Archeological Museum, Athens.

FIGURE 9. Mycenean Seal, *Lion with Calf.*
National Archeological Museum, Athens.

East. This agate from Pylos may also be said to recall, in its subject matter as well as in its vividly precise execution, the description of the brooch Odysseus owned:

> And the brooch upon it was made of gold,
> With twin sockets. And on its face it was skillfully wrought:
> In his front paws a dog was holding a dappled fawn
> And gazed at it while it writhed. All men marvelled to see
> How the one, being of gold, gazed at the fawn he throttled,
> And the other strove to get away as he writhed with his feet.
>
> (19.226–31)

Other seals from Pylos show a feminine cult figure of Circe-like sinuosity (279), and large steers much like the cattle of the sun lying down beside a tree. (275).

To visualize, to express one's visualizations, to think, and to feel, are all activities whose interrelations we have only begun to explore. The similes in the Homeric poems, somewhat fortified by their analogues in corresponding visual objects, testify to a precious level of achievement in the mysterious human enterprise of self-awareness through correlating word or thought and image.

The sort of doubling capacity in art and in literature equally, which I have argued for the Homeric poems, might be considered the normal case, one that obtains in the Western world right to the present day. It is not the only possibility, however. The intense images of the Hebrew prophets, and the very differently structured, elaborately ornamented edifice of Solomon's temple, are more countered than paralleled in the stern biblical injunction against images. The Egyptians would seem to have expended their imaginative energies almost wholly upon the plastic arts, which then spill over into the act of writing but not into a literature to parallel the friezes and statues and coffin lids through that long culture. The early Chinese, on the other hand, have an impressive but limited group of artifacts, to be set beside lyric poems in the Confucian Anthology, poems so sharp and full in their capacity for visual image that similes, in translation at least, seem wholly to disappear. For Homer the simile does by no means disappear; it is a window on the capacity for perception and coordination that is still widening.

Notes

Chapter 1. Thought, Image, and Story:
The Slippery Procedures of Literature

1. So the sophistications of Ingarden, and comparable writers, will end-lessly adjust and calibrate their census of macro- and microconstituents for literature. The accuracy of their description begs the question both of what it is they are describing in general, and more specifically of how such a census would aid an act of interpretation. Ingarden admits as much (Roman Ingarden, "Die Schicht der Bedeutungseinheiten" in *Das Liter-arische Kunstwerk* [Halle: Max Niemeyer, 1931], 60), "Da wir hier keine ausführliche Theorie der Bedeutungseinheiten geben können, so ist es selbstverständlich dass wir mehrere sich aufdrägende Fragen unbeant-wortet lassen und Verschiedenes nur andeutungsweise skizzieren müssen" (Since we can give here no thoroughgoing theory of unities of significa-tion, it has to be understood that we must leave several pressing questions unanswered and sketch in others only by brief indication). Exactly. And these are the very questions that continue to press; if his method can only "andeutungsweise skizzieren" such questions, then *as a method* it stops short of engagingly addressing the title of his work.

2. Charles Altieri, "The Qualities of Action," *Boundary 2*, 5, nos. 2 and 3. Context-dominated approaches like those of Lotman, Eco, Jauss, and Iser, for all their differences, may be assimilated to speech-act theory for their attention to the process itself of communication.

3. Tzvetan Todorov, in *Théories du symbole* (Paris: Seuil, 1977), sum-marizes the varying progression of theories about interactions among two or more of these comparable constituents from Aristotle and the Stoics to

Freud and Jakobson. Of course, a system to explain signs may deploy more than three terms. Peirce has sign, interpretant, represantamen, object, and ground, along with more than sixty "trichotomies" of interaction among them.

4. A. J. Greimas, *Sémantique structurale* (Paris: Larousse, 1966); idem, *Du sens* (Paris: Seuil, 1970); idem, *Maupassant* (Paris: Seuil, 1976).

5. Roland Barthes, *S/Z* (Paris: Seuil, 1970). For Gérard Genette, who allows for other than recursive structures (*Narrative Discourse,* Ithaca: Cornell University Press, 1979; *Figures III,* Paris: Gallimard, 1976), anything else in the "diegesis" is subordinated as "gaps"—and "surprises" (268).

6. Evan Watkins, *The Critical Act* (New Haven: Yale University Press, 1978).

7. Matthew Arnold, "The Study of Poetry," in *Essays: Second Series* (London: Macmillan, 1888), 2.

8. *Image* itself can be a misleading, falsely naïve, or implicitly contradictory term. It can be taken as pairing with, or interacting with, other terms or sets of terms: *word, signification, signifier* and *signified, mimesis, model, object* and *representation, discourse* and *figure, being* and *seeming, emblem* and *expression, sense* and *reference, theme* and *motif.* For a brief discussion of these in the context of painting, see Albert Cook, "Introduction," in *Changing the Signs: The Fifteenth Century Breakthrough* (Lincoln: University of Nebraska Press, 1985).

9. Jacques Derrida ("La Mythologie Blanche," in *Marges* [Paris: Minuit, 1972]) offers five types of metaphor as these may appear in discourse. For poetry these would either falsify the deep topics of the discourse by generalizing too quickly, or else apply only trivially.

10. Adelbert Chamisso, "Das Schloss Boncourt," in *Die Deutsche Romantiker* (Salzburg: Bergland, n.d.), 2:764.

11. René Char, *Les Matinaux* (1950; reprint, Paris: Gallimard, 1978), 76.

12. Jack Hexter, "Historiography," in *International Encyclopedia of the Social Sciences,* ed. David L. Sills (New York: Macmillan, 1968), 6, 368–94; reprinted in *Doing History* (Bloomington: Indiana University Press, 1975). "A general-law explanation cannot tell that story. It is not built to tell stories. . . . General law and narrative are not merely alternative but equally valid modes of explanation."

13. For fiction, Simon O. Lesser, *Fiction and the Unconscious* (New York: Knopf, 1957). For poetry and drama, the works of Norman Holland, as they move back and forth from psychoanalyzing the work to psychoanalyzing the reader's response to it.

14. Irving Massey, "Escape from Fiction: Literature and Didacticism," *Georgia Review* (Fall 1978): 611–30; idem, *The Gaping Pig* (Berkeley: University of California Press, 1976).

15. Claude Lévi-Strauss, *La Voix des masques* (Paris: Plon, 1979), 144.

16. Walter Benjamin, *Der Ursprung des Deutschen Trauerspiels,* in *Gesammelte Werke* (Frankfurt: Suhrkamp, 1974).

Während ein Symbol mit der Verklärung des Untergangs das transfigurierte Antlitz der Natur im Lichte der Erlösung flüchtig sich offenbart, liegt in der Allegorie die facies hippocratica der Geschichte als erstarrte Urlandschaft dem Betrachter vor Augen.

While a symbol transiently presents itself in its transfiguration of decline as the heightened countenance of nature in the light of redemption, in allegory lies the Hippocratic face of history as the stunned landscape before the eyes of the one who observes it.

This of course derives from, while it powerfully transmutes, the standard distinction between allegory and symbol in the German Romantics. Contrariwise, Rudolf Arnheim insists on the necessary spatialization of temporal entities, "any organized entity, in order to be grasped as a whole by the mind, must be translated into the synoptic condition of space" ("Space as an Image of Time," in *Images of Romanticism,* ed. Karl Kroeber and William Walling [New Haven: Yale University Press, 1978], 1–13).

17. Charles Olson, "ABC's 2," in *Archaeologist of Morning,* 1970, as quoted in Charles Boer, "Poetry and Psyche," *Spring,* 1979: "What Olson is advocating is a form of deviant realism . . . a poetry where perception is seen as unmediated (immediate) by a subjectivist ego . . . perception is an unmediated process which constantly picks up information from what we [Boer and Peter Kugler in *Spring,* 1977] call the 'environmental unconscious.' "

Chapter 2. The Range of Image

1. The umbrella phrase *ut pictura poesis* has often been invoked to cover questions common to verbal and visual arts, and it points up our difficulties to notice that in fact Horace had no such question in mind. He was simply making the point, after some musical analogies, that in a long work we may be surprised when Homer nods or a bad poet like Choerilus makes two or three good verses:

> ut pictura poesis; erit quae, si propius stes,
> te capiat magis, et quaedam, si longius abstes.
> Haec amat obscurum; volet haec sub luce videri,
> iudicis argutum quae non formulat acumen,
> haec placuit semel, haec deciens repetita placebat.
> (*Epistulae* 2.3.361–65)

Horace simply says some works please if seen close up, some if far away, some in light, some in dark, some seen once, some seen many times. Other discussions of the limitations on *ut pictura poesis* are to be found in Mario Praz, *Mnemosyne* (Princeton: Princeton University Press, 1970) and Wendy Steiner, *The Colors of Rhetoric* (Chicago: University of Chicago Press, 1983).

2. Jean-Joseph Goux, in *Les Iconoclastes* (Paris: Seuil, 1978), relates iconoclastic strategies to patriarchal organizations, both in their psychological and in their social effects.

3. Ernst Gombrich, *Art and Illusion* (Princeton: Princeton University Press, 1960); Rudolf Arnheim, *Art and Visual Perception* (Berkeley: University of California Press, 1974).

4. Adrian Stokes, *Colour and Form,* in *Collected Works,* vol. 2 (New York: Thames and Hudson, 1978), 7–84.

5. Heinrich Wölfflin, *Principles of Art History* (1932; reprint, New York: Dover, 1950).

6. Edmund Husserl, *Logische Untersuchungen* (Tübingen: Niemeyer, 1913), *passim;* Ludwig Wittgenstein, *Remarks on Color* (Berkeley: University of California Press, 1971).

7. The point is made by André Leroi-Gourhan in *Le Geste et la Parole* (Paris, 1969). I elaborate on it somewhat in *Myth and Language* (Bloomington: Indiana University Press, 1980).

8. See T. A. Van Dijk, *Pragmatics of Language and Literature* (Amsterdam, 1976). The linguistic, psychological, and philosophical dimensions of recent discussion about metaphor may be represented respectively by Samuel R. Levin, *The Semantics of Metaphor* (Baltimore: Johns Hopkins University Press, 1977); Robert L. Rogers, *The Psychology of Metaphor* (Berkeley: University of California Press, 1978); and Paul Ricoeur, *La Métaphore Vive* (Paris: Seuil, 1975).

9. Sigmund Freud, *Die Traumdeutung* (Vienna: Deuticke, 1899), 261. Freud further discusses the use and applicability of images enlisted for abstract thought in general in his discussions of *Darstellbarkeit,* 322ff. The view contemporary with Pindar, however, may be represented by Aeschylus, who speaks of "the forms of dream, confusing all likenesses" (*eike, Prometheus,* 448–51).

10. Elroy L. Bundy, *Studia Pindarica* (Berkeley: University of California Press, 1962). For further inferences see Albert Cook, "Pindar: 'Great Virtues Are Always Many-Mythed,' " in *Myth and Language.*

11. These are the categories adapted from Peirce-like discussions of sign systems by Thomas Sebeok, *Contributions to the Doctrine of Signs* (Bloomington: Indiana University Press, 1976).

12. "Ho de logos / tautais epi suntuchiais doxan pherei," (the scheme / in these circumstances will bear renown), 35. As Farnell says of this passage, "this is the first [*sic*] example of the use of *logos* approaching the later philosophic. We may interpret it as 'the logic of the coincidence,' 'the parity of the reasoning'; near to this is its sense of 'analogy' or 'proportion' in the Herodotean *kata logon*" (L. R. Farnell, *The Works of Pindar* [London, 1930–32], 2:110).

13. Paul de Man, *Allegories of Reading* (New Haven: Yale University Press, 1979) is well able to qualify the systems of Locke, Condillac, and Kant with respect to metaphor by providing subtle analyses of incidental or buried metaphors in their work when they are discussing metaphor. Plato's use of "metaphor" is too integral to submit to such procedures, though as de Man well says, "rhetoric cannot be isolated from its epis-

temological function, however negative this function may be." Of course, Plato's uses here cannot be characterized except incidentally as "rhetoric."

14. I am here following James Adam, *The Republic of Plato* (1902; reprint, Cambridge: Cambridge University Press, 1965), 2:60, 157–71. An unpublished study by Gary Handwerk relates the figural structures of the Sun, the Line, and the Cave complexly to the procedure of the central argument about Justice in the *Republic*. As Handwerk says:

> Platonic imagery serves several purposes. First, it breaks down logically exclusive categories and terms, exposing their rhetorical intentions in the Platonic system. Despite their heterogeneity, the Sun and the Line must be brought together, for they seek to explain the same problem (at least related aspects of it). Second, as a group the images open up philosophical questions a single image would tend to conceal. In its multiplicity, then, the *Republic's* imagery marks the honesty of Plato's discourse. . . . Third, the imagery makes the value judgments problematic which tend to inhibit philosophical progress. Thought is both good and bad; blindness is a matter of where one is coming from. Finally, the Cave shows us what is occurring in the *Republic,* where the movement towards the Good occurs despite, through, and as a means of reconciliation of opposites. This set of images reveals the technique we should apply to other arguments, drawing out from them elaborations towards paradox. . . . The obvious problem here is the discrepancy between what Plato says and what he does; he mounts a sharp philosophical attack on likeness, yet employs it repeatedly.

15. Konrad Gaiser, *Platons ungeschriebene Lehre* (Stuttgart, 1968). According to Gaiser even soul is defined as boundary, in the mathematical sense, for the body in Plato's system, and in it there is a mathematical equivalent for everything. It should be said, in qualification, that Plato classifies mathematics and something of number theory not just under *noesis,* his highest function, but also, overlappingly, under his next highest, *dianoia* (524D–526).

16. Actually I oversimplify. The fictional names Er and Ardrieus (formed also contrary to usual Greek nomenclature) and the invented eschatalogical combinations make a strong element of fiction (the sense of *mythos* as "fable" or "false story") hover persistently over the myth of Er. But the final bearing of the myth, contrastingly, has a supervening force, "the myth was saved . . . and will save us" (621C). So while on the one hand the myth of Er pretends a different actuality from the Cave, which simply allegorizes a perception theory; on the other hand a pretense drops away. The myth purports to offer a vision of what is, not models for what should be. In this light the myth of Er offers the most actual representation in the entire *Republic*.

17. "Fictio retorica musicaque composita," *De Vulgari Eloquentia,* 2.4.20.

18. Inferences from color symbolism, in Nietzsche for example, cannot be confined to this kind of free play, in Heidegger's reading (*Nietzsche* [Pfullingen: Neske 1961], 1.304–5).

19. A different presentation of this argument could have organized it around the voyage imagery—frequent in Pindar and incidental to Pythian 1, derivable from the myth of Er, central to Dante, and recurrent in Rimbaud, as well as at the base of *Le Bateau Ivre.*

20. Raymond Firth, *Symbols Public and Private* (Ithaca: Cornell University Press, 1973); Victor Turner, *Dramas, Fields, and Metaphors* (Ithaca: Cornell University Press, 1974).

21. Valéry, as one instance, declares ("Berthe Morisot," in *Pièces sur l'art* in *Oeuvres* [Paris: Pléiade, 1960] 2:1307–8) that all those who perceive, with the exception of the artist, do so from a particular empirical viewpoint. Looking at a countryside, the philosopher sees phenomena, the geologist a history of physical epochs, a soldier obstacles and occasions, a peasant so many hectares to cultivate . . . and so colors for all of them are *signs* (italics Valéry's). "A l'opposite de cette abstraction est l'abstraction de l'artiste. La couleur lui parle couleur, et il répond à la couleur par la couleur. Il vit dans l'objet, au milieu même de ce qu'il cherche à saisir, et dans une tentation, un défi, des examples, des problèmes, une analyse, une ivresse perpétuels" (As opposed to such abstraction is the abstraction of the artist. Color speaks color to him, and he answers color by color. He lives in the object, in the very environment he seeks to grasp, and in the temptation and challenge of examples, and problems, an intoxication and analysis that are perpetual). Consequently ("Eupalinos," ibid., 2:87), "Il prépar[e] à la lumière un instrument incomparable, qui la répandit, tout affectée de formes intelligibles et de propriétés presque musicales, dans l'espace où se meuvent les mortels" (He prepares for the light an incomparable instrument, which expands the light—one clothed in intelligible forms and nearly musical properties, in the space where mortals move). In a further movement ("Introduction à la méthode de Léonardo de Vinci," ibid., 1:1182), "Cette indépendance est la condition de la recherche *formelle*. Mais l'artiste, *dans une autre phase,* tente de restituer la particularité, et même la singularité, qu'il avait d'abord éliminées de son attention" (This independence is the condition of *formal* research. But the artist, *in another phase,* tries to restore the particularity, and even the singularity, that he at first had eliminated from his attention) (italics Valéry's). These distinctions all resemble very much Husserl's distinction between *empirical* and *abstract* in *Logische Untersuchungen.*

22. Gombrich, *Art and Illusion.* This connoisseur's wide-ranging sensitivity at reconstructing the ellipses and angles of visual presentation tends, when approaching image directly, to impoverish the sense of its rich effect. Does this happen from a sort of nominalist bias? "All artistic discoveries are discoveries not of likenesses but of equivalences which enable us to see reality in terms of an image and an image in terms of reality" (345). This is acute, and neat, in its distinction between likeness and equivalence. But here, and elsewhere, Gombrich's reasoning is circular, and the attention is essentially turned away, from both reality and image. Nor do his terms provide for the hermeneutic circle that would allow us to approach, say, Kandinsky and Matisse—or Constable and van Eyck. In Gombrich a sense of satisfaction at a clear account does duty for the approach to an artistic plenitude.

23. Jean-François Lyotard, *Discours, Figure* (Paris: Klincksieck, 1971).

24. For discussions relating to this question, see Albert Cook, *Thresh-*

olds: Studies in the Romantic Experience (Madison: University of Wisconsin Press, 1985).

25. As a case in point, D. J. Gordon in *The Renaissance Imagination* (ed. Stephen Orgel, Berkeley: University of California Press, 1975) displays the intricate interworkings of Renaissance emblematic conventions in poetry, painting, masque, and architecture. Marvell's poem is in its outward form a poem about an architectural structure (though not a notable one); and yet extrapolations of Gordon's deductions onto Marvell's salmon fishers—or for that matter onto "Upon Appleton House" generally—would yield very little by way of "iconographic" explanation.

26. J. B. Leishman, *The Art of Marvell's Poetry* (London: Hutchinson, 1966), especially 221–91. Ernest B. Gilman, in *The Curious Perspective* (New Haven: Yale University Press, 1978), connects a number of literary phenomena, from figures in Donne to dramatic shifts in Shakespeare, with the contemporary manipulative devices for producing perspectival illusions, through anamorphic, katoptric, and dioptric visual means. He cites many passages where Marvell can be better understood in this light. The *rational Amphibii* of these particular lines echo passages in Thomas Browne and others who use this term to express man's dual ties, to earth and to heaven. Marvell in these lines, to adapt Gilman's notions further, produces a sharp visual illusion or phantasmagoria that is reinforced not by further visual dexterity but rather by the projection of intellectual deductions from the sight. The image, in this sense, transcends metaphor while enlisting the effects of metaphor.

27. Yvonne Sandstroem, in an unpublished study of this poem, indicates many references to the Apocalypse, especially in this passage.

28. See Albert Cook, "Mallarmé: The Deepening Occasion," in *Thresholds.*

29. It is of course antireligious, but its vocabulary remains a religious one—a vocabulary powerful enough to have been instrumental in effectuating the conversion of Paul Claudel.

30. Barbara Lewalski, *Milton's Brief Epic* (Providence: Brown University Press, 1966), 386ff.

31. Stanley Fish, *Surprised by Sin* (London, Melbourne: Macmillan; New York: St. Martin's Press, 1967).

32. Albert Cook, *The Classic Line* (Bloomington: University of Indiana Press, 1966), 288–92.

33. Roland M. Frye (*Milton's Imagery and the Visual Arts* [Princeton: Princeton University Press, 1978], 321) relates the scene around the winepress, and other points of the poem, to the tradition of genre painting. He elsewhere also adduces pastoral. As general iconographic choices we might so classify such images of Milton, but his specific handling lacks the preoccupied attention to abundant detail that characterizes such paintings, as well as the almost exclusively pastoral set of their conception.

34. Cook, *Classic Line*, 282.

35. Roland Frye, *Milton's Imagery*, 4.

36. Roland Frye reproduces this, along with a plate showing the debate

between Christ and Satan in the Holkham Bible, the Sistine Chapel fresco of the Temptation by Botticelli, and a more focused view of the same subject by Tintoretto in the Scuola di San Rocco. However, he cites Gertrud Schiller (*Ikonographie in der Christlichen Kunst,* Gütersloh, 1966–71) as documenting the fact that the Temptation is not an especially prominent iconographic motif in painting, any more than it is in poetry.

37. Erich Auerbach, "Figura," in *Scenes from the Drama of Western Literature* (New York: Meridian, 1959), 11–78.

38. Wayne Shumaker, *Unpremeditated Verse: Feeling and Perception in Paradise Lost* (Princeton: Princeton University Press, 1961), 104–32.

39. F. T. Prince, *The Italian Element in Milton's Verse* (Oxford: Clarendon Press, 1954). Prince points out Tasso's use of the three ancient divisions of style in his *Discorsi.*

40. Wylie Sypher, *Four Stages of Renaissance Style* (New York: Anchor, 1955).

41. For a fuller discussion of Milton's handling of images in this poem, see Albert Cook, "Imaging in *Paradise Regained,*" *Milton Studies,* Summer 1985.

42. Geoffrey Hartman, *Criticism in the Wilderness* (New Haven: Yale University Press, 1981).

43. Albert Cook, "Emily Dickinson's White Exploits," in *Thresholds.*

44. *Semeion,* in *Theologisches Wörterbuch zum Neuen Testament,* ed. G. Kittel and Gerhard Friedrich (Stuttgart: Kohlhammer, 1927–73).

Chapter 3. Aspects of the Plastic Image: Rilke, Pound, and Arp

1. Frank Baron, ed., in *Rilke and the Visual Arts* (Lawrence, Kans.: Coronado Press, 1982), introduces various correspondences between Rilke's poetry and sculpture, especially that of Rodin. It contains a bibliography on Rilke and the arts. Rilke also wrote poems about the paintings of an artist with whom he collaborated, as documented in Karl Eugene Webb, *Rainer Maria Rilke and Jugendstil* (Chapel Hill: University of North Carolina Press, 1978), 13. There is much discussion of Rilke and the plastic arts in Beda Allemann, *Zeit und Figur beim späten Rilke* (Pfullingen: Neske, 1961).

2. "The concept *Ding* was more subtlized as a result of contact with Rodin (it also became more central)" (K. A. J. Batterby, *Rilke and France* [Oxford: Oxford University Press, 1966], 49).

3. All quotations are from Rilke, *Sämtliche Werke,* ed. Ernst Zinn (Frankfurt: Insel, 1955–66). This particular quotation is from 5:252.

4. Rilke combines death, the future, and things, again in the First Duino Elegy:

> Freilich ist es seltsam, die Erde nicht mehr zu bewohnen,
> kaum erlernte Gebräuche nicht mehr zu üben,
> Rosen, und andern eigens versprechenden Dingen
> nicht die Bedeutung menschlicher Zukunft zu geben;
>
> (1:687)

Surely it is strange no more to inhabit the earth,
Scarcely learned uses to exercise no more,
To roses and other self-promising things
Not to give the meaning of a human future;

5. Letter to Witold Hulewicz, November 13, 1925. "Lebens und Todes-
bejahung erweist sich als Eines in den 'Elegien.' . . . Die Natur, die
Dinge unseres Umgangs und Gebrauchs, sind Vorlaüfigkeiten und Hin-
fälligkeiten; aber sie sind, solang wir hier sind, *unser* Besitz und unsere
Freundschaft, Mitwisser unserer Not und Froheit . . . sollen diese Er-
scheinungen und Dinge von uns in einem innigsten Verstande begriffen
und verwandelt werden . . . dass ihr Wesen in uns 'unsichtbar' wieder
aufersteht. *Wir sind die Bienen des Unsichtbaren. Nous butinons éperdu-
ment le miel du visible pour l'accumuler dans la grande ruche d'or de l'Invisible."* (The affirmation of life, and of death, proves to be a unity in the
"Elegies." . . . The things of our acquaintance and use are preliminaries
and perishables; but so long as we are here, they are *our* possession and
our friendship, co-knowers of our need and gladness . . . these appearances and things of ourselves should be conceived of and transformed in
an innermost understanding . . . so that their essence may be resurrected
in us as again "invisible." *We are the bees of the invisible. We hive up
headlong the honey of the visible to accumulate it in the great gold hive of
the Invisible*).

6.   Werk des Gesichts ist getan,
               tue nun Herz-Werk.
        ("Wendung" 2:83)
        Sight-work is done,
               now do heart-work.

7. Otto Bollnow, *Rilke* (Stuttgart: Kohlhammer, 1951), 98–146.

8. See Frances Mary Scholz, "Rilke, Rodin, and the Fragmented Man,"
in Frank Baron, *Rilke and the Visual Arts*, 27–44.

9. The relations among these concepts in Rilke's work are elaborated
extensively in Richard Jayne, *The Symbolism of Space and Motion in the
Works of Rainer Maria Rilke* (Frankfurt: Athenäum, 1972).

10. Letter to Clara Rilke, October 13, 1907. *Dispositions* is in the
plural, as though to allow for the constant play of mind that the still
sculpture records no less than the moving poem. The word for objecthood
does not enlist *Ding;* but rather, it is a term that can also mean objectivity, *Sachlichkeit.*

11. The whole process of change, and the contribution of Gaudier
thereto, is acutely and evocatively described in Hugh Kenner, *The Pound
Era* (Berkeley: University of California Press, 1971). See also Ronald
Bush, *The Genesis of Ezra Pound's Cantos* (Princeton: Princeton University Press, 1976).

12. See Ezra Pound, "How to Read," *The Literary Essays of Ezra
Pound* (New York: New Directions, 1968 [1931]), 24–28.

13. Ezra Pound, *Gaudier-Brzeska* (1916; reprint, New York: New Directions, 1970), 107.

14. W. H. Auden, ed., *The Letters of Van Gogh* (New York: Viking, 1963); "Painting is like algebra: something is to this as that is to the other."
15. Pound, *Gaudier,* 92.
16. Ibid., 94.
17. Ibid., 82–84.
18. Donald Davie, *Ezra Pound: The Poet as Sculptor* (London: Routledge and Kegan Paul, 1964), 155–56, 57.
19. Pound, *Gaudier,* 26.
20. Ibid., 86.
21. Ibid., 28.
22. H. S. Ede, *The Savage Messiah* (New York: Knopf, 1931), 79, 99, 80.
23. Pound, *Gaudier,* 99.
24. Roland Barthes, *S/Z* (Paris: Seuil, 1970), 63.
25. Pound, *Gaudier,* 121.
26. Arp, Hülsenbeck, and Tzara, *Dada in Zürich* (Zurich: Sansouci, 1957), 66.
27. Marcel Jean, ed., *Arp on Arp* (New York: Viking, 1972), 317. The statement was originally made as the last line in a poemlike preface to a Rodin exhibition at the Curt Valentin Gallery, New York, 1954.
28. Quotations are from Hans Arp, *Gesammelte Gedichte* (Zurich: Arche, 1974).
29. A random assortment of egg-sayings will suggest the array of possibilities this image held for him:

in die astlöcher der meilensteine lege ich meine eier
(1:63)
I lay my eggs in the knotholes of milestones

Er schlägt die Eier aus der Frucht
mit einem Frucht- und Eierstock.
Der Fruchtenstock schlägt die Kinderschar
als Segen aus dem Eierrock.
(1:96)
He strikes eggs from fruit
With a fruit-and-egg stick.
The fruit stick strikes the child-flock
As a blessing from the egg-rock.

arps patentiertes eierbrett ist gewissermassen
der phönix des tennisspieles
(1:168)
Arp's patented eggboard is, so to speak,
the phoenix of tennis

das ei aus feuer, das ei aus wasser.
das ei aus wind im seidenen sack.
das ei aus luft . . . das stehende ei. das sitzende ei. das liegende ei.
(1:200)

The fire egg, the water egg.
The wind egg in a silk sack.
The air egg . . . the standing egg. The sitting egg. The lying egg.

und rauchende eier liegen an ihren stellen.

(1:248)

and smoking eggs lie in their places

Aus unscheinbaren grauen Würfeln graue Eier auszupacken.
Einmal entfiel meinen Händen ein solches Ei
fiel zu Boden und zerbrach
und aus seinem Inneren rollte eine
          Unzahl kleiner grauer Würfel
auf denen bunte funkelnde Träume abgebildet
      waren

(2:46)

To unpack gray eggs from invisible gray dice.
Once such an egg fell from my hand
fell to the ground and shattered
and out of its insides rolled a
          huge number of little gray dice
on which sparkling colored dreams were pictured

Auf der obersten Sprosse der Luft sitzt ein Ei, das in nicht endenwollende
"vivat" ausbricht. Ob die Luft eine Leiter sei, wird von den meisten alten Eier-
bändigern verneint. Nach ihrem Dafürhalten können Eier so bequem in der Luft
sitzen wie wir auf einem Stuhl. ("Ein gezähmtes Ei," 2:95)

On the highest sprays of air sits an egg that breaks out in a "vivat" that
wishes no end. That the egg is a ladder to most of the old Egg-group members
deny. So far as they are concerned eggs can sit in the air as comfortably as we
do on a stool. ("A Tamed Egg")

30. William S. Rubin, *Dada, Surrealism, and Their Heritage* (New
York: Museum of Modern Art, 1968), 120.

31. Jean, *Arp on Arp,* 241.

32. Ibid., 282.

Chapter 4. *The Windows of Apollinaire*

1. For a discussion of this aspect of Apollinaire, see Albert Cook, *Prisms*
(Bloomington: Indiana University Press, 1967), 163–70.

2. I owe this point to Margaret Hausman.

3. The image was one to which Apollinaire recurred. "Alfred Jarry . . .
m'apparut comme la personnification d'un fleuve," he said ("Feu Alfred
Jarry," in *Le Flâneur des deux rives* [1928; reprint, Paris: Gallimard,
1975], 88). And in "Océan de terre":

J'ai bâti une maison au milieu de l'Océan
Ses fenêtres sont les fleuves qui s'écoulent
      de mes yeux

I have built a house in the middle of the Ocean
Its windows are the rivers that flow from my eyes

4. Roger Shattuck, *The Banquet Years* (New York: Doubleday, 1961), 279. Anne Hyde Greet and S. I. Lockerbie summarize the details in *Calligrammes* (Berkeley: University of California Press, 1980), 349. Greet and Lockerbie also touch on the general subject I am discussing (350); "Collage, anonymous voices, fragmentation, juxtapositions between space and time are not new in Apollinaire's work, but in 'Les Fenêtres' we find these techniques pushed to an extreme and implicitly associated with the painter's theories on simultaneity." They further point out that *Le Temps* and *La Liberté* are newspapers to which there could be an allusion in lines 14–16. If so, that would intensify the contrast set in the poem between the lingering and the fleeting. In an earlier book, *Le livre du peintre* (Paris: Minard, 1977), Anne Hyde Greet discusses the cross-fertilization between Apollinaire and painters who presented his work in such a way that the resultant book transcends the ordinary illustrated book.

5. Apollinaire, Letter to Madeleine, July 1, 1915, as cited in *Oeuvres Poétiques* (Paris: Pléiade, 1956), 1072.

6. These were questions that interested Klee, who was stimulated by Delaunay.

7. Pléiade, 1071, citing Robert Goffin, *Entrer en Poésie*, 169. "Selon Robert et Sonia Delaunay [le poème] aurait été composé dans l'atelier du peintre et l'on retrouverait une allusion 'au rideau, à la fenêtre, aux oursins et à la vieille paire de chaussures jaunes.' " (Robert and Sonia Delaunay maintain the poem was composed in the painter's studio and that allusion is found there to the curtain, the window, the sea urchins, and the old pair of yellow shoes.)

8. Robert Delaunay, *Du Cubisme à l'art abstrait,* ed. Pierre Francastel (Paris: SEVPEN, 1957), 229.

9. Apollinaire, *Les Peintres Cubistes* (1913; reprint, Paris: Hermann, 1965), 55.

10. Apollinaire makes the connection between Delaunay and the Fauves, "L'Orphisme avec Delaunay . . . jaillit du mouvement des 'Fauves' " ("La peinture moderne," *Der Sturm*, Feb. 1913, 140–49, as reprinted in Delaunay, *Cubisme*, 163).

11. Delaunay, *Cubisme*, 83.

12. Ibid., 104.

13. Ibid., 101.

14. Apollinaire, *Peintres Cubistes,* 50.

15. Ibid., 101.

16. Ibid., 88.

17. Ibid., 52.

18. Ibid., 67.

19. Ibid., 7.

20. Delaunay, *Cubisme*, 56–58.

21. Martin Heidegger, "Der Ursprung des Kunstwerkes," in *Holzwege* (1950; reprint, Frankfurt am Main: Klostermann, 1963); Meyer Schapiro, "The Still Life as a Personal Object," in *The Reach of the Mind: Essays*

in Memory of Kurt Goldstein (New York: Springer, 1968); Jacques Derrida, *La Vérité en Peinture* (Paris: Flammarion, 1979).

22. Robert Greer Cohn, "Les Fenêtres de Mallarmé," *Cahiers de L'Association Internationale des Études Françaises,* no. 27 (May 1975): 289–98. Cohn points out such earlier literary windows as those in the Song of Songs, in *Le lai du laustic* of Marie de France, and in the "Sonnet pour Hélène" of Ronsard.

23. As Michel Butor says (*Les mots dans la peinture* [Geneva: Skira, 1969], 24), "La composition la plus 'abstraite' peut exiger que nous [lisions son titre pour nous] déployer toutes ses saveurs, toutes ses vertus." (The most abstract painting can require us to read its title for ourselves to deploy all its savors and all its properties.)

24. Apollinaire, *Peintres Cubistes,* 53.

25. Jean-François Lyotard, *Discours Figure* (Paris: Klincksieck, 1971).

26. Apollinaire, *Peintres Cubistes,* 57.

27. Ibid., 91.

28. "Concrete" poetry is often associated with minimalist and conceptualist art, and Michael Fried's remarks about that art are evocative for the poetry as well ("Art and Objecthood," in *Minimal Art,* ed. Gregory Battcock [New York: Dutton, 1968], 116–47); "It is . . . as though a work of art—more accurately, a work of modernist painting or sculpture—were in some essential respect *not an object.* There is, in any case, a sharp contrast between the literalist espousal of objecthood—almost, it seems, as an art in its own right—and modernist painting's self-imposed imperative that it defeat or suspend its own objecthood through the medium of shape." The "concrete" poets, and before them Apollinaire, may be said to have inverted this procedure by taking the ordinarily "transparent" medium of printed words and re-rendering it as an aesthetic object. For Apollinaire these objects placed where none had been found before may stand as counterparts to the painting of Delaunay, non-objective in an art that had always represented objects.

For a more positive view of concrete poetry since Apollinaire, see Augusto de Campos, Decio Pignitari, and Haroldo de Campos, *Teoria da Poesia Concreta* (Sao Paulo: Livraria Duas Cidades), 1975. (I owe this reference to Claus Clüver.) I feel these writers, however, extend the term somewhat when they apply it to Pound or even to Cummings. For all his play with letter arrangement, and though Cummings was also a painter, I find little visual interest or conceptual power in his letter arrangements, beyond the initial act of arresting the reader's attention or performing some simple emblematic mimesis.

29. See Albert Cook, "The 'Meta-Irony' of Marcel Duchamp," manuscript.

30. Delaunay, *Cubisme,* 67.

Chapter 5. Surrealism and Surrealisms

1. Dali appeared in this potentially lethal costume at a British Surrealist exhibition in the thirties and was released by the young poet David

Gascoyne, who ran for an emergency monkey wrench. (Incident recounted in a lecture by David Gascoyne at St. John's College, Cambridge, Spring 1982.)

2. Albert Cook, *Prisms* (Bloomington: Indiana University Press, 1967), 108. "[We cannot] reduce *La Cantatrice Chauve* to a fable about the logic of ordinary language. The Firechief does not speak ordinarily, nor do the other characters as they stammer off into surrealistic statements at the end of the play. Trivial chitchat, *Gerede* or *parlerie* in existentialist terms, gathers into its allegorized fits and starts such urgent ultimates as Death (Bobby Watson), Identity (the guests' discovery of their marriage), Love (the maid and her poem about the Firechief), Time (the Clock), and Physical Survival or Chance (Guarding against Fires when *tout prend feu.*)" I have said this in a chapter about allegory, and the capitals emphasize the allegorical nature of the play, though a further reorientation of it towards Surrealism would render inconsequential any significative structure for allegory.

3. Samuel Beckett (with Georges Duthuit), "Tal Coat, Masson, Bram van Velde," *Transition Forty-Nine*, no. 5, 97–103. He speaks of a "vigilant coenaesthesia" that could be taken effectually to cover Surrealism.

4. Alfred H. Barr, Jr., ed., *Fantastic Art, Dada, and Surrealism* (New York: Museum of Modern Art, 1936). Included as comparative material in this show were works from the fifteenth century on. Klee, Kandinsky, and Picasso are classified as "precursors." Aside from those mentioned above, some noteworthy presences in the show include Bellmer, Joseph Cornell, Man Ray, Arp, and Schwitters. Classed as associated "independents" are Alexander Calder, Arthur Dove, Walt Disney, Georgia O'Keeffe, Siqueiros, Rube Goldberg, and James Thurber.

5. Paul Gauguin, *Diverses Choses*, 1896–1897, as quoted in *Theories of Modern Art*, ed. Herschel B. Chipp (Berkeley: University of California Press, 1971), 66, "Color, being itself enigmatic in the sensations which it gives us, can logically be employed only enigmatically. One does not use color to draw but always to give the musical sensations which flow from itself, from its own nature, from its mysterious and enigmatic interior force."

6. Robert Motherwell, in a lecture at Brown University, Dec. 3, 1981.

7. Paul Klee, *Das Bildnerische Denken* (Basel: Schwabe, 1964), 403–29. The same ideas appear translated and in shorter compass in Paul Klee, *Pedagogical Sketchbook* (London: Faber, 1953).

8. Pierre Reverdy in Henri Matisse, *Écrits et propos sur l'art* (Paris: Hermann, 1972), 32.

9. André Breton, *Surrealism in Painting* (New York: Harper and Row, 1971). When Breton does mention Matisse, it is to reject him as an innovator in the line of Surrealism, "Matisse's boldest speculations (*The Piano Lesson, Moroccans*) [did not give] a glimpse of the solution" (52). However, the strange irrational grapefruit-size geometrical bump on the head of the young boy in *The Piano Lesson*, and the outline schematization of his mother (?) in the upper right of the picture, assimilate it

totally to a dream iconography. The same force may be accorded the unnatural spread of color across almost all of *Moroccans at Prayer.*

10. Ibid., 2–4.

11. Wallace Stevens, "The Irrational Element in Poetry," in *Opus Posthumous* (London: Faber, 1957), 216–17.

12. Yury Tynyanov, "Words and Things in Pasternak," in *Pasternak,* ed. Victor Erlich (Englewood Cliffs, N.J.: Prentice-Hall, 1978), 32–33.

13. Inez Hedges, *Languages of Revolt: Dada and Surrealist Literature and Film* (Durham, N.C.: Duke University Press, 1983). Hedges quotes and adapts Marvin Minsky's theory of a frame as a "network of nodes and relations." She speaks of frame-breaking as structural dislocation, as foreground-shift, as decontextualization, and as linguistic dissociation. Per Aage Brandt ("The White-Haired Generator," *Poetics* 6 [1972]: 72–83) sets up three levels of Text, Sleep, and Dream, across which the Surrealist poem moves through contradiction. Compare Albert Cook, *Myth and Language* (Bloomington: Indiana University Press, 1980), 255–56, "a strategy of image-circling . . . is true of surrealism, wherein the positive openness to free combinations of image interacts with the negative exclusion of logical connection between images to produce an illusion of a homogeneous and plenary dream universe . . . the strategy here of circling the image by levelling linguistic procedures at once parallels and reverses the philosophy that is haunted by metaphor."

14. Henri Matisse, "Notes d'un Peintre," in *Écrits et propos sur l'art,* 44–45. "Impressionisme . . . ils rendent des impressions fugitives. . . . Je préfère . . . obtenir plus de stabilité. . . . En s'éloignant de la *représentation* [italics Matisse's] littérale du mouvement on aboutit à plus de beauté et plus de grandeur." (Impressionism . . . they render fugitive impressions. . . . I prefer . . . to obtain more stability. . . . In distancing oneself from the literal *representation* of the movement one arrives at greater beauty and greater grandeur.) "On pourrait reculer les bornes de la théorie des couleurs telle qu'elle est actuellement admise" (We can push back the boundaries of color theory as it is thought of today) (49), "leur pouvoir émotif" (their emotive power) (203).

15. André Breton, *Manifestes du surréalisme* (1924; reprint, Paris: Gallimard, 1975), 8.

16. Other categories suggest themselves too: *Melters* like Yves Tanguy, Arshile Gorky, and Matta, who present elongated vertical swellings or protuberances; *Collocators,* specializing in the collage, like Max Ernst and Joseph Cornell; *Hallucinators* like Dali, who distort the human form or such human artifacts as watches; *Digesters,* like André Masson and William Baziotes, who depict what look like embryo blobs on the canvas, etc.

17. Mary Ann Caws in *The Presence of René Char* (Princeton: Princeton University Press, 1975) produces an expansive list of antithetical images in Char, who can be said therefore to begin with contradictions.

18. Cook, *Prisms,* chapters 1 and 2.

19. Compare André Breton, *Manifestes,* 96. *"Sous sa forme hégélienne la méthode était inapplicable. . . .* Entraîner 'la rose' dans un mouvement

240   *Notes*

qui tient une place singulière dans un rêve, celle impossible à distraire du
'bouquet optique,' celle qui peut changer totalement de propriétés en pas-
sant dans l'écriture automatique, celle qui n'a plus que ce que le peintre a
bien voulu qu'elle garde dans un tableau surréaliste, et enfin celle, toute
différente d'elle-même, qui retourne au jardin." (*Under its Hegelian form
the method was inapplicable* . . . To engage 'the rose' in a profitable
movement of less benign contradictions, in which it might be in succession
the one holding a singular place in a dream, the one impossible to distract
from the 'optic bouquet,' the one that can totally change properties when
it passes through automatic writing, the one no longer possessing that
which the painter wanted to be kept in a Surrealist painting, and finally
the one, wholly different from itself, that returns to the garden.)

20. André Breton, *L'Amour fou* (1937; reprint, Paris: Gallimard, 1976),
128. There are many comparable passages in Breton.

21. "On peut même dire que les images apparaissent, dans cette course
vertigineuse, comme les seuls guidons de l'esprit. L'esprit se convainc peu
à peu de la réalité suprême de ces images. Se bornant d'abord à les subir,
ils s'aperçoit bientôt qu'elles flattent sa raison, augmentent d'autant sa
connaissance." André Breton, *Manifestes,* 52.

22. "Qui étions nous devant la réalité, cette réalité que je sais maintenant couchée aux pieds de Nadja, comme un chien fourbe?" André Breton,
Nadja (1964; reprinted, Paris: Gallimard, 1975), 128.

23. Maurice-Jean Lefebue, *L'Image fascinante et le surréel* (Paris: Plon,
1965). Lefebue discusses dream and duplication, with reference to Borges'
topos about dreaming one is dreaming. He touches on cadavers and masks
as symbols of the hidden and explores repetition as a principle for per-
muting the present with the past in such psychic strategies as rememora-
tion (*ressouvenir*) and losing the past over again (*le passé reperdu*).

24. Hedges, in *Languages,* discusses at length the Surrealists' recourse to
alchemy.

25. "L'incorporation volontaire du contenu latent—arrêté d'avance—au
contenu manifeste est ici pour affaiblir la tendance à la dramatisation et à
la magnification dont se sert souverainement, au cas contraire, la censure."
André Breton, *Les Vases communicants* (1955; reprint, Paris: Gallimard,
1973), 70.

26. René Char, "La Lettre hors commerce," in *Recherche de la Base et
du sommet* (Paris: Gallimard, 1971), 44.

27. Still another direction—so rich are the interpenetrations of one poetry by another—is plotted out by Victor Terras and Karl S. Weimar, between Celan and the Russian tradition of Mandelstam ("Mandelstam and
Celan: Affinities and Echoes," *Germanoslavica,* no. 4 [Fall 1974]: 11–
27). Celan translated Mandelstam and was deeply read in Russian poetry. In quite another direction, one could find certain parallels between
the protosurrealism of Mandelstam's "Slatepencil Ode" ("Grifel'naia
oda") and the work of Wallace Stevens, who could never have read him.

28. Winfried Menninghaus, in *Paul Celan, Magie der Form* (Frankfurt: Suhrkamp, 1980), derives a rich series of predications from Celan's

many self-reflexive statements and tropes about poetic and human speech. Dietlind Meinecke (*Wort und Name bei Paul Celan: zur Widerruflichkeit des Gedichts*, Bad Homburg, 1970), discusses many of the aspects of Celan's transcendence of contradiction through the skillful angling of implied speech theory (47–48): "Nicht nur das Übermittelte, sondern auch das Wortsein selbst eines Übermitteln ist ein Faktor. Die Sinnlichkeit des Wortes und die Wörtlichkeit des Sinnes sind nicht mehr unterscheidbar." (Not only the transmission, but also the verbality itself of a transmission is a factor. The sensuality of the word and the wordiness of the sense are no longer distinguishable.)

29. Peter Szondi, *Celan-Studien* (Frankfurt: Suhrkamp, 1972), 56.

30. Ibid., 77. What Szondi says here is of course fairly loose and effusive.

31. André Breton, *Signe ascendant* (1968; reprint, Paris: Gallimard, 1979), 120–21.

32. André Breton, *Anthologie de l'Humour noir*, 14, as cited and discussed by Ferdinand Aliquié, *La Philosophie du surréalisme* (Paris: Flammarion, 1955), 112ff. As Aliquié well says (113), "la déréalisation n'est pas une fin en soi" (de-realization is not an end in itself).

33. Marie-Louise Gouhier, "Bachelard et le surréalisme," in *Entretiens sur le surréalisme*, ed. Ferdinand Aliquié (Paris: Mouton, 1968), 177–91.

34. Annie Le Brun, ibid., 104. "L'Humour noir . . . une indomptable entreprise de dédramatisation du drame qui naît de l'affrontement du moi et des forces restrictives de l'existence."

35. For Char's own comment on what amounts to such words, see René Char, *Oeuvres* (Paris: Gallimard, Pléiade, 1984), 828–29.

36. Jean-Pierre Richard, *Onze études sur la poésie moderne* (Paris: Seuil, 1964), 95. Compare Philippe Audoin, *Breton* (Paris: Gallimard, 1970), 90. "C'est comme si tout à coup la nuit profonde de l'existence humaine était percée, comme si la nécessité naturelle, consentant à ne faire qu'une avec la nécessité logique, toutes choses étaient livrés à la transparence totale" (It is as though suddenly the deep night of human existence was pierced, as though natural necessity consenting simply to fuse with logical necessity, all things were delivered to total transparence).

37. Ibid., 85.

38. "L'énigme que j'appelle rouge-gorge est le pilote caché au coeur de cette oeuvre dont les situations et les personnages égrènent devant nous leur volonté inquiétante. Le décalogue de la réalité d'après lequel nous évoluons subit ici sa vérification." Hinted at here are the evolutionary ideas of Teilhard de Chardin. Renée Char, *Recherches de la base et du sommet*, 68–69.

39. From Aaron Rosen, *Taps for Space* (New York: Sheep Meadow Press, 1980), 44.

Chapter 6. *William Carlos Williams: Ideas and Things*

1. Did the ancients have separate written titles for their mural painting? Almost surely not. Giotto represents a known scene; the element of illustration and religious reminder obviates a need for any title under the painting. When titles did come in, they remained simply descriptive until the simple irony of Hogarth, the heavier irony of Goya, where a proverb of ironic application is inscribed into the work. Only in modern art does the title interact with the picture. See Michel Butor, *Les Mots dans la Peinture* (Geneva: Skira, 1969); Jean-François Lyotard, *Discours Figure* (Paris: Klincksieck, 1972); Jacques Derrida, *La Verité en Peinture* (Paris: Flammarion, 1978).

2. Much of the detail of the complex interaction between painting and poetry in Williams' work is given in Dickran Tashjian, *William Carlos Williams and the American Scene* (Berkeley: University of California Press, 1978) and Bram Dijkstra, *The Hieroglyphics of a New Speech* (Princeton: Princeton University Press, 1969). In a further collection of Williams' writings on painting, Dijkstra adds a short bibliography of books and articles discussing this element in his work (Bram Dijkstra, *A Recognizable Image: William Carlos Williams on Art and Artists* [New York: New Directions, 1978]).

3. "Vortex," in Dijkstra, *Recognizable Image,* 57. Relevantly, Williams singles out a comparable element in a painting of Charles Sheeler's (ibid., 148), "Classic Landscape owes its effectiveness to an arrangement of cylinders and planes in the distance."

4. Williams never seems to quote Valéry when he transmits this doctrine, as Creeley does not quote either of them when he says form is an extension of content. For further remarks on verbal structures, see W. C. Williams, *The Embodiment of Knowledge* (New York: New Directions, 1974).

5. Joseph Riddel, *The Inverted Bell: Modernism and the Counterpoetics of William Carlos Williams* (Baton Rouge: Louisiana State University Press, 1974); Charles Altieri, "Presence and Reference in a Literary Text: The Example of Williams' 'This Is Just to Say,' " *Critical Inquiry* 5 (Spring 1979): 489–710. Altieri's "presence" stays at one remove still from the surface texture and linear juxtapositions of Williams' poem, and his "reference" confines itself to the prose statement out of which the poem arranges itself.

6. Williams says, *"All* sonnets mean the same thing because it is the configuration of the words that is the major significance" (*Embodiment of Knowledge,* 17).

7. "The object of modern painting was to escape representation. Not so. (It was to escape triteness.) It is to represent nature . . . the writer is to describe, to represent just as the painter must do—but what? and how? . . . The basis is a common one. As thought underlies." ("Painting" in Dijkstra, *Recognizable Image,* 70). Further, "Think of the poem as an object, an apple that is red and good to eat—or a plum that is blue and sour—or better yet a machine for making bolts" (ibid., 1). "I've at-

tempted to fuse the poetry and painting to make it the same thing" (ibid., 3).

8. Dijkstra (*Hieroglyphics,* 169) aptly compares "The Red Wheelbarrow" to a Stieglitz photograph. On the other hand, as Williams says in writing of a photographer ("Walker Evans" in Dijkstra, *Recognizable Image,* 138), bringing the abstract artist into the comparison, "the abstractions he thinks he is freeing are as definitely bound to a place as the work of the most representational artist that ever lived, the only difference being that one sees so much more than the other."

9. Ronald Paulson, *Emblem and Expression* (London: Thames and Hudson, 1975; Cambridge: Harvard University Press, 1975). Paulson traces the evolution of emphasis from emblem to expression in British painting from the eighteenth to the nineteenth centuries.

10. R. P. Blackmur, "Lord Tennyson's Scissors, 1912–1950," in *Form and Value in Modern Poetry* (New York: Anchor, 1957), 374.

11. William Carlos Williams, *Imaginations* (New York: New Directions, 1970), 314. Again, speaking of Juan Gris, Williams says (ibid., 110), "Things with which he is familiar, simple things—at the same time to detach them from ordinary experience to the imagination. Thus they are still 'real' they are the same things they would be if photographed or painted by Monet, they are recognizable as the things touched by the hands during the day, but in this painting they are seen to be in some peculiar way—detached."

12. Ibid., 105.

13. Ibid., 117. Much in Williams' *Embodiment of Knowledge* is relevant to this question.

14. "A marriage has to be seen as a thing." So Williams culminates a complicated account of "Charles Sheeler, artist's" refurbishing of an old farm house for a new wife. "The poem (in Charles's case the painting) is the construction in understandable limits of his life" ("Projective Verse," in *Autobiography* [New York: New Directions, 1951]). In this light we are ill-advised either to hypostatize or to particularize Williams' notion of "thing."

15. Kenneth Burke, "William Carlos Williams' Judgments," in *William Carlos Williams,* ed. J. Hillis Miller (Englewood Cliffs, N.J.: Prentice-Hall, 1966), 47.

16. Wallace Stevens, in ibid., 64.

17. Williams, *Imaginations,* 65.

18. "To vary between knowing and feeling is the artist's purgatory." Williams, "Shakespeare," in *Selected Essays* (New York: Random House, 1954), 56.

19. As Charles Altieri says of this poem, "The words' nominal qualities, combined with their incompleteness and their shared position with the verb 'depends,' also create an effect of substance in action . . . the act is profoundly temporal . . . yet no poem in English is more spatial and timeless." Charles Altieri, "Objective Image and Act of Mind in Modern Poetry," *PMLA* 91 (March 1976): 110–15.

20. Williams, *Imaginations,* 15.

21. Ibid., 81–82.
22. Ibid., 140.
23. See above note 7.
24. Altieri, "Presence and Reference," 502–3.
25. Williams, *Imaginations*, 14.
26. Riddel keeps referring to metonymy in Williams (*Inverted Bell*, 50 and *passim*) but this fashionable term will not do the work of defining Williams' jaggedness. Riddel's other definition is better, "Dr. Paterson moves always between these two inseparable levels of language, the apparently random particulars and the (invisible authentic) speech unlocked by a syntactical shift in their arrangement" (ibid., 120). Williams himself describes the "stain of sense" (*Paterson*, 108) as an analog to the stain in a retort that led to the discovery of radium. "Curie," he elsewhere says, "the image of our age: boiling down the pitch-blende for that stain of radiance" (Yale ms., quoted by Benjamin Sankey, *A Companion to Paterson* [Berkeley: University of California Press, 1971], 133). This emphasizes the force of the particulars, of course. It is the Surrealists who for Williams are, as it were, metonymic, "The simplicity of disorder . . . I avoid your eye merely to avoid interruption" (*Selected Essays*, 91). In another essay, the poem is "a field of action" (280), and the thrust of this phrase is to imply an interaction the term *metonymy* cannot easily cover.
27. Albert Cook, *Prisms* (Bloomington: Indiana University Press, 1967).
28. Riddel, *Inverted Bell*, 27.

Chapter 7. *Maximizing Minimalism: The Construction of Image in Olson and Creeley*

1. George F. Butterick, *A Guide to the Maximus Poems* (1978; reprint, Berkeley: University of California Press, 1980), 3–4. Butterick's quotations show how intricately the phrase is centered on, and bound up with, the likenesses and differences between Olson and Creeley.
2. Charles Boer, "Poetry and Psyche," *Spring*, 1979, 93–101. Boer explains Olson's use of the term, distinguishing it from the Objectivism of Zukofsky and Reznikoff.
3. Albert Cook, "Reflections on Creeley," *Boundary 2* (Spring/Fall 1978):353–64. This essay, from which I have here adapted some paragraphs, also discusses other aspects of Creeley's work.
4. *Olson*, no. 10, Fall 1978. With reference to both Creeley and Olson, see especially "The Act of Image," 73–74.
5. Charles Olson, "ABC's 2," in *Archaeologist of Morning* (London: Cape Goliard), 1970.
6. The equivalent is found in Valéry and Williams in many places, as well as in such formulations as that of Emil Staiger (*Grundbegriffe der Poetik*, 1946). But it appears most pointedly, and almost in Creeley's wording, in an italicized and developed key sentence of Kandinsky's *Über das Geistige in der Kunst* (*1912*), "Die Form ist also die Äusserung des inneren Inhaltes" (So form is the expression of the inner content).

Quotation from 10th edition (Bern: Benteli, 1973), 69. Since by 1915 Pound praised both this book and Kandinsky's painting, Williams could have got the notion explicitly from Pound or directly from the painters with whom he was in constant association after the Armory Show. This twentieth-century commonplace could have come to Creeley, in turn, through many routes—through Williams on the one hand, or through conversations at Black Mountain on the other hand, perhaps from Albers, who long headed Black Mountain and who had been Kandinsky's colleague at the Bauhaus. Or again, he could have got it directly from the translated text of Kandinsky, on sale through the Forties at the Museum of Nonobjective Painting in New York, which reprinted it.

7. Robert Creeley, *Later* (New York: New Directions, 1979), 59.

8. As Jonathan Holden describes it in *The Rhetoric of the Contemporary Lyric* (Bloomington: Indiana University Press, 1980), the "found" quality in a poem is related both to the cutoff of closure and to an omnipresent sense of metaphor.

9. See chapter 5, this volume.

10. Charles Olson, "Equal, That Is, to the Real Itself," in *The Human Universe* (San Francisco: Auerhahn Press, 1965), 117–22. Olson here bases his title on the interpretation of a phrase in a letter of Melville's.

11. Charles Olson, *The Maximus Poems: Volume Three* (New York: Grossman, 1975), 30.

12. Robert Creeley, *For Love* (New York: Charles Scribner's Sons, 1962), 120.

13. Robert Creeley, *Pieces* (New York: Charles Scribner's Sons, 1967), 10.

14. I owe this phrase characterizing Snyder to Jonathan Cook (personal communication).

15. Robert Creeley, *Words* (New York: Charles Scribner's Sons, 1967), 84.

Chapter 8. Expressionism Not Wholly Abstract: Ashbery and O'Hara

1. Marjorie Perloff, in *Frank O'Hara: Poet Among Painters* (New York: Brazillier, 1977), discusses many aspects of O'Hara's relations to painters as they impinge on his poetry.

2. Raymond Roussel, *Nouvelles Impressions d'Afrique* (Paris: Pauvert, 1963), 61.

3. Fred Moramarco, "The Lonesomeness of Words," in *Beyond Amazement: New Essays on John Ashbery,* ed. David Lehman (Ithaca: Cornell University Press, 1980), 279, note 3. "I asked Ashbery specifically about Roussel's influence in *The Tennis Court Oath* poems. At first Ashbery denied any, then said, 'Although come to think of it, in the title poem, the line about the lettering clearly visible in the margin of *The Times* was probably suggested by an episode in *Locus Solus.*'" For Ashbery's own writing on Roussel see also "Re-establishing Raymond Roussel," *Art News Annual,* 1962. This essay is presumably derived from Ash-

bery's abandoned doctoral thesis on Roussel. See also Raymond Roussel, *Comment j'ai écrit certains de mes livres* (1933; reprint, Paris: Pauvert, 1963) and Michel Foucault, *Raymond Roussel* (1957, reprint, Paris: Le Chemin, 1973).

4. David Lehman, "The Shield of a Greeting: The Function of Irony in John Ashbery's Poetry," in *Beyond Amazement*, 101–27. As Lehman says, "Ashbery does not reconcile contradictions; rather, he presents them as though they were parallel lines that cannot be expected to meet in the finite realms we inhabit" (102).

5. Leslie Wolf, "The Brushstroke's Integrity," in Lehman, *Beyond Amazement*, 241. "Ashbery, like de Kooning, 'dares to remove the object further before reconstructing it.'" Quotation from Wylie Sypher, *From Rococo to Cubism* (New York: Vintage, 1960), xxiv.

6. Books by Ashbery are indicated by the following abbreviations: ST, *Some Trees* (New Haven: Yale University Press, 1956); TCO, *The Tennis Court* (Middletown, Conn.: Wesleyan University Press, 1962); SPCM, *Self-Portrait in a Convex Mirror* (New York: Viking, 1975); HD, *Houseboat Days* (New York: Viking, 1977); AWK, *As We Know* (New York: Viking, 1979).

7. See Douglas Crase, "The Prophetic Ashbery," in Lehman, *Beyond Amazement*, 30–67.

8. As Keith Cohen says, in "Ashbery's Dismantling of Bourgeois Discourse," in Lehman, *Beyond Amazement*, 130:

a mint-condition can
of Rumford's Baking Powder, a celluloid earring, Speedy Gonzales,
the latest from
Helen Topping Miller's fertile Escritoire, a shear of suggestive pix on
greige, deckle-edged
Stock.

(*HD* 31)

Note the way the enumeration of each item includes a word that is linguistically alien to that object's "proper place" in the cultural spectrum. "Mint condition" is generally applied to extremely rare, old objects—hardly the case with Rumford's baking powder. [In this instance Cohen may not be up to the minute on the values of "Antiques and Collectibles."] "Celluloid earring" bears its own incompatibility at the level of the signified: as with a plastic corsage or fake pearls, we generally regard any earring as not genuine unless it is made from a rare or semiprecious material," etc. [Also earrings are supposed to be durable, and celluloid ones would wear very badly. They are supposed to be fixed, and celluloid ones would be floppy.]

9. See Albert Cook, "Emily Dickinson's White Exploits," in *Thresholds* (Madison: University of Wisconsin Press, 1985).

10. Cohen, "Ashbery's Dismantling," 136. See also David Rigsbee, "Against Monuments," in Lehman, *Beyond Amazement*, 212; "Consequently, when the poet tells us that the citizens are still 'angry with history,' he merely stresses their dilemma while exposing their collective amnesia as a (necessary) fiction."

11. See Albert Cook, *Prisms* (Bloomington: Indiana University Press, 1967), chapters 1 ("Diffusion") and 2 ("Generality").

12. John Koethe, "The Metaphysical Subject of John Ashbery's Poetry," in Lehman, *Beyond Amazement,* 193–95.

13. For a discussion of this aspect of Char, see Albert Cook, *Prisms,* chapter 6 ("Person").

14. Harold Bloom, "John Ashbery: The Charity of the Hard Moments," in *Figures of Capable Imagination* (New York: Seabury, 1976), 169–209. The general point is made in *The Anxiety of Influence.*

15. All quotations are from Donald Allen, ed., *The Selected Poems of Frank O'Hara* (New York: Vintage), 1974.

16. John Koethe, "Metaphysical Subject," 98. "O'Hara's affinity is with Hume's 'no self' view."

17. Poets of superb achievement beyond the turf of the New York School, poets as different as Anselm Hollo, Tom Clark, and Stephen Rodefer, have learned how to train the O'Hara riff into still newer music—and to keep a trained eye on an ever faster moving object.

Afterword: Visual Aspects of the Homeric Simile in Indo-European Context

1. Émile Benveniste, *Le Vocabulaire des institutions indo-européennes* (Paris: Minuit, 1969).

2. Albert Cook, *The Classic Line* (Bloomington: Indiana University Press, 1966), 98–106.

3. D. J. N. Lee, *The Similes of the Iliad and the Odyssey Compared* (Melbourne: Melbourne University Press, 1964), 7–8. Lee alleges a type 4 of comparisons that do not hold. This class is smaller than he claims, and very likely empty of examples from Homer. Hermann Fränkel, *Die Homerischen Gleichnisse* (1921; reprint, Göttingen: Vandenhoeck and Ruprecht, 1977), 67.

4. Edward M. Bradley, "Hector and the Simile of the Snowy Mountain," *TAPA* 98 (1967): 37–42.

5. The point has been made often before. See C. M. Bowra, "The Simile," in *Tradition and Design in the Iliad* (Oxford: Clarendon Press, 1930), 114–28. Tilman Krischer (*Formale Konventionen der Homerischen Epik* [Munich: C. H. Beck, 1971], 13–90) elaborately classifies the many similes that occur in the narratives of combat. Hermann Fränkel (*Die Homerischen Gleichnisse*) discusses much about the variety and implication of the world of Homeric similes, expanding his remarks in a later study, *Dichtung und Philosophie der frühen Griechentum* (Munich, 1969, 45–49). K. Riezler ("Das Homerische Gleichnis und der Anfang der Philosophie," *Die Antike* 12 [1936]: 253–71), along with many sensitive comments on the contrastive aspects of the similes, extrapolates this function into the more formalized contrasts proposed by the pre-Socratic philosophers. G. P. Shipp (*Studies in the Language of Homer* [Cambridge: Cambridge University Press, 1953], 18–103), finds many evidences of special poetic freedom in the similes (as against the body of the narra-

tive, which he adduces as evidence for the "lateness" of the similes), comparing them to Mycenean art, with citations. Paolo Vivante ("On Poetry and Language in Homer," *Ramus* 2 [1973]: 143–62) states that "Homer's similes mark the high points of what he sympathetically perceives—human actions, above all, whose manifestations seem to converge and blend into one with those of nature" (165). Michael Coffey ("The Function of the Homeric Simile," *Classical Journal*, 1957, 113–32) finds movement, appearance, sound, measurement of space and time, delineation of "situation," and finally "psychology" in the similes. David H. Porter ("Violent Juxtaposition in the Similes of the Iliad," *Classical Journal* 68 [1972]: 11–21) draws compositional conclusions from the remoteness of the domain in the tenor to that of the vehicle, as does D. F. Rauber ("Some Metaphysical Aspects of the Homeric Simile," *Classical Journal* 65 [1969]: 97–103). A whole world scheme hinges on the similes in Olga Freidenberg's conception (Elliott Mossman, ed., *The Correspondence of Boris Pasternak and Olga Freidenberg, 1910–1954* [New York: Harcourt Brace Jovanovich, 1982], 260, October 30, 1946):

An analysis of similes from the *Iliad* shows that the second element of a simile (the plant, animal, cosmic, or everyday-life image, to which the first element is compared) is the one that is extended, independent, and realistic.

Animal comparisons are used to express rage, belligerence, and violence; cosmic comparisons express darkness, death, and destruction. Similes from the *Iliad* do not present images of sunlight, only of storm and tempest.

Moreover, in every extended simile the mythological plane provides the basis for that which is being compared, and the realistic plane provides the basis for that to which it is being compared.

The mythological concept of a simile is based on the idea of a struggle taking place between a totem's two phases: action and nonaction. Both phases are presented concretely and in images as the usual mythological opposites: when the evil force triumphs, it is represented as merely a likeness of the true totem, as its aggressive twin; when the good force triumphs, the false chthonian totem is vanquished and is temporarily silenced (as was the good force in the other instance).

Mythological thinking knows no similes because a simile requires purely conceptual processes of abstraction. Mythological thinking has recourse only to personification, animated by the idea of struggle.

See also her *Mif i literatura drevnosti* (Moscow: Nauka, 1978).

6. Arnold Hirzel, *Gleichnisse und Metaphern im Rig Veda in kulturhistorischer Hinsicht zusammengestellt und verglichen mit den Bildern bei Homer, Hesiod, Aeschylos, Sophokles und Euripides* (Leipzig: Wilhelm Friedrich, 1890). Hirzel asserts, pretty much against his own evidence both positive and negative, that there is a congruence between the figures in the Rig Veda and those in Homer and his followers. In line with my point here, it is apposite to note that Edwin W. Floyd ("Kleos aphthiton: An Indo-European Perspective on Early Greek Poetry," *Glotta* 58, nos. 3–4 [1980]: 133–57) severely qualifies the parallel between *kleos aphthiton* in Homer and *śrávas akṣitam* in the Veda, pointing out that the phrases are differently used in each tradition. This difference in turn raises questions about metrical inferences drawn from the supposed identity of the

two expressions, as in Gregory Nagy, *Comparative Studies in Greek and Indic Meter* (Cambridge: Harvard University Press, 1974).

7. Karl Friedrich Geldner, *Der Rig Veda* (Cambridge: Harvard University Press, 1951).

8. Arthur Macdonnell, *A Vedic Reader for Students* (Oxford: Oxford University Press, 1913), 25.

9. Jan Gonda, *Vedic Literature* (Wiesbaden: Otto Harrassowitz, 1975), 132.

10. Geldner, *Der Rig Veda,* index.

11. Anthony Podlecki calls the similes in the *Odyssey,* this one and others, "similes . . . by which the poet reminds us of an important theme in the poem but with a slight difference of focus or point of view" ("Some Odyssean Similes," *Greece and Rome* 18 [1971]: 81–90, 82). He makes the point that in one simile (21.406–11), Odysseus' stringing the bow is compared to a musician's stringing his instrument (again a predominantly visual simile) and then soon Odysseus spares the rhapsode Phemius from the general slaughter of the suitors (22.330ff.).

12. Erich Auerbach, *Mimesis* (1946; reprint, New York: Anchor, 1957), 1–20.

13. Compare *Il.* 16.297–301:

As when from the lofty crest of a great mountain
Lightning-gatherer Zeus moves a thick cloud
And all the crags show clear and the high headlands
And valleys, and immense bright air breaks from the heavens,
So the Danaans, thrusting the blazing fire from the ships.

14. Kenneth John Atchity, *Homer's Iliad: The Shield of Memory* (Carbondale: Southern Illinois University Press, 1978), 148–87.

15. W. Bedell Stanford, *Greek Metaphor* (1936; reprint, New York and London: Blackwell's, 1972), 135.

16. Hirzel, *Gleichnisse und Metaphern,* 12.

17. Ibid., 17.

18. Paolo Vivante, *The Epithet in Homer* (New Haven: Yale University Press, 1982).

19. See chapter 2, note 1.

20. Cedric Whitman, *Homer and the Heroic Tradition* (Cambridge: Harvard University Press, 1958).

21. Bruno Snell, *The Discovery of the Mind,* trans. T. G. Rosenmeyer (New York: Harper, 1960), 5–8.

22. John Boardman, *Archaic Greek Gems* (New York: Thames and Hudson, 1968).

23. Roland Hampe, *Die Gleichnisse Homers und die Bildkunst seiner Zeit* (Tübingen: Niemeyer, 1952).

24. Bernard Fenik, *Typical Battle Scenes in the Iliad* (Wiesbaden: Steiner, 1968).

25. Scarabs were used as the models for Archaic gems. Emily Vermeule (*Greece in the Bronze Age* [Chicago: University of Chicago Press, 1972], 244), lists the find of thirty Near Eastern cylinder seals at Thebes as one

among many examples of transfer across space. Transfer through time is more difficult to establish but quite plausible.

26. The seals, and their corresponding numbers, are reproduced in Friedrich Matz and Hagen Biesanz, *Corpus der Minoischen und Mykene-ischen Siegel* (Berlin: Mann, 1964).

Index

Adam, James, 229 n
Aeschylus, 11
Albers, Josef, 245 n
Alberti, Rafael, 109, 115
Alexander the Great, 220
Aliquié, Ferdinand, 241 n
Allemann, Beda, 232 n
Allen, Donald, 247 n
Altieri, Charles, 143, 225 n, 242 n,
    243 n, 244 n
Apollinaire, Guillaume, 37, 64–85,
    86, 98, 109, 111, 139, 174, 235 n,
    236 n, 237 n
Arensberg, Walter, 126
Aristotle, 225 n
Arnheim, Rudolf, 8, 227 n, 228 n
Arnold, Matthew, 3, 226 n
Arp, Jean, 37, 38–63, 86, 91, 97, 117,
    234 n, 238 n
Artaud, Antonin, 103
Ashbery, John, 37, 167–202, 245 n,
    246 n
Atchity, Kenneth John, 249 n
Auden, W. H., 234 n
Audiberti, Jacques, 87
Audoin, Philippe, 241 n
Auerbach, Erich, 5, 29, 232 n, 249 n

Bachelard, Gaston, 3

Ball, Hugo, 54
Balthus, 120
Baron, Frank, 232 n, 233 n
Barr, Alfred H., Jr., 238 n
Barthes, Roland, 2, 226 n, 234 n
Battcock, Gregory, 237 n
Batterby, K. A. J., 232 n
Baudelaire, Charles, 3, 80, 83, 109,
    121, 149, 161
Baziotes, William, 239 n
Beardsley, Aubrey, 51
Beckett, Samuel, 6, 87, 238 n
Bellmer, Hans, 238 n
Bembo, Pietro, 31
Benjamin, Walter, 5, 227 n
Benveniste, Émile, 185, 203, 247 n
Berlioz, Hector, 184
Biesanz, Hagen, 249 n
Bishop, Elizabeth, 91–93
Blackmur, R. P., 132, 243 n
Blake, William, 8
Blok, Alexander, 94
Bloom, Harold, 187, 247 n
Bly, Robert, 94
Boardman, John, 249 n
Boer, Charles, 227 n, 244 n
Bollnow, Otto, 233 n
Bonnard, Pierre, 80, 109
Borges, Jorge, 240 n

Bouts, Dirck, 80
Bowra, C. M., 247 n
Bradley, Edward M., 205, 247 n
Brancusi, Constantin, 59, 62
Brandt, Per Aage, 239 n
Braque, Georges, 120, 170
Braudel, Fernand, 158
Breton, André, 37, 55, 56, 57, 86–123, 167, 182, 183, 187, 188, 189, 195, 238–41 nn
Browning, Robert, 9
Bundy, Elroy L., 11, 228 n
Buñuel, Miguel, 87, 103
Burke, Kenneth, 136, 243 n
Bush, Ronald, 233 n
Butor, Michel, 158, 237 n, 242 n
Butterick, George F., 151, 244 n

Calder, Alexander, 238 n
Campos, Augusto de, 237 n
Campos, Haroldo de, 237 n
Cavalcanti, Guido, 20
Caws, Mary Ann, 239 n
Celan, Paul, 20, 37, 111, 112–14, 169, 240 n, 241 n
Céline, Ferdinand, 6
Cézanne, Paul, 41, 126, 131, 148
Chamisso, Adelbert, 4, 226 n
Char, René, 4, 37, 55, 86, 91, 99, 100, 102, 104, 105, 110, 112, 113, 116–21, 169, 187, 226 n, 239 n, 240 n, 241 n, 247 n
Chardin, Jean, 131
Chardin, Teilhard de, 241 n
Chipp, Herschel B., 238 n
Chirico, Giorgio de, 86, 98
Choerilus, 227 n
Clark, Kenneth, 170
Clark, Tom, 247 n
Claudel, Paul, 191, 231 n
Cleveland, John, 21
Clüver, Claus, 237 n
Coffey, Michael, 248 n
Cohen, Keith, 182, 246 n
Cohn, Robert Greer, 237 n
Cole, Thomas, 145
Condillac, Étienne de, 228 n
Confucius, 20
Constable, Arnold, 230 n
Cook, Jonathan, 245 n
Corbière, Tristan, 79
Corneille, Pierre, 190
Cornell, Joseph, 238 n, 239 n

Crase, Douglas, 246 n
Crashaw, Richard, 28
Creeley, Robert, 37, 149–66, 242 n, 244 n, 245 n
Cummings, E. E., 52, 237 n
Curie, Pierre, 244 n

Dali, Salvador, 87, 237 n, 239 n
Dante, 15–16, 20, 48, 163, 229 n
Davie, Donald, 234 n
de Kooning, William, 170, 172, 179, 181, 187, 190, 198, 246 n
de la Tour, Georges, 118, 134
Delaunay, Robert, 69, 71–76, 80–81, 84, 87, 236 n, 237 n
Delaunay, Sonia, 69
Deleuze, Gilles, 101
della Casa, Giovanni, 31
Delvaux, Paul, 98, 108
de Man, Paul, 228 n
Demuth, Charles, 126–28
Derrida, Jacques, 226 n, 242 n
Descartes, René, 47, 185
Dickinson, Emily, 21, 32–36, 180–81
Dijkstra, Bram, 242 n, 243 n
Diogenes, 161
Disney, Walt, 177, 238 n
Donne, John, 20, 231 n
Doolittle, Hilda, 126, 128, 129
Dove, Arthur, 238 n
Dubuffet, Bernard, 161, 170, 172
Duchamp, Marcel, 54, 81–82, 83, 87, 88, 98, 103, 117, 126, 167, 169, 175, 194, 197
Dufy, Raoul, 76
Dumézil, Georges, 203
Duthuit, Georges, 238 n

Eco, Umberto, 19, 225 n
Ede, H. S., 234 n
Eliot, T. S., 9, 84, 163, 179, 190
Éluard, Paul, 37, 55, 86, 91, 97, 101–2, 105, 108, 109, 117, 121, 169, 174, 187, 191
Empson, William, 185
Epstein, Jacob, 49
Erlich, Victor, 239 n
Ernst, Max, 86, 87, 103, 239 n

Farnell, L. R., 228 n
Fenik, Bernard, 221, 249 n
Firth, Raymond, 230 n
Fish, Stanley, 25, 31, 231 n

Floyd, Edwin W., 248 n
Foucault, Michel, 246 n
Francastel, Pierre, 236 n
Fränkel, Hermann, 205, 247 n
Freedberg, Sydney, 189
Freidenberg, Olga, 248 n
Freud, Sigmund, 10, 92, 162, 186,
   226 n, 228 n
Fried, Michael, 237 n
Friedrich, Gerhard, 232 n
Frye, Roland M., 28, 231 n

Gaiser, Konrad, 229 n
Galileo, 32
Gascoyne, David, 238 n
Gaudier-Brzeska, Henri, 47, 53, 126,
   150
Gauguin, Paul, 87, 88, 238 n
Gautier, Théophile, 192
Geldner, Karl Friedrich, 207, 249 n
Genette, Gérard, 226 n
Ghiberti, Lorenzo, 28
Ghirlandaio, Domenico, 80
Giacometti, Alberto, 87
Gilbert and Richard, 187
Gilman, Ernest B., 231 n
Giotto, 131, 242 n
Goethe, Johann Wolfgang von, 62, 71
Goffin, Robert, 236 n
Goldberg, Rube, 238 n
Gombrich, Ernst, 8, 19, 228 n, 230 n
Gonda, Jan, 209, 249 n
Gordon, D. J., 231 n
Gorgias, 207
Gorky, Arshile, 169, 239 n
Gouhier, Marie Louise, 117, 241 n
Goux, Jean-Joseph, 228 n
Goya, Francisco, 242 n
Graves, Robert, 163
Greet, Anne Hyde, 236 n
Greimas, A. J., 2, 226 n
Gris, Juan, 139, 243 n
Grosz, George, 87
Guattari, Félix, 101

H. D. *See* Doolittle, Hilda
Hampe, Roland, 221, 249 n
Handwerk, Gary, 229 n
Hartley, Marsden, 151
Hartman, Geoffrey, 32, 232 n
Hassam, Childe, 151
Hausman, Margaret, 235 n
Haussmann, Raoul, 54

Hedges, Inez, 90, 103, 239 n, 240 n
Hegel, Georg Wilhelm Friedrich, 3
Heidegger, Martin, 112, 118, 127,
   229 n, 236 n
Heraclitus, 13, 104, 119
Herbert, George, 82
Herodotus, 207
Hexter, Jack, 4, 226 n
Heym, Georg, 73
Hirzel, Arnold, 206, 248 n, 249 n
Hogarth, William, 242 n
Holden, Jonathan, 245 n
Hölderlin, Friedrich, 145
Holland, Norman, 226 n
Hollo, Anselm, 247 n
Homer, 10, 20, 26, 34, 36, 192, 203–
   23, 227 n, 247 n, 248 n
Horace, 161, 219, 227 n
Hugo, Victor, 157
Hulewicz, Witold, 233 n
Hülsenbeck, Richard, 234 n
Hume, David, 185, 200, 247 n
Husserl, Edmund, 9, 19, 127, 228 n,
   230 n

Ingarden, Roman, 225 n
Ingres, Jean, 132
Ionesco, Eugène, 87
Isaiah, 31
Iser, Wolfgang, 4, 225 n

Jacobs, Max, 86
Jakobson, Roman, 185, 226 n
Jarry, Alfred, 235 n
Jauss, Hans-Robert, 225 n
Jayne, Richard, 233 n
Jean, Marcel, 234 n
Jerome, Saint, 176
Job, 31
John the Baptist, Saint, 176
Jonson, Ben, 190
Joyce, James, 178
Jung, Carl Gustav, 158

Kandinsky, Wassily, 48, 63, 87, 88,
   169, 230 n, 238 n, 244 n, 245 n
Kant, Immanuel, 13, 185, 228 n
Kenner, Hugh, 47, 233 n
Khlebnikov, Vladimir, 89
Kittel, G., 232 n
Klee, Paul, 55, 74, 88, 124, 236 n,
   238 n
Kline, Franz, 8

Knott, Bill, 110
Koch, Kenneth, 190, 191
Koethe, John, 185, 186, 247 n
Krischer, Tilman, 247 n
Kroeber, Karl, 227 n
Kugler, Peter, 227 n

Lacan, Jacques, 100
Laforgue, Pierre, 79
Lane, Fitz Hugh, 151, 155–56, 161
Lattimore, Richmond, 217
Lautréamont, Comte de, 86, 103
Le Brun, Annie, 117, 241 n
Lee, D. J. N., 205, 247 n
Lefebue, Maurice-Jean, 102, 240 n
Lehman, David, 245, 246 n
Leishman, J. B., 21, 231 n
Leopardi, Giacomo, 35
Leroi-Gourhan, André, 228 n
Lessing, Gotthold, 8, 46
Levin, Samuel R., 228 n
Levine, Philip, 93–94, 111
Lévi-Strauss, Claude, 5, 100, 116, 209, 226 n
Lewalski, Barbara, 25, 231 n
Lewis, Wyndham, 47, 48, 150
Lindner, Robert, 101
Locke, John, 13, 228 n
Lockerbie, S. I., 236 n
Lorca, Garcia, 93, 105–6, 109, 111, 118
Lotman, Yuri, 19, 225 n
Lowell, Robert, 92, 157
Lyotard, Jean-François, 19, 81, 230 n, 237 n, 242 n

Macdonnell, Arthur, 207, 249 n
Magritte, René, 86, 87, 91, 97, 98, 99, 116
Mallarmé, Stéphane, 24, 64, 79–80, 82, 83, 85, 91, 109, 149, 156, 161, 185
Man Ray, 238 n
Mandelstam, Osip, 240 n
Marie de France, 237 n
Marisol, 154, 163, 165
Marvell, Andrew, 20, 21–25, 189, 231 n
Masaccio, 28
Massey, Irving, 5, 226 n
Masson, André, 91, 169, 239 n
Matisse, Henri, 72, 80, 81, 88, 97–98, 109, 119, 190, 230 n, 238 n, 239 n

Matta (Echaurren), 169, 239 n
Matz, Friedrich, 249 n
Mayakovsky, Vladimir, 89
Meinecke, Dietlind, 241 n
Menninghaus, Winfried, 240 n
Merwin, W. S., 37, 91, 113, 118, 157, 163, 169
Miller, J. Hillis, 243 n
Miller, Henry, 181
Milton, John, 9, 21, 25–32, 231 n
Minsky, Marvin, 239 n
Miró, Joan, 86, 87, 88, 97, 98, 121
Mondrian, Piet, 8, 53, 88, 154
Monet, Claude, 243 n
Montale, Eugenio, 156, 157, 185
Moore, Henry, 87
Moore, Marianne, 132, 174
Moramarco, Fred, 245 n
Mossman, Elliott, 248 n
Motherwell, Robert, 88, 238 n
Mukarovsky, Jan, 19

Nagy, Gregory, 249 n
Namier, Lewis, 157–58
Napoleon, 168
Neruda, Pablo, 91, 94, 106–8, 109, 111, 118, 169
Nerval, Gérard, 83
Nietzsche, Friedrich, 104, 131, 229 n
Novalis, 32

O'Hara, Frank, 9, 37, 167–202, 245 n, 247 n
O'Keeffe, Georgia, 238 n
Oldenburg, Claes, 56
Olson, Charles, 5, 37, 149–66, 227 n, 244 n, 245 n
Orgel, Stephen, 231 n

Parmigianino, 189
Pasternak, Boris, 89–90, 91
Pasternak, Leonid, 90
Paul, Saint, 34
Paulson, Ronald, 243 n
Peirce, Charles, 2, 226 n
Péret, Benjamin, 182, 187
Perloff, Marjorie, 245 n
Pershing, John, 129
Picabia, Francis, 54, 87
Picasso, Pablo, 29, 77, 87, 88, 106, 107, 124, 170, 189, 190, 194, 204, 238 n
Pignitari, Decio, 237 n

Pindar, 10–13, 20, 97, 228 n, 229 n
Pirandello, Luigi, 87
Pistoletto, 187
Plato, 13–15, 20, 228 n, 229 n
Podlecki, Anthony, 249 n
Pollock, Jackson, 9, 131, 179, 186, 190
Ponge, Francis, 163
Pope, Alexander, 201
Porter, David H., 248 n
Pound, Ezra, 9, 37, 38–63, 126, 128, 129, 150, 190, 192, 233 n, 234 n, 237 n, 245 n
Poussin, Nicolas, 31, 124
Praz, Mario, 227 n
Prince, F. T., 31, 232 n
Propertius, 192
Proust, Marcel, 8, 23

Quinn, John, 52

Racine, Jean, 190
Ransom, John Crowe, 153
Rauber, D. F., 248 n
Rauschenberg, Robert, 176, 189
Rembrandt, 31, 80
Renoir, Pierre, 140
Reverdy, Pierre, 115, 116, 118, 157, 176, 182, 195, 238 n
Reznikoff, Charles, 139, 244 n
Richard, Jean-Pierre, 118, 241 n
Ricoeur, Paul, 228 n
Riddel, Joseph, 145, 242 n, 244 n
Riezler, K., 247 n
Rigsbee, David, 246 n
Rilke, Clara, 40, 233 n
Rilke, Rainer Maria, 20, 36, 38–63, 114, 171, 172, 191–92, 193, 232 n
Rimbaud, Arthur, 16–18, 20, 24–25, 85, 95, 108, 229 n
Rivers, Larry, 176
Rodefer, Stephen, 247 n
Rodin, Auguste, 39, 41, 42, 43, 47, 232 n, 234 n
Rogers, Robert L., 228 n
Ronsard, Pierre, 236 n
Rosen, Aaron, 121, 241 n
Rousseau, Henri (Le Douanier), 88
Roussel, Raymond, 167–69, 188, 195, 245 n, 246 n
Rubens, Peter Paul, 28, 198

Rubin, William S., 62, 235 n
Runge, Otto, 71, 87

Sandstroem, Yvonne, 231 n
Sankey, Benjamin, 244 n
Sauer, Carl O., 158
Schapiro, Meyer, 236 n
Schiller, Gertrud, 232 n
Schmidt-Rottluff, Karl, 170
Scholz, Frances Mary, 233 n
Schwitters, Kurt, 54, 238 n
Sebeok, Thomas, 228 n
Shahn, Ben, 150
Shakespeare, William, 179, 190, 231 n
Shattuck, Roger, 236 n
Sheeler, Charles, 242 n, 243 n
Shipp, G. P., 247 n
Shumaker, Wayne, 31, 232 n
Sills, David L., 226 n
Siqueiros, David Alfaro, 238 n
Siskind, Aaron, 161
Snell, Bruno, 216, 220, 249 n
Snyder, Gary, 163
Solomon, 223
Sophocles, 133
Spenser, Edmund, 9, 32
Spurgeon, Caroline, 25
Stafford, William, 93, 96
Staiger, Emil, 244 n
Stanford, W. Bedell, 218, 249 n
Steiglitz, Alfred, 135, 243 n
Steiner, Wendy, 227 n
Stendhal, 116
Stevens, Wallace, 3, 9, 33, 88–91, 116, 129, 130, 132, 142, 156–57, 158, 160, 161, 163, 173, 187, 239 n, 240 n, 243 n
Stokes, Adrian, 8, 9, 228 n
Swinburne, Algernon Charles, 53
Sypher, Wylie, 31, 32, 232 n, 246 n
Szondi, Peter, 112, 241 n

Tanguy, Yves, 87, 169, 239 n
Tashjian, Dickran, 242 n
Tasso, Torquato, 31, 32
Tate, James, 110
Tauber, Sophie, 59
Tennyson, Alfred Lord, 9, 53, 80
Terras, Victor, 240 n
Thompson, D'Arcy, 55
Thurber, James, 238 n
Todorov, Tzvetan, 225 n
Toulouse-Lautrec, Henri de, 126

256 *Index*

Trakl, Georg, 20, 95, 114
Turner, Victor, 230 n
Tyler, Parker, 191
Tynyanov, Yury, 89–90, 239 n
Tzara, Tristan, 54, 234 n

Unamuno, Miguel de, 106

Valéry, Paul, 19, 153, 156, 157,
    230 n, 244 n
Vallejo, César, 111
van der Weyden, Rogier, 80
Van Dijk, T. A., 228 n
van Eyck, Jan, 80, 230 n
van Gogh, Vincent, 47, 77
Velasquez, Diego, 134
Vergil, 21
Verlaine, Paul, 83, 90
Vermeer, Jan, 8, 30, 80, 134
Vermeule, Emily, 249 n
Villa, Pancho, 129
Vitrac, Roger, 87
Vivante, Paolo, 219, 248 n, 249 n
Vlaminck, Maurice de, 72
Vuillard, Edouard, 80, 109

Waller, Edmund, 192
Walling, William, 227 n
Watkins, Evan, 3, 226 n
Webb, Karl Eugene, 232 n
Weimar, Karl S., 240 n
Westhoff, Clara. *See* Rilke, Clara
Whitman, Cedric, 220, 249 n
Whitman, Walt, 32, 66
Will, Frederic, 110–11
Williams, William Carlos, 9, 37, 124–
    48, 149, 153, 154, 155, 161, 163,
    164–65, 242–45 nn
Wittgenstein, Ludwig, 9, 187, 228 n
Wolf, Leslie, 246 n
Wölfflin, Heinrich, 9, 228 n
Wordsworth, William, 5, 32, 33, 144,
    145
Wright, James, 94–96

Yeats, J. B., 51, 52
Yeats, William Butler, 52

Zeno, 168
Zinn, Ernst, 232 n
Zukofsky, Louis, 244 n